# SMART TRAINING
## for RUGBY

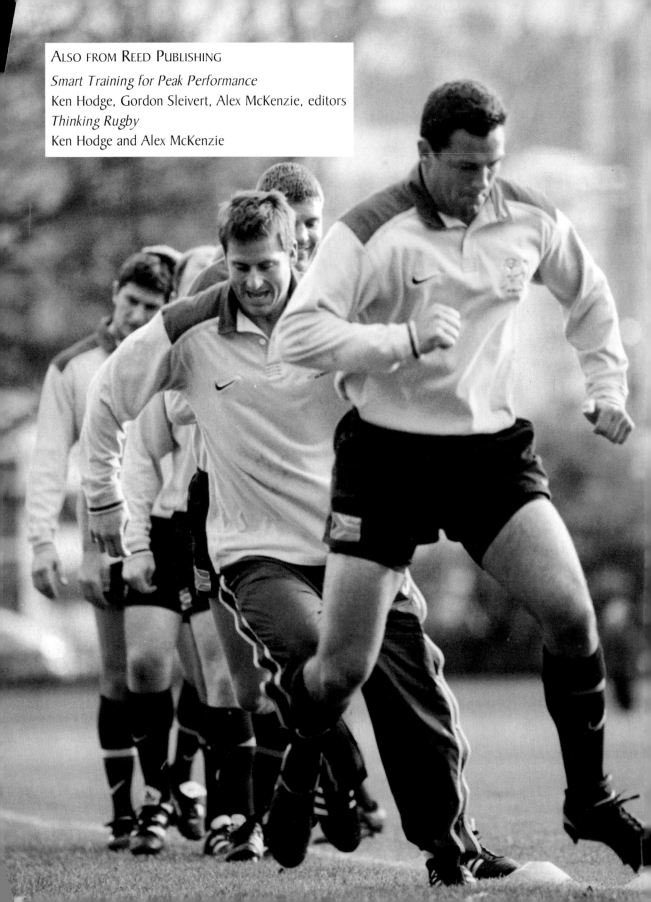

ALSO FROM REED PUBLISHING

*Smart Training for Peak Performance*
Ken Hodge, Gordon Sleivert, Alex McKenzie, editors

*Thinking Rugby*
Ken Hodge and Alex McKenzie

# SMART TRAINING
## for RUGBY

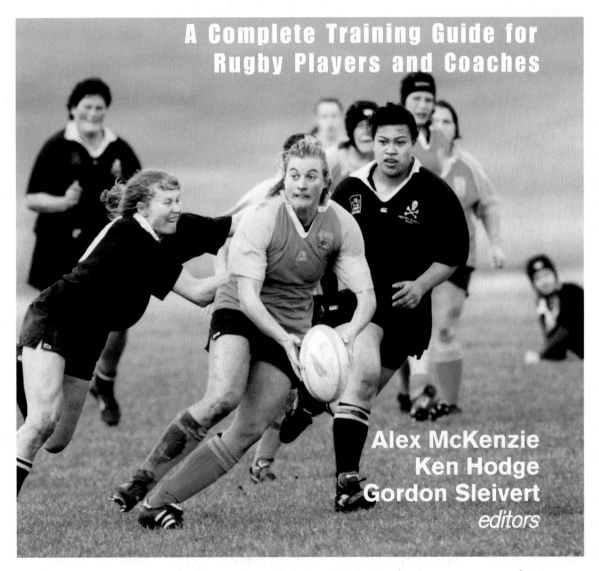

### A Complete Training Guide for Rugby Players and Coaches

**Alex McKenzie**
**Ken Hodge**
**Gordon Sleivert**

*editors*

REED

All photographs are courtesy of the *Otago Daily Times*, except for:
Fotopress: Cover photos; Markus Deutsch: Grunt 3000 (page 61);
Jamie Plowman: Prone bridge hold (page 60), Vertical jump test (62),
Two-step jump test (63), Sit and reach test (64), Plyometric exercises
(87), Overspeed training (88), Horizontal power training (90),
Flexibility exercises (92), Centre of mass (134).

Published by Reed Books, a division of Reed Publishing (NZ) Ltd,
39 Rawene Rd, Birkenhead, Auckland (www.reed.co.nz). Associated
companies, branches and representatives throughout the world.

© 2000 Katrina Darry, Markus Deutsch, David Gerrard, Ken Hodge,
Alex McKenzie, David Pease, Gordon Sleivert

ISBN 0 7900 0721 5

The authors assert their moral rights in the work.

Designed and typeset by Graeme Leather, Island Bridge

First published 2000

Printed in New Zealand

# Contents

# 1 Introduction

*Alex McKenzie, Ken Hodge, Gordon Sleivert*

I have always loved rugby: the physical challenge in which strength and size, speed and endurance, agility and ability are mixed in a team game with tactics and intelligence to produce our national sport. To run the risk of injury in a violent physical confrontation balanced against the sheer exhilaration of using mental and physical capacity to dupe or overpower the opposition.

Rugby is also the contentment of being part of a team which has through mental collusion and diligent training been able to co-ordinate its action to overcome that of 15 [others] with the same ideal.

**Graham Mourie (All Black captain 1977–82, Hurricanes Super 12 coach, 2000– )**

The 'complete player' is a term that is often used to describe a rugby player who excels in all aspects of the game. However, this description means different things to different people. We believe the complete player is more than someone who excels at playing the game. For us, the complete player also ensures that their *preparation* for playing the game is complete! This means that they have examined all aspects of their preparation and performance, identified their strengths and weaknesses, and taken action to build on their strengths and eliminate or reduce their weaknesses.

While it would be fair to say that some people labelled as 'complete players' will have spent considerable time preparing for their performance (especially in terms of off-season training and in-season maintenance of skills and abilities), it would also be fair to say that the label 'complete player' has included many who have not spent an appropriate amount of time preparing for their performance on the field. Many of these players, while excelling at *playing* the game, could be even better if they had *prepared* better. This could mean the difference between being a good player and being a *great* player.

In our experience, rugby players have been notoriously poor at preparing themselves for performance in comparison with athletes in some other sports. This statement may not apply as much at the professional level as it does at the club level, but in general, rugby players do not adequately prepare themselves for the mental and physical challenges the game presents. Doing so could enable them to make the step up to the next level of performance.

So what aspects of preparation are important? In general there are two main factors that influence performance.

**Rugby performance = horsepower + willpower**

This formula indicates that the *physical* basis of rugby performance, including physical ability, physical skill, and physical fitness, represents the *horsepower* required to be a good player. A number of other physical factors also impact upon *horsepower*, including health, injury status, and nutrition. However, the complete rugby player also needs determination, perseverance and motivation to 'train' these physical requirements. In other words, they need a set of psychological skills to enable them

Rugby performance jigsaw.[1]

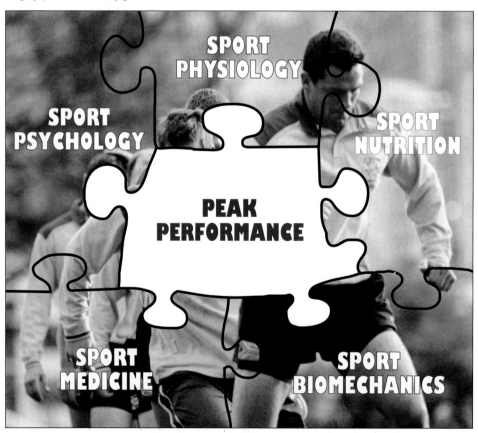

to use these physical attributes when placed under pressure during the game. These *mental* attributes represent the *willpower* aspect of rugby performance. While it is possible to separate these two general factors of performance for training purposes, both factors need to be integrated for consistent rugby performance.

> Australia . . . was the worthiest of champions. Its players not only play with brawn but with brains, and France found the combination too difficult to unlock.
>
> **Brent Edwards (*Otago Daily Times* reporter) on the 1999 Rugby World Cup final**

This integrative and complete approach to training can be likened to assembling a jigsaw. To continually improve in rugby you must identify the pieces of the jigsaw that are important to your performance and develop a plan to complete your 'rugby performance jigsaw' (facing page). Too often players and coaches focus most, if not all, of their training efforts on the 'horsepower' factors of performance (i.e. physiology, nutrition, biomechanics, medicine), and in doing so they neglect the 'willpower' (i.e. psychology) aspects. Often, they simply take this aspect of their performance for granted. Consequently their jigsaw is incomplete.

Elite rugby players often have a number of clear strengths, but the key characteristic that makes them elite is that they have few, if any, clear weaknesses. They carefully plan their training to cater for all their rugby needs — both the 'horsepower' and 'willpower' needs.

This integrated approach to training requires players to adopt an attitude of self-analysis and awareness that enables them to identify their weaknesses as well as their strengths. In doing so they are not dwelling on their deficiencies or taking a negative attitude to their game. Rather, they are being brutally honest with themselves, and actively seeking training methods that will enable them to maintain their strengths and eliminate their weaknesses.

The following example demonstrates the need for such an approach to rugby training.

## Player example

Ben is an openside flanker for a senior club side with aspirations to play regularly for the provincial rep team (he's already had a few games and he wants more!). He has very high levels of endurance fitness, great upper body strength, excellent technique both as a tackler and as a ball carrier, good tactical sense, and an ability to 'read the game'. However, Ben's speed over the first 10–15 metres is only average for a flanker, and he has a bad habit of losing concentration and 'drifting' during the game once he makes a mistake.

At the moment Ben believes that the only way to cope with his lack of speed off the mark is to work even harder on his aerobic fitness so that he will have more energy for all-out sprinting during the game. Consequently, he has increased his endurance training even more than normal, yet now he seems to be getting tired, lethargic and irritable (a sure sign of overtraining). So this doesn't seem to be the answer to his speed problems. As far as his concentration problems are concerned, Ben believes the sure way to prevent losing concentration after mistakes is to stop making mistakes in the first place! So he is now working even harder on his physical skills so that he can 'perfect' them and thus totally eliminate mistakes from his game.

As you can probably guess, this approach to his 'concentration problems' is also doomed to failure — none of us are ever perfect, and we all make mistakes on occasion. Even top provincial players and All Blacks make mistakes, but the difference is that they have developed a number of psychological (psych) skills to help them cope with the pressure that often comes with mistakes. In addition, they have developed their concentration skills to such a level that they are not distracted by mistakes and are able to stay 'in the game'.

Ben's solution to both of his problems was to work harder on his physical fitness and his physical skills (i.e. he only worked on the 'horsepower' aspect of performance). Since neither of his solutions actually matched the problem he was faced with, Ben trained hard, but he didn't train *smart*. You couldn't fault his determination and his motivation to improve his game, but because he wasn't aware of the specific cause of both these problems, he wasn't able to choose training techniques that actually worked on the appropriate solution to each problem.

In this book we will explain how Ben would have been much more successful if he had used some means of performance assessment (e.g. a Peak Performance Profile; see chapter 2), if he had set some training goals for himself (see chapter 3), and if he had then been able to make 'smart' choices about the best training methods for his specific skill needs.

In the following chapters you will see how Ben could have improved his performance if he had: (a) tested his speed and power, then worked on specific speed training drills to improve his power and acceleration; and (b) assessed his concentration skill level and his ability to cope with pressure, then worked on some psych methods (such as self-talk and centring) to improve his concentration and his ability to cope with the pressure that comes with making mistakes during the game. In short, Ben had trained hard, but he hadn't trained *smart*!

You must include *both* the 'horsepower' and 'willpower' factors of performance in designing your training plan. If you want to be the best player you can be, you need to be disciplined enough to plan your training to provide time to train *all* aspects of your performance. Consequently, we provide chapters on separate aspects of the *horsepower + willpower* formula from which you can pick and choose in designing your training plan for peak performance. We also provide a strategy to guide you in the development of your performance plan. The four Ps — Philosophy, Prioritisation, Planning and Periodisation — are central themes in this book. By reading the case studies and examples, and using the worksheets provided, you will be able to:

➤ Identify the key factors for your rugby performance and integrate these factors into your training *philosophy*.

➤ Identify the strengths and weaknesses in your training and performance and *prioritise* those factors that require the most work.

➤ *Plan* sensible and effective strategies to improve your rugby performance.

➤ Integrate your training of the horsepower and willpower aspects of performance into an annual training plan designed to build peak rugby performance. This process is called *periodisation*.

This approach is guaranteed to help you improve your rugby performance by ensuring that you don't just train — you use *Smart Training for Rugby*!

## How to use this book

This book is intended as a planning tool for all those players who are serious about reaching their potential as rugby players. Consequently, our focus is not only on elite players, but on any serious player, whether you are an All Black, a Black Fern, a club player, or a member of the school 2nd XV! The book outlines a step-by-step guide to developing a periodised training plan that is tailored to *your* needs as a player. In doing so, it takes into consideration your age, your physical and psychological characteristics, as well as your playing position, and incorporates these into a training programme that is designed exclusively *for you*, and *by you*!

The chapters that follow provide basic sport science information that you can use to design a new training programme, or to evaluate and/or modify your existing training programme. We make extensive use of worksheets and examples that will make it easier for you to design your own programme. In addition, in chapter II we have provided a number of user-friendly logsheets that you can use to monitor your training, and to evaluate your progress towards your rugby goals.

For various reasons, some players may not wish to invest the time and effort in developing such an extensive training programme as the one that is outlined here. If you think that this applies to you, you may wish to simply pick out the specific information that you want to use. For example, you may wish to complete the peak performance profile in chapter 2, set your goals (chapter 3), and then go directly to chapter 10 and complete the worksheets for your periodised training plan, referring only to the sport science information in the intervening chapters if necessary. Alternatively, you may feel that you are sufficiently knowledgeable in, say, fitness training, and choose only to read those chapters in which you feel your knowledge is lacking (e.g. psychological training and nutrition). The choice is entirely yours.

Having said this, there is no such thing as the perfect rugby player. Every player has areas of weakness that could be improved. If you are committed to reaching your potential as a player, you need to actively work to change those weaknesses into strengths. The challenge then, is to identify your training and performance needs,

and to design a training programme that will overcome your weaknesses and improve your strengths even further, so that you can honestly say you have done all you can to become the best player you can be. It is not sufficient just to work hard and hope it pays off. You need to plan your hard work, *train smart*, and vastly increase the likelihood that you will reach your rugby playing potential. Who knows where that might take you?

Most players hammer themselves in fitness training in the naive belief that [fitness] alone will make them better players. Sure, fitness helps but it is only part of the complete player equation.

**Paul Henderson (All Black 1991–95)**

# 2 Peak performance profiling

*Ken Hodge, Alex McKenzie*

Developing your peak performance profile is a handy way to put together your own peak performance 'jigsaw puzzle'. In conjunction with the goal setting process outlined in chapter 3, the profile will help you to organise a periodised training plan, so that you are more likely to play to the best of your ability more often (i.e. achieve peak performance).

Your peak performance profile will help you identify the various physical, technical, tactical, and psychological requirements for achieving peak performance in your playing position. Examples of rugby qualities that might be included in each area are listed below:

*Physical*

➤ Physiological requirements (e.g. strength, speed, endurance, power, flexibility)

➤ Medical requirements (e.g. general health, injury prevention)

➤ Nutritional requirements (e.g. training diet, pre-game meal, fluid intake)

*Technical*

➤ Techniques for the successful performance of the individual skills for your playing position.

*Tactical*

➤ Strategies for each area of performance in the game (e.g. game plans for various situations)

*Psychological*

➤ Mental skills (e.g. concentration, motivation, confidence, coping with pressure)

The goal setting process outlined in chapter 3 will also help to clarify your peak performance needs, assess your ability in each area, and help you to determine the best methods of improving your abilities. Goal setting is the key to 'smart training', because it will help you to design an overall training plan (see chapter 10) in which you select the appropriate training methods for achieving peak performance.

## Training plan assessment

Effective planning of a rugby training programme first requires assessing the sport of rugby itself. Although certain *team* aspects will need to be accounted for, the assessment of *individual* skills is most important developing an effective personalised training programme. There are a number of ways to assess your individual rugby strengths, weaknesses, and needs, such as coaching observation, match statistics, or video analysis. However, the easiest way to complete a basic assessment of your overall training needs is to complete a peak performance profile.

## Peak performance profile: self-assessment

In identifying your rugby training needs, you have to discover (or rediscover) the essential qualities or skills that contribute to a successful performance in your playing position (i.e. a peak performance profile). Your individuality is emphasised in this profile process, in that *you* decide what is important for you, and *you* evaluate your capabilities in a very personal and individual manner.

The peak performance profile invites you to view yourself as a player involved in the process of developing a general 'jigsaw picture' of yourself and your particular technical, tactical, physical and psychological skill needs (see the peak performance profile forms on pages 21–22). Your jigsaw picture will allow you to design an effective training plan to improve your performance, achieve your goals, and get your brain and body working together as a team. The jigsaw picture you create will be one that readily makes sense to *you*, as opposed to one that has been created for you by your coach or a sport science consultant.[1] Once you have developed your peak performance profile you may wish to share it with your coach so that he or she can help you to refine the profile and design a training plan based upon it.

### PEAK PERFORMANCE PROFILING PHASES [2]

*Phase 1. Understanding the idea*
Be very clear that the profile should be used to help you understand how you

currently feel about your ability to achieve your peak performance. There are no right or wrong profiles — you need to build the profile that you think will best help you achieve your peak performance.

### Phase 2. Identifying performance skills

You need to decide on the important 'performance skills' that you require in order to play well. You should also consider discussing this with your coach and/or team-mates. These skills can usually be categorised as technical, tactical, physical and psychological, although you need to create labels that make sense to you.

Technical skills refer to the specific skills required for your playing position (such as tackling, passing and kicking). Tactical skills are the strategies, patterns and tactics used in your position (you may want to talk to your coach about these options). Physical skills are the endurance, strength, power, speed, flexibility, nutritional and medical requirements of your position, and psychological skills refer to the mental requirements of your position (such as motivation, self-confidence and concentration). These skills collectively represent the jigsaw pieces of a peak performance in rugby.[3]

Each person will have a slightly different set of performance skills, and a slightly different combination of psychological, technical, tactical and physical skills. You must decide for yourself how important each performance skill is to your peak performance jigsaw.

You may wish to identify these performance skills through brainstorming in small groups (four or five players) within your team.[4] If you choose this approach, your task will be to select those skills that you think are appropriate for the team, but also take into account your individual needs. You or your group should consider questions like 'What are the essential qualities of a top level rugby player?' It can also be useful to talk to a former top level player, or invite one to participate in the group discussion.

Don't be limited by the space provided on the profile form. Many players like to use the peak performance skill worksheet on page 19 to write out an extensive list of all the performance skills that they can identify (see the list on page 20 completed by Ben, the flanker introduced in chapter 1). When you have finished the peak performance skill worksheet, you should then select the top three or four skills in each category of performance (e.g. pick out the top three technical skills). Transfer these to either of the peak performance profile forms on pages 21 or 22.

We have included two versions of the peak performance profile for you to choose from. The first one, labelled Peak Performance Profile (1), is a simplified version that includes only two of the four rating assessments (i.e. 'current' and 'best-ever' ratings;

see page 21). The second, labelled Peak Performance Profile (II), is the full version and includes four rating assessments (i.e. 'current', 'best-ever', 'improvement' and 'stability' ratings; see page 22).

### Phase 3. Assessment of the performance skills

You now need to rate yourself on each of the performance skills that you have identified, using the following four scales.[5]

#### Current (right now) performance

Using a scale of 0–10 (with 0 = poor, 5 = average, and 10 = excellent) rate yourself on each of the skills according to how you currently feel (i.e. right now) about your level of skill in each category. You may also want your coach to rate you on these same skills. Your coach's assessment may or may not agree with yours — this can become a basis for greater discussion and understanding between you and your coach.

#### Best-ever performance

Another assessment that you (and your coach) should complete is to rate your best-ever performance in relation to these skills. Most players can recall their best-ever performance, and although that performance may not have been 'ideal', it represents their best so far. Your best-ever profile may not necessarily have ratings of '10' for each skill, because some skills may be important for performance but not absolutely vital for peak performance. Completing a best-ever rating profile helps you decide which skills require and deserve the most work to improve your ability to consistently reach peak performance.[6]

#### Improvement

You should also complete ratings on the skills that need improvement, and determine how much improvement is needed (i.e. 0 = huge improvement needed, 5 = moderate improvement, and 10 = no improvement possible). These ratings are a bit deceptive as the scoring is the opposite of the others; that is, lower scores (e.g. 2 or 3) mean that the player rates him or herself as having considerable room for improvement, while high scores like 8 or 9 mean virtually no room for improvement. Consequently, top level players with well-developed skills will often have high scores on 'improvement', indicating that they have little room for improvement.

The 'improvement' ratings will help you to decide which skill areas have the most room for improvement, which areas you should work on immediately, and which you should leave to a later date. Clearly, the areas that have significant room for improvement and are important for your peak performance are the skills that you should be designing a training programme to improve!

### Stability/consistency

The final rating is of the stability or consistency of your performance skills (e.g. 0 = very unstable, needs control; 5 = moderate stability; and 10 = very stable, maintain). Skills that are unstable or inconsistent are likely to be the most important ones to improve because their instability works against your ability to consistently produce peak performance. For example, as a fullback you may rate yourself as *currently* having good technical skills for punting (rating = 8), and in your *best-ever* performance you rated yourself highly (rating = 9). Unfortunately, your punting is inconsistent from game to game and sometimes between kicks in the same game (rating = 4). At the present time your skill at punting is inconsistent and unstable, possibly due to low levels of psych skills like concentration and coping with pressure.

## *Phase 4. Planning*

You should use your profile ratings to set goals for improving the various skills in your peak performance profile. For example, you may set a goal to improve a technical skill like passing from a 'current' rating of 6 to 8; or set a goal to improve your concentration from 5 to 7. It is important to identify both strengths and weaknesses — then plan your training to *maintain* your strengths and to *improve* on your weaknesses. You should not regard weaknesses as a sign of failure or incompetence — everyone has weaknesses. The key issue is admitting them and working hard to improve them. For example, some people say that Michael Jordan was the greatest ever basketball player. Despite his successful basketball career there were many things that he could not do — he had a number of 'weaknesses':

> I can't skate. I can't swim. If you threw me in the water I'd be able to survive. But I never learned how. I grew up near the beach, but I was never taught to swim as a child. I won't go out on a boat unless it's a big boat. If I'm at a party, I'll make sure to stay away from the edge of the pool. I don't think I ever will learn how. But I do want my children to learn. Any four-year-old boy or girl who's just learning to swim can do something that I can't.
> **Michael Jordan (US basketball player; Chicago Bulls, six-times NBA champions)**

You can also use your profile ratings to gain a greater understanding and agreement between yourself and your coach. To work well together you and your coach must eliminate any major differences in assessments. The profile not only allows your coach to understand you better, but you will gain a greater appreciation of the reasons behind their assessment of your performance profile. As previously mentioned, many players also use the peak performance profile assessment on a regular basis (e.g. weekly or every four or five games) as a detailed form of 'game review' for fine-tuning their training and monitoring their skill levels. On the other hand, you may wish to use the profiling procedure during the 'business end' of the season (e.g. play-offs, semifinals), as repeated profiling can help you assess your progress and degree of readiness for a peak performance.

Once you have identified your training needs you can begin to design your training programme. You need to choose the appropriate methods of training in order to improve the performance skills identified in your peak performance profile.

On page 23 you will see the peak performance profile that Ben completed for himself at the start of this season. Based on this assessment he designed his training programme.

As you can see from Ben's profile, he needs to improve his speed over the first 10–15 metres, tidy up his tackling around rucks/mauls, and improve his running lines on defence. He also needs to take control of his own pre-game 'psych-up', and in particular, to sharpen up his concentration for the full 80 minutes.

Using his profile as a starting point, Ben and his coach Rick were able to design and follow a periodised training programme that allowed Ben to address his skill weaknesses. The first step was to sort his skill needs into different types of training. He labelled his training as follows: fitness/speed training, technical skills practice, and psych skills training. Among his different skill needs he decided his speed over 10–15 metres and his concentration skills were most in need of improvement.

In the following chapters you will see how Ben planned his training so that he 'trained smart', with a focus on improving his areas of weakness, as well as maintaining his strengths.

> Don't accept a weakness without trying to fix it, and always work on multi-skilling yourself. The All Blacks focus on multi-skills in our training, and it's just so important for all players to achieve.
>
> **Martin Toomey (All Black fitness trainer 1992–99)**

# PEAK PERFORMANCE SKILLS: WORKSHEET

Write an extensive list of all the performance skills required for your playing position.

**Name:** ................................... **Playing position:** ...........................

| Technical | Tactical | Physical | Psychological |
|---|---|---|---|
| | | | |

## PEAK PERFORMANCE SKILLS: WORKSHEET

Write an extensive list of all the performance skills required for your playing position.

**Name:** Ben Mills                **Playing position:** Openside flanker

| Technical | Tactical | Physical | Psychological |
|---|---|---|---|
| TACKLING | Reading running lines on defence. | Speed over 10–15 metres. | Commitment to my goals and objectives. |
| Tackling around scrums. | Reading running lines on attack. | Speed to breakdown or in support. | Motivation for skill training. |
| Tackling around rucks/mauls. | Reading opposition attacking moves. | Anaerobic fitness — able to recover during the game. | Motivation for fitness work. |
| Tackling: Cover defence. | Reading holes in opposition defensive pattern. | Aerobic/ endurance fitness. | Concentration for 80 minutes. |
| Ball retention in the tackle. | | Upper body strength. | Ability to shift concentration — focus on the right things at the right time. |
| Body position at 2nd phase. | Options — runner off 2nd phase . | Leg strength and lineout jump height. | |
| Passing in general play. | Options – pick & go off 2nd phase. | Flexibility. | Optimal pre-game psych-up |
| Backline moves; lines and linking. | | Recovery from injuries. | Coping with pressure during the game. |
| Backrow moves; body position on the drive. | | | Confidence for each game. |
| Lineout jumping. | | | |
| Supporting jumpers at lineout. | | | Team cohesion — follow game plan. |

Ben's example

# PEAK PERFORMANCE PROFILE (I)

**Name:** . . . . . . . . . . . . . . . . . . . . . . . . . .    **Playing position:** . . . . . . . . . . . . . . . . . . . . . . . .

List the skills, and rate yourself on the performance of these skills during your *best-ever (peak)* rugby performance, and on your current (right now) level of performance of each skill. Rate yourself according to the following scale:

| | 0 | 1 | 2 | 3 | 4 | 5 | 6 | 7 | 8 | 9 | 10 |
|---|---|---|---|---|---|---|---|---|---|---|---|
| *Current + best:* | Poor | | | | | Average | | | | | Excellent |

| | Current (right now) | Best-ever |
|---|---|---|
| **Technical:** | | |
| . . . . . . . . . . . . . . . . . . . . . . . . . . | I . . . . . . I | I . . . . . . I |
| . . . . . . . . . . . . . . . . . . . . . . . . . . | I . . . . . . I | I . . . . . . I |
| . . . . . . . . . . . . . . . . . . . . . . . . . . | I . . . . . . I | I . . . . . . I |
| **Tactical:** | | |
| . . . . . . . . . . . . . . . . . . . . . . . . . . | I . . . . . . I | I . . . . . . I |
| . . . . . . . . . . . . . . . . . . . . . . . . . . | I . . . . . . I | I . . . . . . I |
| . . . . . . . . . . . . . . . . . . . . . . . . . . | I . . . . . . I | I . . . . . . I |
| **Physical:** | | |
| . . . . . . . . . . . . . . . . . . . . . . . . . . | I . . . . . . I | I . . . . . . I |
| . . . . . . . . . . . . . . . . . . . . . . . . . . | I . . . . . . I | I . . . . . . I |
| . . . . . . . . . . . . . . . . . . . . . . . . . . | I . . . . . . I | I . . . . . . I |
| . . . . . . . . . . . . . . . . . . . . . . . . . . | I . . . . . . I | I . . . . . . I |
| **Psychological:** | | |
| . . . . . . . . . . . . . . . . . . . . . . . . . . | I . . . . . . I | I . . . . . . I |
| . . . . . . . . . . . . . . . . . . . . . . . . . . | I . . . . . . I | I . . . . . . I |
| . . . . . . . . . . . . . . . . . . . . . . . . . . | I . . . . . . I | I . . . . . . I |
| . . . . . . . . . . . . . . . . . . . . . . . . . . | I . . . . . . I | I . . . . . . I |

## PEAK PERFORMANCE PROFILE (II)

**Name:** ............................... **Playing position:** ...........................

List the skills, and rate yourself on the performance of these skills during your *best-ever (peak)* rugby performance, and on your *current (right now)* level of performance of each skill. Also rate the level of improvement needed, and the consistency of each skill. Rate yourself according to the following scale:

|  | 0 | 1 | 2 | 3 | 4 | 5 | 6 | 7 | 8 | 9 | 10 |
|---|---|---|---|---|---|---|---|---|---|---|---|
| *Current + best:* | Poor | | | | | Average | | | | | Excellent |
| *Improvement:* | Improvement needed | | | | | | | No improvement necessary | | | |
| *Stability:* | Very unstable | | | | | | | | | | Very stable |

|  | Current | Best-ever | Improvement | Stability |
|---|---|---|---|---|
| **Technical:** | | | | |
| ............................ | I......I | I......I | I......I | I......I |
| ............................ | I......I | I......I | I......I | I......I |
| ............................ | I......I | I......I | I......I | I......I |
| ............................ | I......I | I......I | I......I | I......I |
| **Tactical:** | | | | |
| ............................ | I......I | I......I | I......I | I......I |
| ............................ | I......I | I......I | I......I | I......I |
| ............................ | I......I | I......I | I......I | I......I |
| **Physical:** | | | | |
| ............................ | I......I | I......I | I......I | I......I |
| ............................ | I......I | I......I | I......I | I......I |
| ............................ | I......I | I......I | I......I | I......I |
| ............................ | I......I | I......I | I......I | I......I |
| **Psychological:** | | | | |
| ............................ | I......I | I......I | I......I | I......I |
| ............................ | I......I | I......I | I......I | I......I |
| ............................ | I......I | I......I | I......I | I......I |
| ............................ | I......I | I......I | I......I | I......I |

Ben's example

# PEAK PERFORMANCE PROFILE (II)

**Name:** *Ben Mills*      **Playing position:** *Openside flanker*

List the skills, and rate yourself on the performance of these skills during your *best-ever (peak)* rugby performance, and on your *current (right now)* level of performance of each skill. Also rate the level of improvement needed, and the consistency of each skill. Rate yourself according to the following scale:

|  | 0 | 1 | 2 | 3 | 4 | 5 | 6 | 7 | 8 | 9 | 10 |
|---|---|---|---|---|---|---|---|---|---|---|---|
| *Current + best:* | Poor | | | | | Average | | | | | Excellent |
| *Improvement:* | Improvement needed | | | | | | | No improvement necessary | | | |
| *Stability:* | Very unstable | | | | | | | | | | Very stable |

| | Current | Best-ever | Improvement | Stability |
|---|---|---|---|---|
| **Technical:** | | | | |
| *Body position at breakdown* | 8 | 9 | 5 | 7 |
| *Tackling in general* | 9 | 10 | 8 | 8 |
| *Tackling around rucks/mauls* | 5 | 7 | 4 | 7 |
| *Passing/link play* | 8 | 9 | 8 | 9 |
| **Tactical:** | | | | |
| *Reading running lines on attack* | 8 | 9 | 7 | 8 |
| *Reading running lines on defence* | 5 | 8 | 6 | 8 |
| *Options: choosing runner moves* | 8 | 9 | 8 | 9 |
| **Physical:** | | | | |
| *Speed over 10–15 metres* | 3 | 7 | 5 | 8 |
| *Upper body strength* | 10 | 10 | 10 | 10 |
| *Aerobic fitness/endurance* | 9 | 10 | 8 | 8 |
| *Leg strength & lineout leaping* | 8 | 9 | 7 | 8 |
| **Psychological:** | | | | |
| *Pre-game psych-up (activation)* | 5 | 9 | 3 | 2 |
| *Commitment* | 8 | 10 | 7 | 7 |
| *Concentration* | 4 | 8 | 3 | 5 |
| *Motivation for training* | 7 | 9 | 8 | 10 |

# 3 Goal setting

*Ken Hodge, Alex McKenzie*

Goal setting is the starting point for planning your training for peak performance. If you have your goals clear in your mind then peak performance becomes achievable on a regular basis. This philosophy is perhaps best expressed by former All Black captain and current Wellington Hurricanes coach Graham Mourie, who said that:

Performing well at any level is possible providing the individual has his goals clear in his mind and is prepared to do the work necessary to reach them.

**Graham Mourie (All Black captain 1977–82; Hurricanes Super 12 coach 2000– )**

Briefly, a goal is an aim, objective, target, or dream. More specifically, a goal is a particular standard of performance that is usually to be attained within a specified time limit.[1] When deciding upon the areas in which to set goals, you need to select the skills from your peak performance profile that you believe to be the most important, or those that most need to be improved.

## Why set goals in rugby?

Achieving your goals shows that you are making improvements in both your training and your playing performances, and as a result helps to maintain your motivation.

Your levels of self-confidence, anxiety and stress are also affected, and appropriate goal setting will help you to maintain optimal levels of each of these psychological skills.[2] For example, when a player is only focused on the *outcome* of a game (i.e. winning), unrealistic and unattainable expectations can often result. These can lead to lower self-confidence, increased anxiety and decreased effort. The overall result is *poor performance*.

Goal setting also helps you to manage the *time* you have available for training. You need to make the most efficient and effective use of your training time — goal setting will help you to prioritise the use of your time.

---

### Goal Setting and Time Management

'Time is nature's way of making sure everything doesn't happen at once.'

---

The process of goal setting also helps you to identify your strengths and weaknesses, which is the ideal starting point for designing your training plan. Goals help you to determine what is important in your training. They do this by providing direction and forcing you to prioritise your needs.[3] Goal setting is like a road map: the long-term goal is the destination, while the short-term goals are pit stops along the way, and the goal achievement strategies, such as the training methods, are the choice of route.

Goal setting definitely works. I've found that if you write down your goals and what you've done, see what you've achieved, you feel your goals are more attainable.

**Zinzan Brooke (All Black 1987–97)**

# What types of goals should you set?[4]

### PERFORMANCE GOALS

Set performance goals rather than outcome goals. These should be based on the peak performance skills identified in your profile. In top level rugby there is enormous pressure from many sources, especially the media, to set outcome goals such as winning against a particular opponent. Indeed, coaches sometimes emphasise and teach outcome goals. However, outcome goals are not within your control, and consequently can become a major source of anxiety, which in turn can lead to poor performance.[5] Therefore, rather than setting outcome goals, you should set performance goals.

> All I want to do is play well and enjoy it. The only thing I can do is to play as well as I can. The rest of it is out of my control.
>
> **Todd Blackadder (All Black 1996–98; Canterbury captain 1996– )**

Performance goals differ from outcome goals in that they focus on a 'task-mastery' definition of success — they are all about mastering specific tasks or skills. The nuts and bolts of playing well and being successful depend on doing these basic tasks and skills correctly (e.g. passing, kicking, tackling, scrums, lineouts, second phase ball retention). If you succeed in performing these tasks well then you are likely to achieve the outcome you are seeking. Consequently, performance goals encourage you to focus on 'how to win' rather than winning itself. The beauty of these goals is that you have control, because the goals are based on measuring your mastery of specified tasks or standards of performance, such as making sure that your passes are as accurate as possible.[6]

> Winning was not the most important thing any more. Winning wasn't the point. Playing the best rugby was the point, and winning was the by-product. The distinction is real.
>
> **David Kirk (All Black 1983–87) talking about the approach of the All Blacks to the 1987 World Cup**

With performance goals the criterion for success is being better than you were last time at a specified task, such as the number of first-time tackles, the percentage of accurate lineout throws, or the percentage of correctly executed backrow moves, passes, or kicks for touch. Rather than comparing yourself with your opponent(s) to determine your success, performance goals allow you to compare yourself with your own previous performance. You have more control over these goals, and they are also a very honest and demanding way to measure success. For example, even when you win easily against a poor opponent, your performance goals provide a more demanding evaluation of your 'real' success on the day. On the other hand, when you lose against a good opponent you still have a measure of success that provides you with information about performance improvements and about the effectiveness of your training. Outcome goals are just too crude and imprecise as a useful measure of success.

## LONG-TERM AND SHORT-TERM GOALS

A long-term goal is a 'dream' goal. It is the ultimate objective, and provides direction for your periodised training plan. Short-term goals allow you to see regularly how much you have improved, and can increase your intensity in training and competition. Achieving short-term goals is also useful in that you can reward yourself for effort and hard work in training and competition.

We took this season just step-by-step, establishing short-term goals as we went along.

**Todd Blackadder (All Black 1996–98; Canterbury captain 1996– ) talking about the 1997 Canterbury team that won the NPC 1st Division**

## SPECIFIC MEASURABLE GOALS

These are goals that are easy to measure and thus make it simple to determine whether or not you have achieved them. They need to be very specific to the skill that you are trying to improve, and you need to write down a detailed description of each goal so that you can see whether you've attained it or not.

*Examples of specific, measurable goals*

POOR GOAL: As a halfback I want to be faster breaking away from the scrum base.

GOOD GOAL: I will reduce my time for a 20-metre standing start sprint by 0.5 seconds.

POOR GOAL: I want to improve my upper body strength to help my scrummaging.

GOOD GOAL: Before the start of the season I will be able to perform 3 x 8 reps of 100 kg in bench press, and 3 x 8 reps of 30 kg in neck extensions.

POOR GOAL: I want to be more accurate in my passing.

GOOD GOAL: I will be able to hit a 30-cm-square target, on the run, 9 times out of 10 after receiving a pass from another player.

### DIFFICULT BUT REALISTIC GOALS

Aim to stretch your capabilities by challenging yourself with difficult but realistically achievable goals. Know your own limitations, and remember that goals must be 'out of reach but not out of sight'. They should be achievable if you put the work in. If you set goals that are unrealistic and too difficult to achieve then you are virtually guaranteeing failure, rather than increasing your chances of success.

POOR GOAL: I want to make 100 percent of my tackles in next Saturday's game.

GOOD GOAL: Because the tackling rates of the best All Black players in my position are around 80 percent, and because my tackling rate last Saturday was 60 percent, I will strive to successfully make at least 70 percent of my tackles in next Saturday's game.

> There's no point in having an unachievable vision — but it has to be big enough to be a little frightening, big enough so that there is a fear it won't be achieved.
> **David Kirk (All Black 1983–87)**

### POSITIVE GOALS

Set positive rather than negative goals. For example, instead of saying to yourself 'I will not blow my cool every time a refereeing decision goes against me,' say 'Whenever a refereeing decision goes against me I will remain composed and stay focused on my game.' Or instead of saying 'I will not miss any more than 10 percent of my lineout throws,' say 'I will hit my jumpers with 90 percent of my lineout throws.' That is, instead of focusing on 'I won't fail,' focus on 'I will succeed'.

## In what areas should goals be set?

The areas in which to set goals are physical, technical, tactical and psychological.

### PHYSICAL GOALS

Health and fitness (e.g. improving endurance, power, strength, flexibility, weight, diet, sleep patterns).

### TECHNICAL GOALS

Goals that relate to performance of the particular skills of your position (e.g. keeping shoulders relaxed when sprinting, passing accurately with both left and right hands, following through when goal-kicking).

### TACTICAL GOALS

These goals relate to an understanding and appreciation of appropriate tactics, such as attacking and defensive strategies, and game plans (e.g. improving your ability to 'read' opposition backline defensive patterns and quickly identify the best point of attack; improving the ability to read the right 'lines' to run in support).

### PSYCHOLOGICAL GOALS

Psych skills and methods (e.g. planning to practise mental preparation techniques, practising imagery of performance in pressure situations, coping with poor refereeing or criticism from your coach).

## Goal-setting staircase

The steady progression through your short-term goals allows you to reach your long-term goals. First choose the key areas in your peak performance profile that need improvement, and set long-term goals for each area. Then set short-term sub-goals for each long-term goal. Each key area should have its own staircase of sub-goals (see page 30 for an example of a sub-goal staircase).

## Assessing your training needs

Before you go any further, make sure you have asked yourself some key questions regarding your rugby performance. These should include 'Where am I now?', 'Where do I want to be in a week, next month, in six months, two years?', 'What are my strengths and weaknesses?'

Goal-setting staircase (example only).

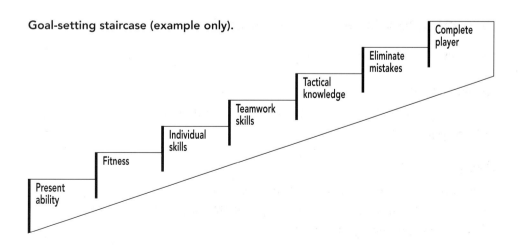

**Sub-goal staircase for strength fitness.**

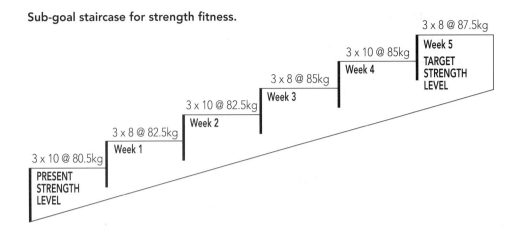

## TALK TO YOUR COACH AND PRIORITISE YOUR NEEDS

The next thing to do is talk to your coach about the results of your peak performance profile (see chapter 2). Using your coach's advice, set long-term and short-term goals for each area. Then, based on these 'priorities', use the SMART system to actually 'set' your goals.

# SMART goal setting

## HOW TO SET SMART GOALS[7]

| | | |
|---|---|---|
| **S** | = | Specific |
| **M** | = | Measurable |
| **A** | = | Adjustable |
| **R** | = | Realistic |
| **T** | = | Time-referenced |

*Specific*

Set specific goal(s). These need to be difficult to reach, but still realistic. They should be *performance* goals, stated positively, and should involve a detailed description of the goal so that it can be measured.

*Measurable*

Set numerical goal(s). If you state your goals in readily measured, numerical terms it makes it simple to determine whether or not you have achieved them. For example, you could set goals in terms of such things as:

➤ Percentage of tackles made

➤ Number of rucks hit in good body position

➤ Number of accurate passes made

➤ Number of successful backrow moves executed

➤ Percentage of times that specific moves made the advantage line or tackle line

➤ Number of accurate lineout throws

➤ Exact times for specific sprint or endurance distances

➤ Amount of weight lifted for specific weight room exercises

## Adjustable

Goals and goal schedules may need to be adjusted or changed as you work through them. For example, sickness or injury may interfere with progress. In addition, you may find the goals you initially select are too hard or too easy. You must be prepared to modify and change goals, strategies, and target dates as required. As with any new activity it will take time to develop effective, accurate and realistic goal setting.

## Realistic

Set difficult, but realistic goals (see example on page 28). Don't set goals that are beyond your capabilities. On the other hand, don't set goals that are too easy to achieve, because they will not present a sufficient degree of challenge to ensure that you make an effort to achieve them. Consequently you won't perform as well as you are able and you are unlikely to reach your potential peak performance level.

POOR GOAL:   I want to make 100 percent of my goalkicks from within 40 metres.

GOOD GOAL:   Because I'm currently only making 50 percent of my kicks from within 40 metres, my goal is to be successful with 75 percent of my kicks from within 40 metres over the next five games.

## Time-referenced

Set target dates for achieving your goal(s). Again, these should be difficult but realistic. If you don't set a target date, you can always use the excuse that you're still working towards achieving the goal if somebody asks you how you're progressing. But if you have a target date, then the closer to that date you find yourself, the more effort you are likely to put into making sure you achieve the goal.

### A GOAL STRATEGY

After you have set your SMART goals you must outline a strategy of training methods to achieve them. Be specific. For example, a goal strategy for improving passing accuracy for a halfback might be: 'I will practise an extra 30 passes from the ground (as if from a scrum or ruck) and 30 passes from the air (as if from a lineout or maul) after training on Tuesdays and Thursdays. I will also ask for an hour of one-on-one coaching each week from the coaching development officer in my province.'

## Complete the goal achievement worksheet

To help you think through the key questions mentioned above you should fill out the worksheet on pages 35–36. This will help you 'think through' your goals in depth as you strive to express yourself in writing. Make sure the goals you set follow the SMART goal guidelines, and that you include a specific training strategy to achieve each goal (record these in your training logbook: see chapter 11).

## Ensure your commitment to your goal(s)

> Through Otago University rugby I became more convinced of the need
> . . . to set high standards and be ruthless and proud in executing them.
> **Josh Kronfeld (All Black 1995– )**

You must have the desire, motivation and commitment to pursue your goal strategies. Writing a 'contract' with yourself can be helpful (see the worksheet on page 36). Social support from significant people in your life is also vital (e.g. team-mates, parents, partner, friends, boss). Make sure you inform these people about your goals and training plan — they can't support you if they don't know what you are trying to achieve and why it matters to you!

After following these guidelines, you should insert your performance goals and goal strategies (training methods) into a training plan (see chapter 10).

## Self-monitoring

To ensure your commitment to your goals and your training plan you should do the following:

> ➤ *Write out* your long-term and short-term goals (see facing page).
> ➤ *Write down* at least one achievement strategy for each short-term goal. Use

the goal achievement worksheet on pages 35–36 to record this information (photocopy extra worksheets as you need them).

➤ *Write down* target dates as well, because deadlines provide an added incentive and help to plan the time frame of your goal achievement.

➤ *Finally,* your goal evaluation procedures should also be recorded for use with your training log.

| | |
|---|---|
| **SKILL/AREA NEEDING IMPROVEMENT** | Tackling performance |
| **SPECIFIC GOAL** | I will successfully make at least 70% of my attempted tackles during games. |
| **GOAL ACHIEVEMENT STRATEGY** | 1. After training on Tuesdays I will complete 15 minutes of tackling practice with a team-mate, using tackle bags.<br><br>2. I will practise 10 minutes of tackling imagery each day, making sure that I imagine making tackles from the side, in front and behind. |
| **TARGET DATE/EVALUATION** | 18 May. Then reset goal to 75% by 15 June.<br><br>Team statistician to write down team and individual tackling preformance statistics for each game. |

*Remind yourself of your goals by maintaining a training log* (see chapter II). Other options include making a wall poster as a visual reminder of your goals, target dates, and overall training plan. You may want to write your goals on index cards and display them somewhere such as on your mirror or the fridge door. Ask yourself: 'What did I do today to become a better player?'

Remember, monitoring is your job, not your coach's, and self-monitoring and self-evaluation lead to self-motivation. Be organised, be responsible, be committed and be assertive. Have the attitude: 'If it's to be, it's up to me!'

## Evaluate your goal attainment

*Monitor your progress regularly.* Not only should you monitor your progress, but you should check your target dates as well. They may need to be adjusted according to how well you are progressing towards your goals. Your training methods/strategies should also be reviewed periodically for their effectiveness. Remember, setting goals does not in itself improve performance. The hard work and training detailed in the strategy is what enables you to achieve your goals and subsequently improve performance.

————

**Common goal-setting problems**

Goals that are not specific.
Goals that are not realistic.
Setting too many goals at one time.
No goal achievement strategy.
Poor goal monitoring/evaluation.
Lack of commitment.

————

## Summary: goal setting for peak performance

Once you have identified your peak performance needs and written them out as 'performance goals' you can begin to design your periodised training plan. You need to choose the appropriate training methods to develop or improve the performance qualities identified in your peak performance profile.

Goal setting is the first step in prioritising your needs for your training plan. To achieve your goals, you must next identify the specific training methods you will need to put into action. Read the relevant sport science information in this book to identify the scientific basis for your choice of training methods.

> If all you care about is winning, if you aren't enjoying the play — if the relief of not losing is the biggest emotional gain — then the best of it is lost.
> **David Kirk (All Black 1983–87)**

# GOAL ACHIEVEMENT WORKSHEET

**Name:** ..........................................................................................................................

• **Specific statement of** *performance* **goal:**

..........................................................................................................................
..........................................................................................................................
..........................................................................................................................
..........................................................................................................................
..........................................................................................................................

• **Target date for goal achievement:** ........................................................................

• **What is the 'payoff' from achieving my goal?**

..........................................................................................................................
..........................................................................................................................
..........................................................................................................................
..........................................................................................................................

• **What are the consequences of** *not* **achieving my goal?**

..........................................................................................................................
..........................................................................................................................
..........................................................................................................................
..........................................................................................................................

• **What is my** *strategy* **to achieve my goal?**

..........................................................................................................................
..........................................................................................................................
..........................................................................................................................
..........................................................................................................................

*Continued*

• Possible *obstacles* in the way of achieving my goal:

.................................................................................................
.................................................................................................
.................................................................................................

• Strategies for *overcoming* these obstacles:

.................................................................................................
.................................................................................................
.................................................................................................
.................................................................................................

• What *excuses* do I usually make?

.................................................................................................
.................................................................................................
.................................................................................................

• Is it worth the time, effort, and commitment to reach my goal?

Yes . . . . . . . No . . . . . . . Why? . . . . . . . . . . . . . . . . . . . . . . . . . . . . . . . . . . . .
.................................................................................................
.................................................................................................
.................................................................................................
.................................................................................................

## GOAL-SETTING CONTRACT

I . . . . . . . . . . . . . . . . . . . . . . . . . . . . . . . . . . . . . . . . . . . pledge that I am committed to achieving the goal that I have set out above. I will achieve this goal by following the goal achievement strategy that I have developed and outlined above. I am fully committed to this goal and my achievement strategy.

**Signed:** . . . . . . . . . . . . . . . . . . . . . . . . . . . . . . . . . . . . **Date:** . . . . . . . . . . . . . . . . . . . . . . .

**Witness:** . . . . . . . . . . . . . . . . . . . . . . . . . . . . . . . . . . **Date:** . . . . . . . . . . . . . . . . . . . . . . .

# 4 Fitness profiling

*Markus Deutsch, Gordon Sleivert*

> I was always conscious that the older I got, the harder I had to train and, being captain, I never wanted to be seen to be unfit. I was always prepared to put the work in and I did so . . . I put in a lot of time.
>
> **Sean Fitzpatrick (All Black 1986–97; Captain 1992–97)**

## Specific physical demands and fitness requirements

One of the defining features of top rugby players is that they have plenty of horsepower. However, this description is not precise enough to describe the variety of physical attributes required for an 80-minute, intermittent, high-intensity game. Although all rugby players need to be physically fit, there are large differences in the horsepower requirements between positions, and different players require different types and levels of fitness. It is not enough to be physically fit — today's player needs to be *rugby fit*!

To understand which aspects of fitness are most important to your performance it is first necessary to review the different components of fitness that are important to rugby.

### ENERGY FOR RUGBY

Whether driving forward in a scrum, running wide down the wing or kicking a penalty, all work in rugby requires a continual supply of energy in the muscles. This energy is supplied in the form of a chemical called ATP (adenosine triphosphate), which is stored in muscle. Unfortunately there is only enough ATP in the muscle for several seconds of work, and it must be continually replenished by several different energy supply systems utilising different fuels.

Which system supplies energy for any particular activity depends on the intensity and duration of the activity, and its frequency.[1] For example, on average a forward may have to perform 5 seconds of high-intensity work, followed by 40 seconds of slow jogging, walking, or standing still, during which time their body rests and attempts to recover before the next work bout. This means that on average the period of time a forward will rest between high-intensity activity is eight times longer than their previous work bout. In technical terms this is described as a work/rest ratio of 1:8. In backs, this rest period is longer and more likely to be in the range of 80–100 seconds, so most of their work/rest ratios will be between 1:15 and 1:20. That is, backs will rest for 15–20 times as long as their previous work bout before they exercise again.

Although these figures represent the *average* demands of the game, there will be times during the game when these typical rest periods are not available, increasing the energy demands even further. For instance, although the average work/rest ratio for a forward may be 1:8, up to 20 percent of their work periods will be followed by a rest period of the same or shorter duration (i.e. work/rest ratio ≤ 1:1). As will be explained shortly, it is the intensity of the work, the length of the work periods, and the work/rest ratios that determine how the energy for exercise is provided.

## ENERGY SUPPLY SYSTEMS

There are three dominant energy supply systems that are used during a rugby match. One energy system requires oxygen, and is called the aerobic system (aerobic = with oxygen). The other two systems can supply energy whether oxygen is available or not, and are therefore classified as anaerobic systems (oxygen independent). The two anaerobic systems are used during short bursts of play or high intensity phases. The aerobic system (also known as the cardiovascular system) is important during sustained phases of play and critical during the recovery phases of a rugby game.

### *The anaerobic systems (short-term power)*

#### 1. Phosphagen system

For very high-intensity exercise of short duration (less than 10 seconds) the phosphagen system supplies the majority of energy. Phosphagens are high-energy substances that are stored directly in the muscle. This energy system is the fastest and most direct method of providing energy. Its fuel, creatine phosphate, is stored directly in muscle and can most accurately be described as 'rocket fuel'.

Although this rocket fuel can support very high-intensity exercise it is used up very quickly (in less than 20 seconds),[2] and other energy supply systems must also be used to maintain horsepower over longer phases of play. Fortunately, creatine phosphate can be rapidly replenished during recovery periods.

### 2. Lactic acid system

This anaerobic system can produce energy at a similar rate to the phosphagen system, but has the advantage of being able to supply energy for several minutes, rather than seconds.[3] It uses a 'high-octane' fuel called carbohydrate (sugar) and produces lactic acid as a waste product. Lactic acid contributes to muscle fatigue, which is why this system cannot be used for longer. It is probably of most importance for forwards during rucks and mauls, or in any period of sustained high-intensity play. Forwards must have the ability to continue working

Phosphagen stores supply the bulk of the energy for backline sprints.

when lactic acid has accumulated in muscle. This is called lactic acid tolerance. It hurts!

Although it can cause fatigue, lactic acid is a 'necessary evil' in sports such as rugby. When there is not enough rest between bouts of work, or other conditions prevent the recovery of the creatine phosphate system, the lactic acid system is the only way players can sustain a high power output. This is discussed more in the next chapter.

### *The aerobic system (recovery)*

The aerobic system cannot supply energy very quickly, and in rugby it is primarily used for recovery between hard phases of play. An aerobically fit player can replenish creatine phosphate more quickly between high-intensity sprints and does not accumulate lactic acid as quickly during high-intensity phases of play. Additionally, when lactic acid does accumulate in a game and starts to cause fatigue, a player who has high levels of aerobic fitness can clear the lactate from the muscle more quickly and therefore sustain intensity better than a player who has a lower level of aerobic fitness.[4]

Aerobic fitness enables forwards to recover rapidly from scrums and other intensive set plays.

In rugby, the aerobic system mainly uses carbohydrates as fuel. The burning of this fuel requires that oxygen be present. Since oxygen is carried to the working muscles in the bloodstream, a large strong pump (heart) and good pipes (blood vessels) are critical in ensuring that oxygen delivery is optimised. This is why aerobic fitness is often referred to as cardiovascular fitness. A fit rugby player is 'all heart'!

## MUSCULAR ENDURANCE, STRENGTH AND POWER

Strength is the peak force developed during the maximal contraction of a muscle or muscle group, and can be expressed in two ways.

### Absolute strength

Absolute strength is the maximum amount of force that can be exerted. It is probably most important in tackles and scrums, where high forces must be exerted to overcome the size and momentum of opposing players. As most of these intense activities are performed while standing still or moving slowly, it is important that players in these situations can exert large forces on other players (or groups of players), but also be able to move themselves efficiently. Most of these activities require this strength to be controlled and sustained, and thus the speed of these movements is relatively slow (e.g. scrummaging). Since larger muscles are able to exert more force than smaller muscles, large individuals generally have higher levels of absolute strength and are selected for positions requiring this attribute.

### Relative strength

This is the highest level of strength possible relative to body size. It is most relevant in situations where the bodyweight must be propelled or accelerated. It is important in forwards, who must constantly reposition themselves to stay with the play, and is particularly important to loose forwards and backs. Relative strength therefore plays a large role in activities such as getting up off the ground, changing direction from forwards to backwards, and accelerating (i.e. speed off the mark).

### Muscular endurance

Muscular endurance is related to strength and is the ability to perform repeated muscular contractions with minimal fatigue (loss of force). As with strength, muscular endurance has both absolute and relative components, and is important in all activities that require repeated or sustained muscular contractions. An example of this is when a team must perform several defending scrums in quick succession, or when players are required to perform multiple phases of rucking and mauling without recovery.

### Muscular power

Muscular power is best described as a combination of strength and speed, or the ability of the muscles to contract both forcefully and quickly. Players and coaches often refer to this quality as explosive strength. When rugby fans think of power, they think of Jonah Lomu. Jonah is an excellent example of a powerful player.

Power directly influences starts, stops, direction changes, jumping ability and the ability to control any external forces (such as opposing players) that may be encountered. A high level of muscular power allows for faster starts, quicker direction changes, higher jumps and harder tackles. Passing and kicking also require muscular power.

### SPEED

Speed can be split into two parts: acceleration and maximum velocity. Acceleration reflects a player's ability to increase speed quickly and is the most important speed attribute for rugby players. This is because most plays occur within 2–10 metres and good acceleration may mean the difference between allowing a player to break through an opening or providing great cover defence.

In an open sprint most players continue to accelerate for up to 40 metres, and only rarely in a game do players reach top speed (maximum velocity). The ability to reach a high maximum velocity is most important for backs and only rarely important for forwards, as most phases of play in which they are involved occur within 10–20 metres. Several other fitness components have an effect on speed, including strength and power. It is important to remember, however, that it is difficult to turn a donkey into a thoroughbred. Although speed is somewhat trainable, it is mostly an attribute that players are born with. If you are slow, you can blame your parents!

## SPEED/POWER ENDURANCE (REPEATED SPEED)

As rugby involves between 40 and 100 work periods during a match (depending on position), the ability to repeatedly produce speed and power is very important. Especially in forwards, whose short recovery periods often do not allow for the recovery of the creatine phosphate system, the lactic acid system becomes the most important for this aspect of fitness. In fact, this element of fitness is of more importance than the ability to produce pure speed or power in the fully recovered state. This is explained in more detail in chapter 5.

## FLEXIBILITY

Flexibility is the range of motion available in a joint or series of joints. It reflects the ability of the muscles and tendons around that joint to lengthen. Good flexibility may help prevent muscle strains and tears, and may also play a role in improving skills where range of motion is important. It is possible to have too much flexibility, and this can cause instability around certain joints. For example, players who are very flexible in the shoulder may be more likely to suffer shoulder separation injuries. In our experience, however, most rugby players are not overly flexible and could benefit from a more regular whole-body stretching routine.

Stretching before and after training and games helps to prevent injuries and enhance skills.

## BODY COMPOSITION (MUSCULARITY vs FATNESS)

Rugby players come in all shapes and sizes, and this is indeed necessary for success. Forwards tend to carry more muscle and fat than backs. This provides them with a number of advantages. Higher body mass makes them difficult to move out of the way, and a large muscle mass increases their absolute strength. A little bit of extra fat also provides padding and some resistance against the knocks and blows experienced on a regular basis. Too much fat, however, is just extra baggage that must be carried around the paddock, and rapidly wears a player down.

Backs must regularly perform long sprints, and have to attain high running speeds during both defence and attack. Obviously fat will slow backs down, but so too will extra muscle. Excessively large muscles that are not directly involved in propelling a player (i.e. upper body muscles) just increase the load they have to carry around. For this reason, successful backs are generally light for their height when compared to forwards as they carry less muscle and fat.

The fitness components that are important to rugby performance are illustrated in the 'rugby fitness jigsaw' below. Not all fitness components are equally important for each position or player, and most players have their strengths and weaknesses. Our

**Rugby fitness jigsaw.**

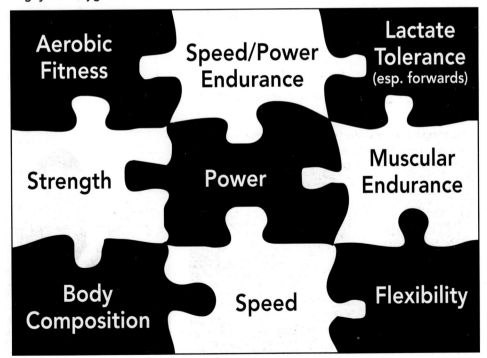

openside flanker, Ben, has filled in the worksheet to the right to identify the fitness components that are important to his position and his style of play. He can use this to evaluate his current strengths and weaknesses, using the information in the following section. You should make up a similar worksheet to list the attributes that are important to your own, or your players', performance; this can then be used as a guideline in order to decide which fitness components require further objective evaluation.

**Worksheet for Ben (openside flanker)**

| Fitness component | Importance (1–5)* |
|---|---|
| Aerobic fitness | 3 |
| Speed | 1 |
| Power | 1 |
| Strength | 3 |
| Speed/power endurance | 2 |
| Muscular endurance | 5 |
| Lactate tolerance | 2 |
| Flexibility | 4 |
| Body composition | 2 |

* 1 = important, 5 = unimportant.

## Evaluating rugby-specific fitness

You have already subjectively evaluated your fitness using the peak performance profile (chapter 2). Fitness testing will complement this by enabling you to determine your level of fitness objectively, and make it easier to set specific and measurable goals (chapter 3).

Most commonly, players are tested for fitness using field tests at their club ground or a local athletics track. Although laboratory tests can be performed at many sport science institutions, field-based testing is more practical, as large numbers of players can be tested together, and less expensive equipment is required.

In the following section some simple tests are outlined that can be used to test aspects of physical fitness that are important to rugby performance. In addition, some new rugby-specific fitness tests that have been developed at the University of Otago are outlined. These tests will help you to evaluate your strengths and weaknesses and provide you with a fitness profile. This may also help you to decide where to concentrate your training, and give you some baseline measurements for goal setting, and subsequent evaluation of whether you have reached your training goals.

Tables are provided so that you can rank your level of fitness. The fitness level that you are able to attain depends on a number of factors, including your age and gender, so you should consider this when interpreting your fitness scores.

*Age categories are not included in the tables; rather, the fitness categories are provided for athletes of average age (e.g. 20–35 years old). If you are older or younger than this your fitness scores may be a little higher or lower. For example, a young player who is smaller than usual may do well on an aerobic fitness test, yet may not do as well on a test of absolute strength or power.*

In the tables that follow, you will notice that forwards have been split into two groups. Props and locks have been grouped together, as their on-field movements are similar, and both are largely responsible for a team's scrummaging performance. Hookers have been grouped with loose forwards, as they often play a loose forward role around set plays such as lineouts.

### AEROBIC FITNESS TESTING

Based on laboratory studies, it has been shown that performance in high-intensity intermittent sports such as rugby can be improved when an athlete is able to use oxygen to produce ATP very quickly. The faster a player can use oxygen during a game, the greater their overall work rate will be and the faster their recovery during rest periods.

Your aerobic fitness is best assessed by measuring your maximum rate of oxygen consumption ($VO_2$max). This is a direct test of how fast you are able to bring oxygen into the lungs, transport it through your bloodstream to the working muscles, and use it to provide energy for exercise.[5] It is generally expressed as a volume measure corrected for bodyweight, correctly known as *relative* aerobic fitness. For example, an elite back might be able to consume a maximum of 60 ml of oxygen ($O_2$) per minute for every kilogram of their bodyweight. Their $VO_2$max would therefore be expressed as 60 ml/kg/min.

Unfortunately $VO_2$max tests require expensive equipment and technical expertise so they are not generally available to the majority of rugby players. Fortunately, there are a number of simple tests that you can use to predict your aerobic fitness. Although these tests are not quite as accurate as the laboratory $VO_2$max test, they are highly reliable and will give you consistent results when you perform repeat testing over time.

There are two popular field-based tests that have been designed to estimate $VO_2$max in the field: the Multistage Fitness Test, and the three-kilometre run. As both these tests measure a player's ability to move their own bodyweight, they are both tests of relative aerobic fitness, and can estimate a player's score in ml/kg/min. For tight forwards especially, absolute aerobic fitness is also important, as most of their work is done against other players. This is discussed further later in this chapter.

## The Multistage Fitness Test (the Beep Test)[6]

The Multistage Fitness Test (also called the Multistage Shuttle Run, or the 'Beep Test') involves repeated 20-metre shuttle runs until exhaustion. The players are required to pace themselves according to an audible beep played on a cassette. The test begins slowly, and the pace gradually quickens until the player can no longer keep up with the tempo of the recording. Once the player fails to complete two consecutive shuttles, the test is over. Their test score is the last level they reach before they fail to maintain the necessary speed

GOAL:        To complete as many 20-metre shuttle runs as possible.

EQUIPMENT:    20-metre shuttle run tape.

             20-metre measuring tape.

             Pylons or markers.

             Tape player.

**The Multistage Fitness Test.**

| Level | Run speed (km/h) | $VO_2$ max |
|-------|------------------|------------|
| 4     | 10               | 26.4       |
| 5     | 10.5             | 29.8       |
| 6     | 11               | 33.3       |
| 7     | 11.5             | 36.7       |
| 8     | 12               | 40.2       |
| 9     | 12.5             | 43.6       |
| 10    | 13               | 47.1       |
| 11    | 13.5             | 50.5       |
| 12    | 14               | 54.0       |
| 13    | 14.5             | 57.3       |
| 14    | 15               | 60.8       |
| 15    | 15.5             | 64.3       |
| 16    | 16               | 67.7       |
| 17    | 16.5             | 71.1       |
| 18    | 17               | 74.6       |

PROTOCOL:

1.  This test requires you to run between two lines (20 m apart) at a pace dictated by the cassette recording. Before you start the test you must follow the instructions on the cassette to ensure that it has not stretched and the cassette player is operating at the correct speed. The test should be performed on a consistent surface, and careful attention must be paid to ensuring that you run the full 20-metre distance in time with the voice recording.

2.  The running pace starts slowly (8.5 km/h) and increases gradually (0.5 km/h) each 1-minute stage. This is a progressive test and it will require a maximum effort by the end of the test.

3.  Your foot should cross the line in time with each beep. If you arrive at the line before a 'beep', you must wait for it before you recommence running.

4.  The test is finished when you can no longer continue or when you do not reach the end line fast enough twice in a row. Remember your last completed stage. This will be announced on the shuttle run cassette.

5.  Your test is scored by counting the number of 20-metre laps successfully completed. You can predict your $VO_2$max by referring to the table at the bottom of the previous page, and determine your fitness category from the table below.

**Fitness categories for relative $VO_2$max (ml/kg/min).**

| Position | Gender | Excellent | Average | Needs improvement |
|---|---|---|---|---|
| Props & locks | Male | > 53 | 45–50 | < 45 |
| | Female | > 45 | 40–45 | < 40 |
| Hookers & loosies | Male | > 55 | 48–52 | < 48 |
| | Female | > 48 | 42–47 | < 42 |
| Backs | Male | > 57 | 50–55 | < 50 |
| | Female | > 50 | 44–49 | < 44 |

## Three-kilometre time trial

This test involves completing a 3-km run as fast as possible on a set track. The test is best performed on a consistent surface such as an athletics track. However, it can be done on the field if the ground conditions are firm and even. The benefit of this test is that once again whole teams can be tested at once, and only a stopwatch and tape measure are needed.

GOAL:        To complete the 3-km run as fast as possible.

EQUIPMENT:    Stopwatch.

PROTOCOL:

1. Ensure you are sufficiently warmed up by performing 10 minutes of light exercise, or at least enough to break into a sweat.

2. Complete the 3 km as fast as possible and record your time to the nearest second.

3. Target lap times should be provided for players who are unfamiliar with time trials. Once players become familiar with this test they develop an appreciation of the lap times they can sustain.

4. Your $VO_2$max may be calculated using the following formula:[7]

   $VO_2$max = 0.2 (speed in metres per minute) + 3.5 (ml/kg/min)

   For example, if you completed the 3000 metres (3 km) in 15 minutes your speed is 200 m/min (3000 m / 15 min):

   $VO_2$max = 0.2 (200) + 3.5

   = 40 + 3.5

   = 43.5 ml/kg/min

5. Determine your category of fitness from the table on page 47. A value of 43.5 ml/kg/min would place you in the 'Needs improvement' category if you are a male forward, and in the 'Average' category if you are a female forward.

It is important to note that these tests are measuring your *relative* aerobic fitness, as they only involve running and therefore performance is weight-dependent. If you play in a position where much of your work must be done against other players (i.e. forwards), it is important that your weight is also taken into account. Absolute aerobic fitness may be calculated by converting the relative $VO_2max$ score expressed in ml/kg/min to the units of L/min, which ignores body mass.

For example, if relative $VO_2max$ is measured as 43.5 ml/kg/min in a 100-kg player, it can be converted to an absolute score as follows:

Step 1: relative $VO_2max$ x body mass = 43.5 ml/kg/min x 100 kg
$$= 4350 \text{ ml/min}$$

Step 2: 4350 ml/min / 1000 ml/L = 4.35 L/min

Recommended standards for absolute $VO_2max$ in forwards are shown below

**Fitness categories for absolute VO$_2$max (L/min) (based on average bodyweights of 110 kg (male), 80 kg (female) for props and locks; 100 kg (male) and 75 kg (female) for hookers and loosies).**

| Position | Gender | Excellent | Average | Needs improvement |
|---|---|---|---|---|
| Props & locks | Male | > 6.0 | 5.5 | < 5.2 |
| | Female | > 3.8 | 3.5 | < 3.2 |
| Hookers & loosies | Male | > 5.5 | 5.1 | < 4.8 |
| | Female | > 3.6 | 3.3 | < 3.0 |

## ANAEROBIC FITNESS TESTING

### Speed

As previously mentioned, the most important aspect of speed for rugby players is acceleration over distances of 5–20 metres. Occasionally, however, players are required to sprint longer distances, so speed is generally tested over distances of 40 metres. Split times may also be measured at 10-metre intervals to gauge acceleration. To make the test specific to rugby, the sprint may also be performed holding a ball in both hands.

It is particularly important that sprint testing is done on a consistent surface, as wet ground, and even wind, can greatly affect test results. The table on page 51 provides rankings for acceleration and speed over various distances.

---

### 40-metre running sprint test

GOAL:  To test acceleration, speed and fitness of the phosphagen anaerobic system.

EQUIPMENT:  2–3 stopwatches.

Tape measure.

PROTOCOL:

1. Ensure you are adequately warmed up.

2. Measure 40 metres on a running track or flat surface.

3. From a standing start, have two or three people time you over 40 metres (and splits) to the nearest 0.1 second. Calculate the average time; this will minimise any errors by the timers, and be more reliable than if only one tester is used.

4. Keep a record of your results and compare your completion times as your training progresses. See which fitness category you are in by checking the table on the facing page.

---

Another component of fitness that can be calculated from speed testing is *momentum*. Momentum is the product of speed and body size, and is important for players who want to use their size and speed to break tackles or run the 'crash ball'. Calculations of momentum are usually based on 10-metre times, as follows.

Calculation of momentum from 10-metre sprint time and body mass:

STEP 1  Convert 10-m time to speed in metres/second
Speed (m/s) = 10 (m) / time (s)

STEP 2  Multiply speed by body mass (kg)
Momentum (kg m/s) = speed (m/s) x body mass (kg)

**Speed standards (time in seconds) for rugby players.**

| Position | Gender | Sprint Distance (m) | Excellent | Average | Needs improvement |
|---|---|---|---|---|---|
| Props & locks | Male | 0–10 | < 1.9 | 2.1–2.0 | > 2.2 |
| | | 0–20 | < 3.2 | 3.5–3.3 | > 3.6 |
| | | 0–40 | < 5.7 | 6.0–5.8 | > 6.2 |
| | | 10–20 | < 1.6 | 2.0–1.8 | > 2.1 |
| | Female | 0–10 | < 2.1 | 2.3–2.1 | > 2.3 |
| | | 0–20 | < 3.4 | 3.7–3.5 | > 3.75 |
| | | 0–40 | < 6.0 | 6.2–6.0 | > 6.3 |
| | | 10–20 | < 1.8 | 2.2–2.0 | > 2.25 |
| Hookers & loosies | Male | 0–10 | < 1.8 | 2.0–1.9 | > 2.1 |
| | | 0–20 | < 3.1 | 3.4–3.2 | > 3.5 |
| | | 0–40 | < 5.6 | 5.9–5.7 | > 6.1 |
| | | 10–20 | < 1.5 | 1.9–1.8 | > 2.0 |
| | Female | 0–10 | < 2.0 | 2.2–2.0 | > 2.2 |
| | | 0–20 | < 3.3 | 3.6–3.4 | > 3.65 |
| | | 0–40 | < 5.9 | 6.1–5.9 | > 6.2 |
| | | 10–20 | < 1.75 | 2.1–1.95 | > 2.15 |
| Backs | Male | 0–10 | < 1.7 | 1.9–1.8 | > 2.0 |
| | | 0–20 | < 3.0 | 3.3–3.1 | > 3.4 |
| | | 0–40 | < 5.5 | 5.8–5.6 | > 6.0 |
| | | 10–20 | < 1.4 | 1.8–1.7 | > 1.9 |
| | Female | 0–10 | < 1.9 | 2.1–1.95 | > 2.1 |
| | | 0–20 | < 3.2 | 3.5–3.3 | > 3.55 |
| | | 0–40 | < 5.85 | 6.0–5.8 | > 6.1 |
| | | 10–20 | < 1.70 | 2.0–1.85 | > 2.05 |

FOR EXAMPLE:

If a 110-kg prop covers 10 metres in 1.6 seconds:

Speed     = 10 / 1.6
         = 6.25 m/s

Momentum = 6.25 x 110
         = 687.5 kg m/s

**Some standards for typical momentum scores (kg m/s).**

| Position | Gender | Excellent | Average | Needs improvement |
|---|---|---|---|---|
| Props & locks | Male | > 600 | 530–560 | < 500 |
| | Female | > 420 | 380–400 | < 350 |
| Hookers & loosies | Male | > 540 | 480–500 | < 460 |
| | Female | > 400 | 370–390 | < 360 |

## Speed endurance

Speed endurance tests involve a series of sprints separated by short recovery periods.

GOAL: To test ability to maintain speed over repeated sprints.

EQUIPMENT: Stopwatch(es).

Tape measure.

PROTOCOL:

1. Ensure you are adequately warmed up.

2. Measure 40 metres on a running track or flat surface.

3. The speed endurance test involves 10 x 40-metre sprints, with 30 seconds total given for each sprint. For example, if the player completes a sprint in 5 seconds, they will have 25 seconds recovery before the next sprint. The test set-up is shown at right. The player sprints 40 metres, then jogs a further 40 metres, then turns and waits for the next 30-second period to start.

4. The time taken to complete the 40-metre sprint is recorded, and the procedure is repeated until each player has completed 10 sprints (five in each direction).

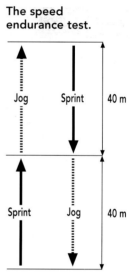

The speed endurance test.

Two or three people are required to administer this test. The first person controls the rolling time and tells the player when they are required to sprint again, the second writes down the sprint times, while the third ensures the clock is reset after each sprint. As for speed testing, the results will be more accurate if you use two timers to measure the sprints and average the times for each sprint.

To make the speed endurance test easier, eight repetitions can be performed rather than ten and a 40-second turnaround can be used.

Two results can be determined from this test:

1.  Speed decrement (%) = $\dfrac{\text{slowest 40 m} - \text{fastest 40 m} \times 100}{\text{fastest 40 m}}$

2.  Speed endurance = average time over 10 sprints

Recommended standards are listed in the table below. Rapid fatigue may be the result of a number of factors, including low levels of aerobic fitness or lack of training history with repeated high-intensity sprints (see chapter 5).

**Speed endurance test (40-metre sprint every 30 seconds) standards for rugby players.**

| Position | Gender | Fatigue index | Excellent | Average | Needs improvement |
|---|---|---|---|---|---|
| Props & locks | Male | Speed decrement (%) | < 7% | 8–12% | > 12% |
| | | Mean speed (s) | < 5.9 | 6–6.2 | > 6.3 |
| | Female | Speed decrement (%) | < 8% | 9–13% | > 13% |
| | | Mean speed (s) | < 6.2 | 6.3–6.4 | > 6.4 |
| Hookers & loosies | Male | Speed decrement (%) | < 6% | 7–11% | > 11% |
| | | Mean speed (s) | < 5.8 | 5.9–6.2 | > 6.2 |
| | Female | Speed decrement (%) | < 7% | 8–12% | > 12% |
| | | Mean speed (s) | < 6.1 | 6.2–6.4 | > 6.4 |
| Backs | Male | Speed decrement (%) | < 5% | 6–10% | > 10% |
| | | Mean speed (s) | < 5.7 | 5.8–6.0 | > 6.1 |
| | Female | Speed decrement (%) | < 6% | 7–11% | > 11% |
| | | Mean speed (s) | < 6.0 | 6.1–6.3 | > 6.3 |

This speed endurance test must be considered along with absolute speed results because it is possible to have a very good fatigue ratio but be consistently slow. In fact, the fastest players often have the largest speed decrements. Their well-developed anaerobic energy supply systems allow them to run fast, but these systems also generate lactic acid, which causes fatigue — hence a high fatigue ratio.

For example, Ben has performed this test and averaged 5.9 seconds over 10 x 40-metre sprints. His fastest sprint was 5.7 seconds and his slowest was 6.3 seconds. We can calculate his fatigue ratio as:

Fatigue ratio (%) = (slowest time − fastest time) / slowest time x 100

$$= (6.3 - 5.7) / 6.3 \times 100$$

$$= 9.5 \%$$

Ben's flatmate, Jack (a prop), has also performed the test and averaged 6.4 seconds over the 10 x 40-metre sprints. His fastest time was 6.2 seconds and his slowest 6.5 seconds. When the fatigue ratio is calculated as above it comes to 4.6%. Although Jack's fatigue ratio is much better than Ben's it can readily be seen that even Ben's slowest time is practically equivalent to Jack's fastest time. Therefore it can be inappropriate to compare fatigue ratios between players. Rather, it is most appropriate to use this test as an index of change within yourself, or one of your players. As fitness improves you should observe lower fatigue ratios.

To compare yourself with others or to compare players, it is probably most appropriate just to calculate average sprint time in this test. Not only does this indicate something about speed, but it also indicates relative speed endurance. For example, Ben's average sprint time in the speed endurance test was 5.9 seconds compared to Jack's average time of 6.4 seconds. This indicates that on average Ben can maintain a higher speed than Jack, despite a higher speed decrement in this test (6.4 vs 4.6%). In training Ben may still want to aim to increase his speed endurance, and Jack could benefit from working on his acceleration and sprint speed.

Another option is to combine the speed endurance test with the speed test by simply taking the first sprint in the test as the speed result. The advantages of this are that two fitness tests can be combined into one, and it ensures that players are sprinting as fast as possible on the first sprint of the speed endurance test.

Speed endurance can also be tested using a 400-metre run. However, as this test involves only one longer work bout, it is more a test of lactate tolerance than of the ability to perform repeated short sprints. Although it is not as specific to rugby it still provides useful results and is a somewhat easier test to administer, particularly to large groups.

## 400-metre run

GOAL:         To test speed endurance.

EQUIPMENT:   Stopwatch.

PROTOCOL:

1. Ensure you are adequately warmed up.

2. From a standing start run 400 metres as fast as possible on a running track or flat surface and record your time to the nearest 0.1 second.

3. Keep a record of your results and compare your completion times as your training progresses.

4. Compare your time with those recorded below to see which fitness category you are in.

**400-metre run standards (time in seconds) for rugby players.**

| Position | Gender | Excellent | Average | Needs improvement |
|----------|--------|-----------|---------|-------------------|
| Props & locks | Male | 68 | 74 | 79 |
|  | Female | 72 | 77 | 83 |
| Hookers & loosies | Male | 66 | 71 | 75 |
|  | Female | 69 | 75 | 79 |
| Backs | Male | 68 | 74 | 79 |
|  | Female | 72 | 77 | 83 |

## Muscular strength, endurance and power

### Strength

As mentioned earlier, there are two ways that we can look at strength: absolute strength and relative strength.

➤ *Absolute strength* can be measured using weights, machines, or even concrete blocks! The most common way is to measure the maximum amount of weight a person can lift for a given number of repetitions, also known as a repetition maximum (RM). For example, if a prop could bench press only three times with a weight of 100 kg, we would say that player had a 3 RM of 100 kg. It is possible to assess strength with anything from a 1 RM test to, say, a 5 RM test. Although the 1 RM test is a better measure of absolute strength, this kind of lifting can be dangerous to players who aren't used to these sorts of loads during training. In many cases, a 3 or 4 RM test will give more consistent results and be safer for the player. With younger players, either relative strength tests or high-repetition (e.g. 12 RM) strength tests should be used for safety.

➤ *Relative strength*, as explained earlier, is strength relative to a player's bodyweight. The easiest way to test relative strength, therefore, is to use your weight as the resistance. Examples of these tests include chin-ups, push-ups, abdominal tests, and dips. The aim of such tests is to see how many repetitions of each exercise a player can do.

The best strength tests are those that are specific to the activities encountered during a game. For example, a bench press will tell you about a player's strength at fending off tacklers, while a close grip chin-up will mimic a ripping or wrestling movement. The following are some recommended strength tests for rugby:

➤ Bench press

➤ Close grip reverse chin-up

➤ Upright or bent-over row

➤ Half squat or lunge

It is important to note that these exercises should also be used as part of the players' weight-training regime, so that when it comes to testing, all the players are equally familiar with them.

## Absolute strength: Four-repetition maximum (4 RM) strength test

GOAL: To determine the maximum amount of weight that can be lifted four times for a given exercise.

EQUIPMENT: Universal gym-type equipment or free weights (free weights preferable).

PROTOCOL:

1. Ensure you are adequately warmed up.

2. You can test either upper body (bench press, chin-up, or row) or lower body strength (half squat or lunge).

3. Start the test by performing 4 repetitions slowly and in control, with a weight that can be lifted 8–10 times (8–10 repetitions maximum [RM]).

4. After 3 minutes' rest, increase the weight by one plate (about 5 kg) and again attempt 4 repetitions.

5. Repeat this procedure until 4 repetitions cannot be completed.

6. The last weight that was successfully lifted for 4 repetitions is the 4 RM weight for that exercise and represents the absolute strength score. This value divided by bodyweight gives strength-to-weight ratio and is the relative strength score. Check your strength fitness category in the table below and the tables on page 58.

**Absolute strength rankings for bench press.**

| Bodywt (kg) | 4 RM Bench Press (kg) | | | | | |
| | Excellent | | Satisfactory | | Needs improvement | |
| | Male | Female | Male | Female | Male | Female |
|---|---|---|---|---|---|---|
| 60 | 63 | 44 | 53 | 37 | 46 | 32 |
| 70 | 73 | 51 | 62 | 43 | 54 | 38 |
| 80 | 84 | 59 | 70 | 49 | 62 | 43 |
| 90 | 94 | 66 | 79 | 55 | 69 | 49 |
| 100 | 105 | 73 | 88 | 62 | 77 | 54 |
| 110 | 115 | 80 | 97 | 68 | 85 | 59 |
| 120 | 125 | 88 | 106 | 74 | 92 | 65 |

*(CONTINUED)*

Absolute strength rankings for half squat.

| Bodywt (kg) | 4 RM Half Squat (kg) | | | | | |
| | Excellent | | Satisfactory | | Needs improvement | |
| | Male | Female | Male | Female | Male | Female |
|---|---|---|---|---|---|---|
| 60 | 103 | 72 | 86 | 60 | 76 | 53 |
| 70 | 120 | 84 | 101 | 71 | 88 | 62 |
| 80 | 137 | 96 | 115 | 81 | 101 | 71 |
| 90 | 154 | 108 | 130 | 91 | 113 | 79 |
| 100 | 171 | 120 | 144 | 101 | 126 | 88 |
| 110 | 188 | 132 | 158 | 111 | 139 | 97 |
| 120 | 205 | 144 | 173 | 121 | 151 | 106 |

Relative strength rankings for bench press and half squat tests.

| | Bench Press | | Half Squat | |
| | Male | Female | Male | Female |
|---|---|---|---|---|
| Excellent | 1.1 | 0.8 | 2.0 | 1.8 |
| Satisfactory | 0.90 | 0.5 | 1.7 | 1.5 |
| Needs improvement | 0.75 | 0.4 | 1.4 | 1.2 |

## Muscular endurance tests

Local muscular endurance is generally tested using calisthenic-type tests such as push-ups, sit-ups, or a prone bridge hold. Your scores on these tests can be used to monitor changes in endurance of the upper body and trunk region (abdominals).

Jonah Lomu is not only strong in the weight room, he uses this strength to dominate the opposition.

## Push-ups or sit-ups

GOAL: To perform as many push-ups/sit-ups as possible using correct technique and in a controlled manner.

EQUIPMENT: Metronome set for 50 beats per minute (25 push-ups or sit-ups performed per minute). If you don't have a metronome you can estimate this pace by counting (e.g. 'Up - 1 - 1000, down - 1 - 1000, up - 2 - 1000, down - 2 - 1000').

A flat surface and a mat.

PROTOCOL:

*Push-ups*

1. Start face down, hands placed so that your thumbs are under your shoulders, arms fully extended and feet together.

2. Lower your body until your elbows are bent to a 90-degree angle then push up, pivoting on your toes to the beat of the metronome (down on one beat, up on the next).

3. Continue until you can no longer keep pace with the metronome or can't continue with proper technique. Record the total number of repetitions.

*Sit-ups*

1. Lie on your back, with your knees bent at 90 degrees, hands beside your ears and elbows pointed forward.

2. Curl up on one beat so that your elbows touch your thighs, while keeping your buttocks and heels on the floor. Lower your body on the next beat so that your shoulder blades touch the floor.

3. Continue until you can't keep pace with the metronome or you violate one of the following test rules three times: (a) lose pace with the metronome; (b) hands come in front of your ears; (c) elbows do not touch thighs; (d) buttocks come off floor; (e) feet come off floor. Record the total number of repetitions.

4. Compare your scores with those in the table on page 60 to determine your current level of muscular endurance.

## Prone bridge hold

GOAL: To hold a prone bridge for as long as possible using correct technique and in a controlled manner.

EQUIPMENT: A flat surface and a mat.

PROTOCOL:

1. Lie on your stomach with your feet together and your forearms on the ground at shoulder width.

2. Look forward, and raise your trunk off the ground so that your back is flat and your weight is supported on your forearms and on your toes (as for a push-up).

3. The aim of the test is to maintain a flat back and strict posture for as long as possible.

4. Record the time (seconds) it takes until a flat back can no longer be maintained, and you either raise or lower your hips.

**Fitness categories for muscular endurance.**

| | Sit-ups (no. of reps) | | Push-ups (no. of reps) | | Prone Bridge (min) | |
|---|---|---|---|---|---|---|
| | Male | Female | Male | Female | Male | Female |
| Excellent | > 32 | > 25 | > 30 | > 25 | > 3.0 | > 2.5 |
| Satisfactory | 25–32 | 15–25 | 20–30 | 15–25 | 2.0–2.5 | 1.8–2.2 |
| Needs improvement | < 25 | < 15 | < 20 | < 15 | < 2.0 | < 1.8 |

### Muscular power tests

Power is the combination of strength and speed. Once again, it has absolute and relative components. Players who are more powerful (in absolute terms) than other players are more likely to be successful in the contact parts of the game (tackling, rucking, mauling). Players who are powerful for their size (relative power) will be better equipped for accelerating and changing direction quickly. There are a range of field tests for both relative and absolute power.

Relative power can be measured using tests that are bodyweight-dependent, such as the vertical jump and standing long or broad jumps. To get accurate results, it is important that players are shown the correct techniques. Absolute power tests must always contain an external object that players push against. Examples include a medicine ball throw and powerlifting.

A new development for testing absolute power in rugby players is known as the GRUNT 3000. This piece of equipment accurately measures power output for activities such as rucking and mauling, and absolute strength for static pushing as in scrums. The benefit of this system is that it measures power as it is specific to rugby, and can thus be used as a tool for testing, training and coaching.

When choosing power tests, it is important that the movements used in the tests are also used during training. Otherwise some players will improve without actually getting more powerful. They will just get better at the test!

You can assess your muscular power quite simply through a jump test. These are particularly useful in the assessment of leg power since they primarily utilise the buttock and thigh muscles, which are instrumental in many sports activities. These tests are best used to monitor changes in muscular power throughout a training year, so testing must be performed regularly.

The GRUNT 3000 test is a new development in power testing for rugby players.

## The vertical jump test

GOAL: To jump as high as possible.

EQUIPMENT: A smooth wall of sufficient height.
Measuring tape.
Chalk.

PROTOCOL:

1. Ensure you are sufficiently warmed up.

2. Mark the fingertips of your dominant hand with chalk.

3. Position yourself parallel to a mark measured 20 cm from the wall, and reach as high as possible with your dominant arm to mark the wall, while keeping your feet flat on the ground and the opposite arm at the side of your body. This measure is considered to be your standing reach.

4. Assume the jump position; i.e. bend your knees to 90 degrees, extend both arms behind your body, and keep your arms and legs still.

5. Once in the jump position, jump and mark the wall as high as possible. Three trials are given, the first being a practice trial.

6. Measure the difference between standing reach height and maximal jump height and record to the nearest centimetre. This value is the *vertical jump score*. Check your score against those in the table on the facing page to see which fitness category you are in.

Standing phase.

Squatting phase.

Jumping phase.

## The two-step jump test

This test is an appropriate measure of explosive horizontal power.

GOAL:            To jump as far as possible.

EQUIPMENT:    Adequate floor space.
                 Masking tape.
                 A 10-metre measuring tape.

PROTOCOL:

1. Ensure you have adequately warmed up.

2. Tape a jump starting line to the floor and fix the 10-metre measuring tape at 90 degrees to this line.

Stride start.

3. Starting with one foot forward and from a one-foot take-off, jump as far as possible, landing on the opposite foot and immediately pushing off with the landed foot to jump as far as possible onto both feet. Three trials are given, the first being a practice trial.

One-footed landing.

4. After landing, the distance from the starting line to the athlete's heels is recorded to the nearest cm. The best of the last two trials is taken as the final score. Check your score against those in the table below to see which fitness category you are in.

Double-footed finish.

**Fitness categories for muscular power.**

|  | Vertical Jump (cm) | | Two-step Jump (cm) | |
| --- | --- | --- | --- | --- |
|  | Male | Female | Male | Female |
| Excellent | > 62 | > 47 | > 500 | > 375 |
| Satisfactory | 55–62 | 41–47 | 425–500 | 320–375 |
| Needs improvement | < 55 | < 41 | < 425 | < 320 |

## OTHER ASPECTS OF FITNESS

There are many other aspects of anaerobic fitness that are important for rugby.

### Flexibility

Since flexibility is joint-specific there is no one test that is relevant for all sports. The most common assessment is a test of trunk, back and hamstring flexibility, since this is thought to be especially important in the prevention of lower back problems.

---

### Sit and reach test

GOAL: To bend as far forward as possible using the correct form, in order to assess the flexibility of the trunk, back and hamstrings.

EQUIPMENT: Metre stick.
Bench.
Block of wood.

PROTOCOL:

1. Ensure you are adequately warmed up then sit on the floor with the bottom of your feet flat up against the legs of the bench and your knees locked straight.

2. Attach the metre stick to the bench so that the '0' end is closest to you and the soles of your feet are at the 26-cm mark.

3. Bend forward very slowly, exhale, and with your arms extended push your fingers along the metre stick. Keep your knees straight and the push smooth, not jerky.

4. Have someone measure the distance that you have been able to push your fingers, to the nearest cm, and take the best of two trials as your flexibility score. Check the table below to see which flexibility category you fit into.

| | Excellent | Satisfactory | Needs improvement |
|---|---|---|---|
| Male | > 40 | 31–40 | < 31 |
| Female | > 41 | 32–40 | < 32 |

## Body composition

Simply knowing a player's weight does not tell us much about body composition, but tests exist that can estimate how much of our body's mass is fat and how much is muscle. One problem, however, is that these tests require a high degree of expertise on the part of the tester in order to get reliable results.

The most common method of assessing body composition is skinfold testing (or a 'pinch test'). This involves measuring the thickness of fat deposits at various sites on the body, and using these measurements as an indicator of how much body fat a player has. If you would like one of these tests, contact your local sport-science service provider.

## The Rugby-Specific Fitness Test (RSFT)

The RSFT is an example of how sport science is entering the game of rugby. Developed at the University of Otago, the RSFT is a military-style circuit test that has been designed to mimic the demands of 10 minutes of high-intensity match play. The test involves a variety of movements and directional changes, sprints over various specific distances, and measurements of specific power and strength using the GRUNT 3000 (page 61). There are tests for forwards and backs, based on data from time-motion analysis studies conducted at Otago.

The advantage of the RSFT is that it gives a measure of actual rugby fitness, rather than testing each element of fitness in isolation, as happens with the tests on the previous pages. Although it is important to see how each element is improving, it is match fitness that is most important at the end of the day.

As the RSFT requires a lot more equipment than most of the tests already described, it may not be accessible to many players at the non-elite level. The concept behind the RSFT, specificity, should be applied to all levels of rugby when choosing fitness tests, and especially when putting together training plans. How this can be done effectively is discussed in the following chapter.

# 5 Improving fitness

## *Gordon Sleivert, Markus Deutsch*

No words of ours can express too emphatically what we consider to be the extreme importance to the player of Rugby Football who aspires to skill and honour, of regular and consistent training on a sound and sensible system.

**Dave Gallaher and Billy Stead (All Black captain and vice captain 1905)**

This chapter is designed to provide 'a sound and sensible system' to help you achieve your fitness potential. First, though, we'll review some general training principles so you can ensure that your rugby training is *smart training*.

## Training principles

### THE OVERLOAD PRINCIPLE

In order for any fitness component to improve it must be overloaded.
To obtain optimal improvement and prevent injury, overload must be individualised and progressive.

The overload principle is the most important of the training principles. 'Overload' means exercising your body beyond the level to which it is accustomed. For example, if you are used to running 3 km every second day, continuing your training programme without increasing the intensity or duration of your run will not cause further improvements in your aerobic fitness. You are not overloading your aerobic system. To improve your fitness you need either to increase the duration of your runs, or to increase their intensity (i.e. run harder). When you overload your body through regular physical activity it does not wear out and become weaker, rather it becomes stronger and fitter.

It is often thought that for a session to be productive, the player must be fatigued by the end of it. This may be true if you are trying to improve endurance or lactate tolerance, but it does not apply when training some other aspects of fitness. For example, if the goal of a session is to increase sprint speed or scrummaging power, then in order to overload that element of performance, long rest periods must be taken between repetitions, so that the player can concentrate on *high-quality*, powerful movements. They may not be breathless for the whole session, or be fatigued at the end of it, but they will still have overloaded a particular element of fitness.

There are a number of different ways to overload any one fitness component. In each case there are four main factors that you must consider. These form the basis of the FITT principle.

## THE FITT PRINCIPLE

---

Optimal training overload relies on the proper manipulation of the frequency (F), intensity (I), time (T) and type (T) of training.

---

Training *frequency* is the number of weekly training sessions you do for any particular fitness component. You must train regularly if you are to improve fitness; it is not enough to load a particular fitness component once every few weeks. Optimal training frequency varies according to your level of fitness and what fitness component you are training. In general, to improve aerobic fitness you need to exercise at least three days a week, but if you are less fit you may notice improvement when training as little as twice a week. Muscular strength, speed and power may be improved by training these components two to three times a week.

Training *intensity* represents the degree of physical effort required in a training session, i.e. how hard you work or how vigorous an activity is. Aerobic system intensity is usually measured by monitoring your pulse (heart rate) or perceived exertion (how difficult does this feel?).

In weight training, intensity refers to the load that is being lifted. For example, if you can bench press 40 kg ten times then that load is equal to an intensity of 10 repetitions maximum (10 RM). Most general strength training programmes recommend training with a load that can be lifted 8–12 times (8–12 RM).

The measure of training intensity for most anaerobic sprint training is based either on perceived exertion or a known pace, e.g. you might run 150 metres at 30 seconds

**Optimal training zone.**

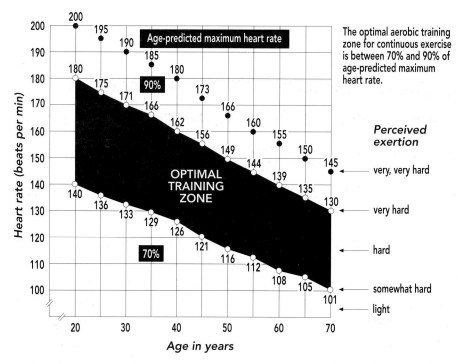

pace. It is very important to monitor your training intensity. Many players train at either too low or too high an intensity, but you cannot adjust your training programme (e.g. increase or decrease intensity) if you don't know what intensity you are training at.

The *time* you spend training is generally used as an indicator of how much training you are doing in a particular session. In aerobic and sprint training both time and distance are frequently monitored. In weight training, time is generally not monitored; instead the number of repetitions and sets of repetitions give an indication of training duration.

Time or distance can also be monitored for individual exercise intervals to help target the training of particular energy systems within the body. Activities of very short duration (5–10 seconds) primarily load the short-term phosphagen anaerobic systems, while slightly longer training times (20 seconds to 1 minute) primarily load the lactic acid anaerobic system. Exercise intervals longer than 2 minutes primarily load the aerobic system.

It is important to remember, however, that with any exercise interval you are not just training one energy system. This is because the energy systems are used

Depending on your training goal, the load lifted during resistance training should vary.

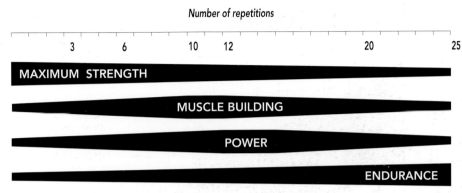

Number of repetitions

concurrently; for example, even during a 5-second interval the aerobic system is supplying a small amount of energy, the lactic acid system is supplying some energy and the phosphagen system is also being used (see figure below). It is therefore not surprising that a certain amount of cross-training occurs between energy systems during high-intensity work. You can, however, use time or distance as a guide to which energy system you are primarily overloading, assuming you are exercising as hard as you can over a given distance. By using a mixture of distances, two or more energy systems can be overloaded within one session.

The *type* of training you do is obviously important — it doesn't make sense to train fitness components that are not relevant to your sport. Similarly, it makes little

**Energy systems used during maximal effort runs of various lengths.**

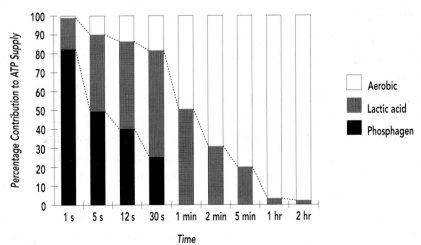

sense to train muscles that are not involved specifically in the movements used in your sport or position, or to train relevant muscles in a non-specific fashion. This is the basis of the 'specificity principle'.

## THE SPECIFICITY PRINCIPLE

———

The characteristics of the training load must be specific to the movement, muscles and energy systems of the sport you are training for.

———

Basically, the specificity principle states that if you want to improve in an activity, then performing that activity is the best way to do it. It has repeatedly been shown that fitness improvement is specific to the muscles and movements used in the training programme. It is therefore important to try to keep your training as rugby-specific as possible, regardless of what fitness component you are training. While it is obviously not practical for players to play a game two or three times a week, if you can use specific elements of the game in training, then the on-field benefits clearly will be greater.

Specificity has two main elements — energetic and mechanical. 'Energetic' refers to the particular energy system(s) supplying most of the energy, and to the intensity and duration of both the work and rest periods. 'Mechanical' refers to factors such as body position, impacts, and changing from one muscle group to another. When planning training, both these elements need to be taken into account.

The physical demands of rugby are unique and complex. Rugby players need to be fit in many areas, such as strength, power, speed, aerobic fitness, and so on. They need to use all of the major muscle groups, and must constantly switch from lower to upper body exertion. Rugby is also a very inefficient activity, with players having to swap from one movement to another. All these factors must be considered when putting together specific training for rugby players.

There are times when it is not possible to apply the specificity principle directly. For example, if you are injured you may not be able to run and you may have to perform some alternative exercise. Keeping the specificity principle in mind, aqua-running would be a better choice than cycling, but cycling would still be better than doing nothing. If you have to cross-train because of injury, try to mimic rugby movements closely. If you are a large and heavy rugby forward weighing in excess of 120 kg, aspects of your training may also require some variation from the specificity principle since long-duration high-impact activities such as running may put you at risk of injuries such as shin splints. In this situation an activity such as stair climbing

All Black prop Carl Hoeft training in the water.

or circuit training would be reasonably sport specific while avoiding the potentially risky repeated impacts associated with running.

When you overload your body through exercise training, its initial response is breakdown and fatigue. The exercise session generally causes some depletion of the fuels stored in muscle, and can even cause some tissue damage. This is not a bad thing. It is a necessary step toward improving your fitness. With adequate recovery, for example an easy day between hard training sessions, the various systems of the body respond to this general breakdown by replenishing fuel stores and repairing tissue damage. In fact, you are rebuilt to be stronger and more fit so you are better able to handle your next exercise session and any damage it may cause.

That is why, if you are to maximise your training gains, you must gradually increase your training. If you keep the training durations and intensities the same, after a while your body will be able to cope with it and the training will no longer be effective for improving fitness.

Remember, however, it is possible to have too much of a good thing. That is, if you apply too much overload too quickly your body will not be able to adapt and you may become injured or overtrained. Introduce changes in the length or intensity of your exercise sessions gradually. Similarly, remember that recovery is as important as exercise! It is not recommended that you train hard every day. By interspersing hard and easy physical training days you will allow your body time to recover and adapt to increasing exercise durations and intensities. This is the basis of the 'rest principle'.

## THE REST PRINCIPLE

———

To optimise fitness improvements, training sessions must be interspersed with rest sessions.

———

Rest does not always mean complete time off, but you can build recovery into your training programme by having light days and using a variety of training methods. In addition to interspersing rest through your training week, you should also incorporate rest weeks regularly throughout your training year. For example, after two or three weeks of hard training you should insert an easier training week.

The difficulty with this is often translating planning into action. It is not easy to talk yourself into a recovery week when your training has been going really well and you are feeling highly motivated. Conversely, when they are feeling tired, or perhaps nursing a niggling injury, motivated players will often try to squeeze out one more good week of training. This can be counterproductive.

Don't use the need for rest as an excuse to take it easy, but remember — *listen to your body*. If you start to notice negative trends in your training logbook (e.g. restless sleep, persistent fatigue or poor workouts), by all means *train smart* and use the rest principle.

**Optimal recovery allows the body to realise maximum fitness gains with every training session.**

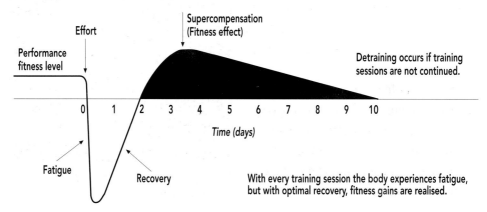

# Amount of training

Considering the previous discussion, you might ask 'How much training should I do?' In the early part of the off-season you may have a relatively small training load, but as the season progresses the load will increase. So, how do you know how much training to undertake during the various training periods? How much training is too much?

There is a fine line between being in excellent condition and performing well, and being just over the line and performing poorly because niggling injuries, extreme tiredness, or viral infections hamper your training. You want to be in the best condition possible at competition time, but the more you push yourself in training the more likely it is that you will become vulnerable to illness and injury. There is a limit to how much of a training load you can sustain from day to day. We call this limit your 'overtraining threshold'.

The idea is to train just below your threshold, so that you get maximum returns from your training without overtraining. It's okay to undertake brief (up to one week) periods of a high training load above your threshold, but if you train very hard for too long (more than a couple of weeks) you may end up with long-term (chronic) overtraining problems. The classic warning signs of imminent overtraining are a loss of confidence, mood swings (beyond normal), frequent depression or irritability, loss of appetite, or diminished quality of sleep. You may also experience long-term medical problems (such as flu, colds, chest or throat infections). Often you won't notice these warning signs yourself, so make sure you listen to your coach, training partner, or family if they become aware of such signs.

Stress in other areas of your life can also contribute to chronic or ongoing overtraining, and it is important to be aware of this danger. For example, viral infections (e.g. colds, flu) and increased mental stresses at work, with a partner

Training too hard is counterproductive; aim to train just below your threshold.

Naturally gifted athletes like Christian Cullen enjoy a headstart in the training stakes, but still need to apply themselves to building up fitness.

or because of financial problems can all have the effect of lowering your overtraining threshold. If you are under greater stress than normal, be prepared to reduce your training load so you don't overtrain.

Since we are discussing the flexibility of your training programme it is appropriate to consider how you individually respond to training, and therefore how your training programme can be individualised. The same programme will not be equally effective for everyone since people respond to training in different ways. There are 'high' and 'low' responders to physical training.[1] With the same amount of training, 'high responders' are capable of improving fitness greatly, while 'low responders' will improve to a much lesser extent.

Similarly, there are 'early' and 'late' responders to training. Some people show improvement early in a training programme, while others take much longer to improve. Of course we all wish to be both high and early responders to training, but this is rarely the case. Therefore, you need to be both flexible and patient when designing and implementing your training programme.

If you notice in your training logbook that your fitness is improving very quickly, you may be able to introduce longer training sessions or increased intensities sooner than you had planned. Alternatively, you may have to delay increases in the duration or intensity of training if you find that improvements are small or are taking a long time. Don't despair — be patient. You have to work with the body you've been given!

### THE INDIVIDUALISATION PRINCIPLE

———

Training benefits are optimised when programmes are planned
and if necessary adjusted to meet your individual needs
and capabilities.

———

Individuals who have been training for a number of years will be closer to their fitness potential than those who have just begun; with less room for improvement, they will receive only small improvements in fitness for large investments of training time. If you fall into this category your fitness goals should reflect this, and should be conservative. Often, players who have been training for a number of years will be very close to their genetic ceiling in one area (e.g. aerobic fitness), but have a large potential for improvement in other areas (e.g. flexibility, anaerobic fitness). By training their weak areas they can vastly improve their performance.

If you are an experienced player it might pay to examine your peak performance profile (chapter 2) or your fitness test results to see whether this is true for you. On the other hand, if you haven't done much targeted training then you will probably improve by doing almost any physical training.

## THE CEILING PRINCIPLE

---

As fitness levels increase, the relative and absolute improvements
in fitness will decrease — even with progressive overload.

---

It can be difficult to overload all the components of fitness that are important to rugby. If you are not well trained, it is not advisable to try and train your aerobic fitness, strength and speed all at once. For one thing you would simply run out of time, and you would also become fatigued and overtrained very rapidly. Yet rugby demands fitness in a variety of areas, and players usually need to train a number of fitness components. Well-trained players with long training histories actually train a number of fitness components concurrently because they are not looking for major gains in their fitness base. This type of training allows greater emphasis to be placed on speed and anaerobic development since strength and aerobic fitness are already well developed and require less attention.

For young or developing players a sequenced training programme is best. The major emphasis in the off-season should be to improve aerobic fitness and strength. As the rugby season approaches, more emphasis is placed on developing anaerobic fitness, speed and power. During these latter training periods, aerobic and strength fitness is simply maintained, not overloaded. In fact, during the competitive season all fitness training may simply be maintenance training, and the total amount of training may actually be reduced. This is necessary to ensure adequate recovery — not only will your body be fatigued from physical training sessions, but games and practices will contribute to overall fatigue.

In general, to maintain a particular fitness component for up to three months, the frequency of training of that component may be cut by two-thirds as long as the intensity and duration of each workout is maintained. For example, if you are strength training three times a week you can decrease your training frequency to once a week and maintain strength as long as you don't change the amount of weight you are lifting, the number of repetitions you perform with that weight, or the number of sets of repetitions you perform in each session. If you drop the intensity of the training, rather than the volume, then the strength you have developed will not be maintained.

### THE MAINTENANCE PRINCIPLE

———

Loss of fitness may be prevented by maintaining the intensity and duration of exercise sessions while decreasing frequency by two-thirds.

———

# Tapering

Tapering is the process of physical 'fine-tuning' immediately prior to competition. It is traditionally used in individual sports where major competitions are infrequent. During a taper the duration of physical training is gradually reduced by the same amount each day, while intensity is maintained, until only a competition warm-up or light skills session is completed the day before competition. This type of taper has been shown to provide a three to five percent improvement in performance, as opposed to a taper that reduces duration while intensity is only moderate.[2]

Since rugby involves regular competition it is impossible to taper in the same way as in other sports, but the principle of tapering is still important. Each week your preparation should consist of a high training load at the beginning of the week, tapering through to the next competition. Again, you should reduce the duration of the physical training as the taper progresses, but maintain the intensity. During the taper the emphasis should shift from physical training sessions at the start of the week to less taxing skills sessions and mental/tactical preparation by the end of the taper. In this way you can be sure to maximise your fitness and minimise your fatigue before each game.

For example, Ben, our flanker, has had a hard game on Saturday afternoon, and has to play again the following Saturday. During the week, he wants to do one hard weights session and one interval session, and he has two team skill sessions. After a bruising encounter like Saturday, he can only do some low-intensity pool work on Sunday before his first team training on Monday night. His interval and weights sessions must then be done on Tuesday and Wednesday, before a light team run on

While running is a core part of rugby training, strength training and whole body fitness are also vital.

Thursday and a complete rest on Friday ahead of the Saturday game. By allowing adequate recovery, Ben will be fresh for the hard but short sessions mid-week, but will have Thursday and Friday to recover for Saturday's game.

You are now familiar with the training principles that should guide you in the development of your personalised physical training plan. You may already have a good understanding of the physical training needs of your playing position and your current development in each of the relevant fitness components. However, in case you have never designed your own training programme, some specific guidelines are provided here to get you climbing the staircase to peak performance.

## The aerobic system

Training can improve your aerobic fitness by as much as 30 percent, depending on your initial fitness level. There are two main methods of training: continuous training and interval training. As rugby is traditionally known as a running game, most aerobic training tends to focus on running activities. However, since the upper body is also used in most rugby activities, training should also target these muscle groups (specificity principle). A third type of training, called functional endurance training, is designed to improve your whole body aerobic fitness in a rugby-specific manner.

### CONTINUOUS TRAINING

Continuous training is useful if you have little experience with aerobic training. It involves sub-maximal exercise performed at a moderate to high intensity for sustained periods. This means you should train at a heart rate between 70 and 85 percent of your maximum.[3] Once you can perform 45 minutes of continuous aerobic exercise then you can begin to insert some interval training into your programme. In fact, since rugby is really an 80-minute interval workout we believe the bulk of your aerobic training should be interval based. This provides the added bonus of training the anaerobic energy systems to some degree at the same time as training aerobic fitness. Remember that rugby is an intermittent, high-intensity sport, so long runs at slow speeds will not be as effective for developing your rugby fitness.

Continuous training can be useful for players who need to lose weight and improve their general fitness, because this low-intensity work is less likely to cause injuries. An element of specificity can still be included by varying the movements and using both upper body and lower body exercises.

### INTERVAL TRAINING

Interval training involves spacing exercise and rest periods (easier exercise) so that you can complete a large amount of high-intensity exercise with little fatigue. The pattern of spacing can best be described by a work:rest ratio. If this ratio is 1:1 then exercise and rest periods are equal in duration (e.g. one minute of hard exercise followed by one minute of easy exercise). A 2:1 work:rest ratio implies two minutes of exercise followed by one minute of rest.

A typical interval workout might consist of one minute of hard exercise at a heart rate of 185 beats per minute (work interval) followed by one minute of easy jogging (relief interval), repeated up to ten times. This would enable you to exercise for ten minutes at a heart rate that you could not sustain if you used continuous exercise. Generally, the work phase of an interval workout is performed at an intensity sufficient to raise heart rates from 85 percent of maximum up to maximum (see optimal training zone diagram, page 68).

Usually when we think of interval training we think of running-based workouts, simply because we have borrowed these training methods from sports like athletics. Using other high-intensity activities such as boxing or wrestling, or combining these activities with running, will enable a greater degree of specificity to be maintained. Even more specificity can be maintained by using functional endurance training.

### FUNCTIONAL ENDURANCE TRAINING

This involves the use of many different muscle groups in many different movements, similar to the aerobic demands of the game itself. The movements can either be highly specific to rugby (tackling, scrummaging, driving, etc.) or they can simply contain a range of fitness elements such as power or strength work (e.g. medicine balls, push-ups, etc.). You can also vary the length of the work and rest intervals, depending on whether you want to overload training time, intensity, or both.

Remember that work:rest intervals during rugby are varied, and even more varied between positions. So keep this in mind when putting these sessions together. The diagram below is an example of a functional endurance course.

**A functional endurance session. Note that the session includes upper and lower body movements, directional changes, and rest stations.**

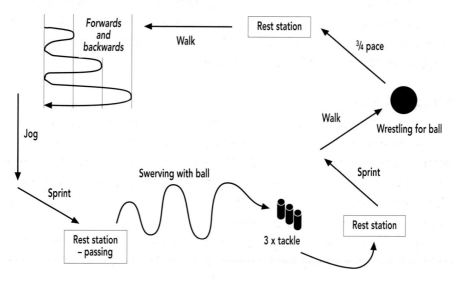

The table below provides some general aerobic training guidelines. Of course, sufficient warm-up and cool-down periods should be used before and after each workout.

**Aerobic training guidelines. Short continuous runs of 20-30 minutes can be used for recovery sessions. In order to elicit changes in fitness, however, runs of at least 30-40 minutes are required.**

| Training Factors | Continuous Training | Functional Endurance Training | Interval Training |
|---|---|---|---|
| Intensity | 70–85% max heart rate | 85–95% max heart rate | 85–100% max heart rate |
| Duration | 20–60 mins | 40–50 mins (5 sec–1 min work intervals) | 35–45 mins 1:1 work:rest ratio (1–5 min work intervals) |
| Frequency | 3–5 times/week | 2–3 times/week | 2–4 times/week |

# The anaerobic systems

## CONTEMPORARY TRAINING

To train the phosphagen and lactic acid anaerobic systems requires interval training in order to complete sufficient high-intensity work to bring about improvement. There are two approaches to training the lactic acid system. The traditional approach is to use high-intensity intervals that cause substantial accumulation of lactic acid in the blood and muscle, and to combine this with near-complete recovery between work intervals. An alternative approach is to use 'lactate stacking' intervals. These intervals are somewhat shorter, and although maximum blood and muscle lactic acid levels do not occur in one exercise interval, complete recovery is not provided. Therefore, waste products such as lactic acid 'stack up' or accumulate over the duration of the interval set, in a similar fashion to what might be experienced during a sustained phase of high-intensity play. Very short (5–10 second) intervals with active recovery (jogging, walking) can be used to train lactate production rather than tolerance, as these short bursts allow high power outputs to be maintained without early fatigue.

## CROSS-TRAINING

It has recently been demonstrated that lactic acid training can also improve aerobic fitness.[4] Even though we may use the anaerobic systems predominantly during work bouts, the aerobic system is still responsible for providing energy for recovery during rest periods. In addition, as previously discussed, both anaerobic systems will be recruited together so it is almost impossible to train one anaerobic system without training the other.

A large component of the adaptation to anaerobic training occurs in the neuro-muscular system. This is similar to strength training in that the muscles become bigger and stronger. With this type of training players may learn to accelerate better and improve speed to a small extent. It is difficult to turn a donkey into a thoroughbred, however, so if you are not fast don't expect to become a Christian Cullen overnight. Nevertheless, anaerobic training does benefit rugby players and is a time-efficient method of training because it develops so many fitness components concurrently.

**Guidelines for interval training the anaerobic phosphagen system and training acceleration.**

| Prescription Factor | Intervals |
|---|---|
| Work phase | 3–5 sec |
| Work/rest ratio | 1:10 up to 1:25 |
| Intensity (% max effort) | 98–100% |
| Repetitions | 4–6 |
| Sets | 2–3 |
| Rest between sets | 5–10 min light exercise |

Guidelines for interval training the lactic acid anaerobic system and training speed.

| Prescription Factor | Traditional Intervals | Lactate Stacking |
| --- | --- | --- |
| Work phase | 5–60 sec | 30–60 sec |
| Work/rest ratio | 1:3 | 2:1 |
| Intensity (% max effort) | 80–85% | 80–85% |
| Repetitions | 4–6 | 5–15 |
| Sets | 1–4 | 1–3 |
| Rest between sets | 5–10 min | 5–10 min |

A word of caution, however, before you become too enthused about this training method. It is known that too much anaerobic training over too long a period can overtrain an athlete and lead to injury. We generally recommend a maximum of two anaerobic training sessions each week, although for short periods (a maximum of three weeks) athletes can benefit from three sessions each week.

## FUNCTIONAL TRAINING

The interval training methods outlined are two ways of specifically overloading the anaerobic systems. When training the anaerobic phosphagen system, and therefore maximum acceleration, we typically use very short work bouts and allow for complete recovery between repetitions, so that each sprint can be done under ideal conditions (see table below). When training the lactic system, we typically use longer intervals than those in games, so that we train our resistance to fatigue under highly anaerobic conditions.

As mentioned in the previous chapter, the actual demands of rugby fall somewhere in between. With average work bouts of five or six seconds, and average rest periods

Guidelines for interval training repeated speed and the lactic acid system.

| Prescription Factor | Forwards | Backs |
| --- | --- | --- |
| Work phase | 4–8 sec | 4–8 sec |
| Work/rest ratio | 1:5 up to 1:15 | 1:10 up to 1:25 |
| Intensity (% max effort) | 98–100% | 98–100% |
| Repetitions | 10–20 | 10–15 |
| Sets | 3–4 | 2–3 |
| Rest between sets | 3–5 min light exercise | 5–10 min light exercise |

of 30–90 seconds being the most common, it is actually our ability to make lactic acid during work periods, and then remove it during rest periods, that is most important. This type of fitness is known as *repeated speed* or *speed endurance*. While doing longer intervals will help speed endurance by developing a player's resistance to fatigue, we also need to do some work which requires the repeated production of high-power bursts by the lactic acid system. The table on the bottom of page 81 gives some guidelines for training repeated speed in forwards and backs. It is good to use a mixture of workouts in this range to develop all-round match fitness.

Once again, as for functional aerobic training, not all of these intervals need to be done running. In fact, a higher intensity can probably be maintained if a mixture of upper and lower body exercises are used. This is particularly beneficial for forwards, who will often have to switch from upper to lower body movements during a game. This type of session can even take the form of a functional endurance circuit, as long as careful attention is paid to ensuring adequate recovery between intervals, so that high power outputs can be maintained throughout the session.

## Muscular strength and power

To improve muscular strength and power, the neuromuscular system is usually trained through resistance training, although, as previously mentioned, anaerobic training can cause many similar improvements. The way you train is critical if you are to effectively target strength, endurance or power.

**Appropriate weight-training exercises for rugby forwards and backs. All techniques should be thoroughly assessed, and some should not be used by junior athletes.**

| Body Area | Forwards | Backs |
|---|---|---|
| Upper body | Chin-ups (reverse grip), lat pull-downs, shoulder press, bench press, dumbbell press, upright rows, cable rows, internal/external shoulder rotations | Chin-ups (wide grip and reverse), bench press, dumbbell press (and single arm), cable rows, cable crossovers, tricep extensions |
| Core | Crunches, leg raises, prone bridges, Swiss ball work, woodchops, dead lifts | Rotation crunches, woodchops, Swiss ball work, dead lifts |
| Legs | Reverse hack squat (facing machine), full squats, half-squats, calf raises | Half-squats, lunges, split squats, calf raises |
| Advanced whole-body | Olympic lifting — power cleans, dead lifts, etc.* | |

* Many advanced techniques such as Olympic lifting require years of training. In most cases, field-based power work will be more time effective.

For example, in training for power and acceleration the positive part of a lift (e.g. the pushing component of a bench press) is performed explosively, but the negative part of the lift (lowering) is performed slowly and in control. However, when training for strength both the positive and negative parts of the lift are performed slowly and in control. These factors and other important training requirements are summarised in the table on page 84, which should help you to select the appropriate weight-training programme for your needs.

Remember to choose weight-training exercises that are as sport-specific as possible. Examples of exercises that use similar muscles and movements to those used by rugby players in different positions are provided in the table on the facing page.

The following is a brief description of the four most relevant weight-training programmes for rugby players at various levels.

## BEGINNER

As explained earlier, resistance-training programmes must follow a progression, otherwise injury and illness will result. For the developing rugby player (under 16 years old), many exercises that are used by senior players can result in injuries, as certain areas of the body may be too weak to support large external weights. The beginner should therefore focus on a good foundation before attempting heavy weight training. Emphasis should be on developing correct techniques, rather than lifting as much weight as possible. The best way to ensure safety with young athletes is to use exercises that use only the player's bodyweight as resistance, such as push-ups, chin-ups, dips, abdominal work, or single-legged squats. The development of abdominal and back strength is particularly important for players at this stage.

## STRENGTH AND MUSCLE BUILDING

A common objective of weight training for rugby players is to increase body size. The best type of resistance training to achieve this is one that provides the optimal combination of volume (sets and reps) and intensity (weight). On average, this combination occurs at about 70–80 percent of a person's maximal lift (1 RM); at this weight the player should be able to complete about 8–12 lifts per set. This combination will result in the greatest amount of damage to the muscle's structure, and therefore the most growth in response.[5]

## MAXIMAL STRENGTH

As maximal strength training places large forces through the body, we recommend you should have at least a year's training experience before attempting this type of programme. You need to be experienced with the techniques to be used, and should have developed sound core (abdominal and back) strength. The focus for maximal strength training is not to do a large volume of lifts, but rather to perform quality movements that will transfer to performance on the field.[6] Maximal strength training should use techniques that involve large muscle groups, and even ones that combine upper and lower body strength. By doing this, you can work all muscle groups in the body without having to use as many exercises.

## MAXIMAL POWER

Powerful movements involve the optimal combination of force (strength) and speed of movement. For this training you therefore use a moderate weight (about 50–60 percent of 1 RM), and perform the movements as quickly as possible.[7]

Once again, it is important to have sufficient training experience before attempting power training. Players often use poor technique when trying to perform movements fast, which can lead to serious injury. You will also notice that, although you use a relatively light weight, you only need to perform as few as five repetitions per set. The reason for this is that, unless performed in a fresh state, movements will not be performed powerfully, so they will no longer be overloading that element of fitness. To maximise the relevance of power training to game performance, you should select exercises that use large muscle groups and that are specific to the movements performed in rugby.

Guidelines for resistance training.

| Programme Variables | Beginners or <16 yrs old | Strength & Muscle Building | Maximal Strength* | Maximal Power |
| --- | --- | --- | --- | --- |
| Intensity | 30 RM** | 10–12 RM** | 3–6 RM** | 15–20 RM** |
| Repetitions | 15–25 | 8–12 | 1–6 | 5–15 explosive reps |
| Sets | 3–5 | 3–5 | 3–5 | 3–5 |
| Rest between sets | 0.5–1 min | 1.5–2 min | 3–5 min | 3–5 min |
| Exercises per workout | 8–10 | 8–10 | 1–4 | 4–6 |
| Frequency | 2–3 times / week / muscle group | 2–3 times / week / muscle group | 2 times / week / muscle group | 2 times / week / muscle group |

\* You should not attempt this programme without sufficient weight-training experience.
\*\* RM = Repetition Maximum = the load that can be lifted with correct technique the indicated number of repetitions but no more.

As weight training is relatively new to the rugby world, we have tended to borrow our weight-training techniques from other athletes such as sprinters and body-builders. For example, many rugby players select high-volume, split routines, as used by body-builders. There are several potential problems with this. First, many of the exercises used by body-builders are aimed at developing small muscle groups, so they probably do not transfer well to sport-specific strength. Also, these programmes require a player to go to the gym between six and eight times a week. Although this may be possible during the off-season, it is not realistic during the season.

As discussed earlier, rugby players need to be fit in many different areas, unlike the athletes we have borrowed our training methods from. Rugby players should therefore focus on large-muscle-group, sport-specific exercises that will develop whole-body strength. In this way players can get large benefits from two to three trips to the gym per week and still have time to develop the other elements of fitness.

## Plyometrics

Plyometrics is a form of jump or throw training aimed at improving power output and speed through overloading the elastic properties of muscle. Put simply, stretching a muscle is like stretching an elastic band; energy is stored within an active stretched muscle that can be released when the muscle contracts. Most rugby movements involve the active stretch of a muscle followed by a contraction (shortening) of that muscle, and these linked events are referred to as a stretch-shortening cycle. For example, during sprint running the quadriceps muscle is first stretched during the impact of the foot with the ground but subsequently shortens to help propel the body forward. The elastic energy stored in the stretch is released during the propulsion phase, so this is a very effective method of increasing the force and velocity characteristics of the quadriceps during sprinting.

In plyometric training the stretch aspect of the stretch-shortening cycle is over-loaded more than usual through bounding, hopping, jumping off elevated boxes and other activities that increase the ground reaction force of landing. Plyometric training may also be used for the upper body, using throws with equipment such as medicine balls, so the muscle is able to generate greater amounts of force during shortening.

Although plyometric training has not been thoroughly studied, a few studies have indicated that it may improve power, acceleration and/or speed.[8] This type of training has a reputation for causing injury, but these injuries have largely come from weak athletes performing rebound jumps from excessive heights or performing advanced level plyometric training without an adequate strength base.

*Plyometric training should not be performed by rugby players with less than a four-month strength training base, by players with musculo-skeletal injuries or weakness, or by players who have not yet physically matured.*

## PLYOMETRIC TRAINING SURFACE

Plyometric training should be performed on a fairly hard surface because the coupling time between the stretch of a muscle and the shortening of the muscle must be short. If the surface is too soft then all the elastic energy that is stored in a stretch will be lost before the muscle shortens. Ideal surfaces for plyometric training include an athletics track, grass or artificial turf, or a sprung gymnasium-type floor. Concrete and asphalt surfaces, although hard, may not be forgiving enough and may increase the chances of lower limb injury. A good supporting shoe must also be worn.

## INTENSITY

The intensity of plyometric exercise can be controlled in several ways. The most common progression is to begin with double leg hops or jumps and progress to single leg hops. With double leg hops body mass is absorbed between both legs upon landing while single leg hops have a much greater impact and subsequent stretch load. Dropping from fixed heights and then exploding into a vertical jump upon landing is another method of increasing intensity for lower limb plyometrics. For upper body plyometrics (e.g. medicine ball throws) the intensity can be changed through changing the weight of the ball, changing the throw velocity (or distance of throw), and changing the base of support. Intensity can be increased by moving from standing on two legs with a wide stance, to narrowing the stance, to kneeling. The less stable forms of support require greater utilisation of the stretch-shortening cycle by the upper body musculature involved in the training movement.

## VOLUME

The volume of the training stimulus is set by the number of foot contacts or throws experienced in a training session. Generally plyometric training is practised in two to three sessions per week. Initial volumes should be in the range of 80 foot contacts, increasing to no more than 150 foot contacts over eight to ten weeks. On the facing page are plyometric exercises suitable for a senior rugby player.

## EXECUTION OF EXERCISES

In all exercises the muscles should be slightly flexed on ground contact or when catching the medicine ball. The main emphasis should be on spending as little time

**Four examples of plyometric exercises.**

Bounding.                                      Heavy bag thrust.

Zig-zag.                                        Lateral medicine ball pass.

as possible in contact with the ground or ball. Each movement should be performed as explosively as possible. The analogy of landing on a frying pan is often used.

## SAFETY AND INJURIES

Because of the high impacts sustained by the body during plyometric exercises the likelihood of injuries to the muscles of the lower legs is considerable if factors such as programme design, ground surface, and the player's strength-training background and injury history are not considered. Progression from low- to higher-impact exercises, and low- to higher-volume sessions over eight to ten weeks, will minimise the chance of injury. Players with recent injuries should obtain medical clearance before beginning a plyometric programme.

## Overspeed sprinting

Overspeed training involves training at a faster speed than is voluntarily possible by using towing systems or running on slight downhill grades. Athletes have experimented with being towed behind motor vehicles (not recommended), pulled along by winch systems, towed by other players and towed by bungy cords secured between players.

The principle behind this training is that by running full-tilt downhill or being towed overspeed a player will learn to increase stride frequency and therefore increase running speed. There has been little research into how well this approach works, but what results have been obtained suggest it may increase speed, although perhaps no more so than standard sprint training.[9] The use of bungy cords is popular in New Zealand, but it is difficult to estimate the degree of stretch that should be placed on the bungy cord, and the actual period of overspeed training may be quite short for each sprint. It seems that training on a slight downhill slope (a two to three percent gradient) over 20–40 metres has the greatest potential for improving stride frequency and speed.

### SESSION VOLUME

Training volume in an assisted session is usually determined by the total distance covered, which should not exceed 300 metres.

Resisted sprint training.

Overspeed training (downhill running).

## SAFETY CONSIDERATIONS AND INJURY

This type of sprinting can be dangerous. If the slope is too steep or the towing strain too high, a player will sprint outside their comfort zone and begin to brake at high speed, causing high-impact forces. In a recent study in our laboratory about ten percent of rugby players who participated in sprint-assisted training experienced pain or injury in the leg at the knee or below.

## PROGRESSION OF EXERCISES

Assisted sprinting requires a gradual increase in the overspeed stimulus (i.e. the amount of assistance). The amount of assistance is dictated by the pre-stretch placed on the bungy cord, or the slope of the gradient in downhill running. Regardless of the equipment used, it is important that the pre-stretch does not provoke overstriding (obvious when the athlete is leaning too far back or being pulled forward while running).

# Resisted sprinting

This type of speed training involves sprinting under load, either through uphill sprinting or through towing weighted sleds, old tires or other players using ropes or bungy cords, or even specially designed parachutes. The principle behind it is that the extra resistance encountered through working against gravity or having to tow a weight increases the strength of the working muscles in a sprint-specific manner, and to a greater extent than is usually possible.[10]

As with sprint-assisted training there is little research indicating the effectiveness of this technique, but the small amount of research that has been completed indicates that it may increase stride length to a small extent and increase speed in a similar fashion to standard sprint training.

## SESSION VOLUME

Training volume in an assisted session is usually determined by the total distance covered, which should not exceed 300 metres.

## SAFETY CONSIDERATIONS AND INJURY

Provided a general strength and speed programme precedes resisted sprinting it is relatively safe, with a low potential for injury. It is important that the connecting rope between the harness and the sprint sled has no slack in it when performing the explosive start of the sprinting movement.

## PROGRESSION OF LOAD AND EXERCISES

Loads of between 10 and 22.5 percent of bodyweight appear to be ideal (the condition of the surface — wet or dry — will dramatically affect the required load.) Variation within this weight range, the distance over which the weight is towed, and the use of contrast training, where the load is immediately removed during sprinting, can be used to provide variety to the training schedule. Essentially, shorter distances dictate greater loads, and longer distances dictate smaller loads.

Sprint training, assisted training or resisted training may all improve speed in rugby players, but there is little evidence that one system is superior to another. The wise player, coach or parent will use a variety of approaches to develop speed. Certainly assisted training should be performed with caution, but when used sparingly with other training methods, speed training can be both fun and effective. Remember that variety is the spice of life, and this certainly holds true when sprint training on a regular basis.

# Horizontal power training

Time-motion analysis research at Otago University has shown that movements requiring horizontal power and strength, such as rucking, mauling, scrummaging and tackling, form crucial parts of a rugby team's performance. For forwards, these activities contribute about 80–90 percent to the total amount of high-intensity work performed, while sprinting only contributes about two percent! Even in backs, 20–30 percent of their high-intensity work is in rucking and mauling.

Horizontal power training.

For forwards especially, spending a lot of training time developing sprinting speed is probably unnecessary. Training to maximise power outputs during rucking, mauling and scrummaging is likely to have a much greater effect on match performance. Although weight training and plyometrics may improve horizontal power, these techniques often train players to produce strength and power in the vertical direction. We have already mentioned tools such as the GRUNT 3000, which has been developed specifically for developing horizontal power and strength. Although most players will not have access to this type of equipment, there are other methods that can be used to develop horizontal strength and power. These include performing strength or power movements on your club's scrum machine, against other players, or even in the gym if you can modify the equipment to get into a specific horizontal position. You can even find a sandpit and perform explosive horizontal jumps, as long as you do them safely. The trick is to be inventive, but always remember to keep good body position, and not to perform too many repetitions to avoid injury.

## Flexibility

The most effective way to improve flexibility is to stretch after exercise, since your muscles are already warm and supple. A variety of techniques are recommended, but players should avoid ballistic stretches, as these involve fast bouncing movements at the end of the stretch and are most likely to cause tearing injuries. You should use slow movements and hold your stretches for 20–60 seconds. The table below suggests specific guidelines, and a suggested stretch programme is outlined on page 92.

There are also several advanced stretching techniques. The most popular is PNF, proprioceptive neuromuscular facilitation. This involves a muscle group being stretched by a partner until the player indicates they are at the limit of their flexibility. The stretch is then held in this position for several seconds, or the player then opposes the direction of movement in which they are being stretched. This action desensitises several mechanical receptors that exist in the muscle so that it relaxes. The partner can then provide a little more stretch to increase range of motion, and this process may be repeated two or three times.

This is an advanced technique which should only be performed under the supervision of a qualified strength and

**Guidelines for improving flexibility.**

| Flexibility Programme | |
| --- | --- |
| Frequency | 3–5 times / week |
| Intensity | Stretch until there is moderate tension |
| Duration | 20–60 seconds |
| Repetitions | 2–3 |
| Type | 8–12 position-specific stretches |

Standard flexibility exercises for rugby training.

conditioning specialist or physiotherapist. However, it is effective at increasing range of motion. PNF stretching should not be performed immediately before a sprint session or competition, as some evidence suggests that this extreme type of stretching may impair the rate at which force can be developed in muscle and therefore impair power production.[11]

## Summary: Improving fitness

By now you have identified which fitness components are important to your performance, and hopefully evaluated yourself in these areas. You have also been exposed to some general guidelines for improving your fitness. Your next step is to build a general training plan for the year, considering your strengths and weaknesses in each area and the goals that you have set (see chapter 3). You can then start planning some of the specifics of your training programme using the principles outlined in this chapter.

Remember to regularly re-evaluate your fitness, and revisit your goals. This will ensure that your training is goal-directed, and keep you climbing up the staircase to peak rugby performance.

# 6 Mental toughness training

*Alex McKenzie, Ken Hodge*

Mental toughness is an essential requirement for any top level rugby player. I believe that my mental skills have been the 'key' to my ability to cope with the pressure of playing international rugby. Mental toughness is a skill that takes time to learn and develop; it is not about being 'macho tough' or aggressive, instead it is about being a 'thinking' rugby player.

**Anton Oliver (All Black 1995– )**

Coaches often refer to 'mental strength' and 'mental toughness' when attempting to describe that elusive quality that distinguishes great performers from good ones. But what does mental toughness mean and what can a player do to develop this quality?

Sport psychology focuses on teaching practical psychological (psych) skills and methods to players so that they can develop their psychological abilities (i.e. mental toughness) to the same high level as their physical abilities.[1] Indeed, the key difference between a good performance and a poor performance may be a player's psychological skill level rather than their physical skill level.[2] This does not mean that psychological skills are more important than physical, tactical, or technical skills.

They are equally important, which means that all the pieces of the peak performance 'jigsaw puzzle' need to be in place. Psychological skills represent just one of those pieces, and like physical and technical skills they need to be taught correctly, fine-tuned by the player and coach, and then practised regularly.

---

The real contest is in the mind.

---

Psychological skills training (PST) is designed to help players improve their psychological skills to a level that matches their physical skills. It is important to realise that this focus on PST is not just for All Blacks or elite players. These skills are equally appropriate and important for players and athletes of all ages and levels of physical performance. PST is just as useful for the 40-year-old Golden Oldies player, the 16-year-old age-group player and the average club player as it is for an All Black. In fact, anyone who wants to consistently perform to the limits of their physical capabilities, and to thoroughly enjoy their rugby, can use PST to help them.

---

Champion players are not extraordinary people, they are
ordinary people who do extraordinary things.

---

## Why do you need psych skills?

Top rugby players have well-developed physical and technical skills, and are fit and healthy, but many believe that what sets them apart from those who have not reached the same level of achievement is their psychological skills.

Most players know that they should relax, be positive and confident, and stay focused. However, they don't always know *how* to do this. When PST skills and methods are explained to experienced players they often respond by saying, 'I wish I'd had this information when I first started competing. I do most of this stuff now but it took me years of trial and error to figure it out!'

Many players already use these psychological skills in some form or another, but it is the haphazard and often lengthy learning process they had to endure that PST is designed to eliminate. The PST programme seeks to teach players basic psych skills and methods that have both an intuitive appeal and a sound scientific basis.[3] As such, PST is an integral part of smart training.

To quote an old coaching saying, we are 'trying to put an old head on young shoulders'. PST is designed to ensure that the old head is a 'smart' one!

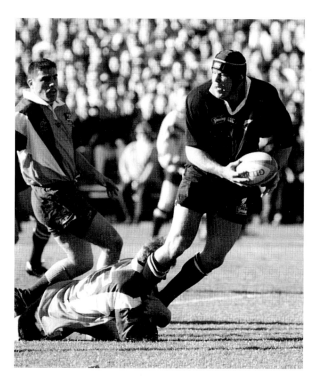

Guys still put their bodies on the line, but in every area far more thought goes into it. Mental and physical preparation is at a higher level.

**Josh Kronfeld (All Black 1995– )**

## Objectives of psychological skills training [4]

The PST programme outlined in this chapter has three major objectives:

➤ To help you consistently perform to the best of your ability — performance enhancement.

➤ To help you enjoy rugby more by reducing stress and improving performance.

➤ To help you develop psychological skills for use in other life situations (e.g. concentration, coping with pressure, stress management).

## The psychological skills training (PST) programme

All players have the potential to improve some aspect of their psychological abilities. Consequently PST is a key piece of your peak performance jigsaw puzzle, along with the physical, tactical, and technical pieces of the puzzle. The challenge is for you to identify your particular PST needs and then design a PST programme for yourself. You need to have all the pieces of the peak performance jigsaw puzzle in place. The aim is to have the brain and the body working together as a team.

## PST SKILLS vs PST METHODS[5]

The distinction between PST skills and PST methods is vitally important for a successful PST programme, but it is usually overlooked by players and coaches.

### PST skills

In the context of PST, a skill is a competency, capability, or ability level (e.g. peak concentration). PST skills are developed through the use of a number of PST methods (see Hodge & McKenzie 1999 for details of PST skills for rugby).[6] The major PST skills are:

➤ Motivation

➤ Self-awareness and self-esteem

➤ Self-confidence

➤ Peak physical activation

➤ Peak mental activation

➤ Peak concentration

### PST methods

A method is a technique to help a player develop a particular skill just like a physical 'drill' is used to develop a particular physical skill.[7] A method in this sense means a procedure, technique or drill (e.g. imagery). The major PST methods are:

➤ Goal setting (see chapter 3)

➤ Mental preparation

➤ Self-talk

➤ Centring/relaxation

➤ Imagery

# *The* PST programme?

Ideally the PST programme is an individually designed combination of PST methods selected to attain your PST skill needs. There is no 'set' or 'packaged' PST programme for any one playing position or any one type of player — it needs to be tailored to *your* needs (see Hodge & McKenzie 1999 for details).[8]

It is important to approach your PST programme with the same commitment to planning as you would put into your physical training. Ideally, this requires a period-ised plan that takes into account all periods of the season (see chapter 10), although specific weaknesses may be addressed at any stage. The PST skills and methods must be integrated into your skill and team training in order to simulate their use during a game. Often you will need to do additional PST practice by yourself, in the same way as extra physical practice is usually needed for fine-tuning physical skills.

Our flanker Ben's first step in designing his PST programme was to select those psych skill needs that required the greatest improvement. These were:

(i) concentration, and

(ii) pre-game psych-up = peak activation.

Then, based on this skill assessment, Ben concluded that he first needed to identify some psych methods that would help him improve his concentration. He chose to use the methods of self-talk and imagery.

Once Ben saw some gains in his concentration, he was in a position to work on some PST methods to enhance his pre-game psych-up. He chose to combine the use of mental preparation, imagery and self-talk to work on this performance skill.

# Planning your PST programme for mental toughness

### PST PROGRAMME FOR THE TEAM (SQUAD)

The team will have some general or common needs such as cohesion (teamwork, team spirit), awareness of team-mates' needs, leadership, and communication skills. You may need to take these into account before you finalise your own PST programme.

### PST PROGRAMME FOR EACH INDIVIDUAL

The key aspect of any effective PST programme is that it needs to be personally designed and individually tailored to your PST skill needs. Like physical skills and methods, psychological skills and methods need to be learnt properly, adapted or modified to fit your strengths and weaknesses, fine-tuned following initial use, and then *practised, practised, practised*.

# Psychological skill needs: common areas

Listed on the facing page are some of the common PST skills that players find they need to work on after completing a peak performance profile. We have also included some suggested PST methods that we have found useful in developing these particular skills.

However, don't feel you have to use all or even any of the suggested PST methods for a particular PST skill. You should make your own choice of methods based on your needs and preferences.

## SELF-CONFIDENCE

This involves the feelings and images you have about what you believe you can and can't do. You need to develop and maintain a stable, realistic level of self-confidence.

PST METHODS:

➤ Goal setting

➤ Positive self-talk

➤ Mental preparation

➤ Imagery

## MOTIVATION

Motivation is both 'wanting to' and 'having to' do something. You must identify rugby goals you 'want to' achieve (this is the long-lasting fuel for goal accomplishment), but also be realistic enough to realise there will be times when you will need to motivate yourself to do something because you 'have to' do it (e.g. training motivation). When you reach the stage of having to do something rather then wanting to do it, you will need strong self-discipline and mental toughness to 'tough it out'.

PST METHODS:

➤ Goal setting

➤ Positive self-talk

## CONTROLLING ACTIVATION

This deals with controlling your psych-up levels through the management of motivation and activation. You need to psych yourself up without psyching yourself out by being overactivated.

PST METHODS:

➤ Centring

➤ Relaxation

➤ Mental preparation

## COPING WITH PRESSURE

This skill involves being able to cope with the pressure that comes with a commitment to achieving challenging goals.

PST METHODS:

➤ Centring

➤ Relaxation

➤ Mental preparation

➤ Self-talk

## CONCENTRATION CONTROL

This deals with the ability to 'tune in' what's important to your performance and 'tune out' what's not. It includes being able to maintain concentration as well as the ability to shift focus when needed.

PST METHODS:

➤ Imagery

➤ Centring or relaxation

➤ Self-talk

## COMMUNICATION AND TEAM COHESION

These are the tools that allow you to interact and communicate effectively with other players, team-mates, coaches, and managers.

PST METHODS:

➤ 'Key words' for team communication

➤ Teamwork (task cohesion), team spirit (social cohesion)

# Steps in learning psychological skills

## EDUCATION

When learning PST skills, you should initially focus on increasing your awareness of PST, increasing your understanding of PST principles, developing realistic expectations of PST, and understanding the need for PST. The peak performance profile is vital in this self-education process. Indeed, you have already taken an important step by reading this book. Recommended Reading and Resources on page 244 contains references for a number of other practical books about PST — in particular, Hodge and McKenzie's *Thinking Rugby* (1999) is a rugby-specific book on sportpsych.

## ORGANISATIONAL CONSIDERATIONS

There are a number of important organisational questions that must be answered when planning your PST programme.[9] First, who should conduct the programme (sportpsych consultant, coach, or you)? Second, when to implement the programme (pre-season, early season)? Third, when to practise the methods (at home, before practice, after practice, during practice)? Fourth, how much time should be spent on mental training (possible clash with physical practice time)? Fifth, how to assess your psych skill needs (when, who, how much assessment)? And sixth, what PST skills to include, what methods to learn, and what sequence to learn them in?

There are no set answers to any of these questions. You must have an attitude that allows you to be assertive and confident enough to make these decisions yourself. After learning the basics of the PST programme you should be in a position to make an informed decision on these matters — trust your own knowledge of yourself, your abilities, your strengths and weaknesses, your playing position, and now your knowledge of PST.

However, given our experience of teaching PST, we offer the following recommendations. To learn PST properly, you should ideally work initially with a sport-psych consultant. There are currently few coaches who have enough knowledge or experience with PST to teach it effectively. Nevertheless, it is important that your coach gains a basic understanding of your PST programme so that they can reinforce what you are doing and lend advice and support.

In addition, it is important to approach your PST programme with the same commitment to planning that you would put into planning your physical training. This requires a simple periodised plan that takes into account all periods of the season (see chapter 10 for details of periodised plans). Ideally, PST should begin in the off-season and develop through the pre-season and early season with the goal of peaking for the important games in the season.

Experience has taught us that PST methods are best learned and practised during normal physical training or practice time. PST skills and methods must be integrated into physical training in order to simulate their use during competition. However, you will often need to do additional PST practice by yourself, just as extra physical practice is usually needed for fine-tuning your physical skills.

## PST PRACTICE CONSIDERATIONS

In learning PST methods you need to understand the reasoning behind the PST programme. In other words, you should provide the what, why, when, and how of mental training for yourself as a player. You must also structure your team and individual situation to allow for PST practice. In doing so, it is vital to stress personal responsibility and commitment as a player — you must do the hard work and practice yourself. In addition you must be flexible and individualise your programme and learning procedures to take into account the team and your particular situation.

### EVALUATING THE PST PROGRAMME

As with the development of any new skill, your initial PST programme will probably not be perfectly matched to your individual needs. Consequently there is a need for frequent evaluation during the learning and practice of PST methods (e.g. repeated use of peak performance profiles). There must also be a post-season evaluation, so that you can make future recommendations, improvements and modifications.

## Summary

Remember, PST is not intended to overcomplicate your rugby performance. Indeed, you will not need all of the skills and methods to enhance your rugby performance and enjoyment. The task before you is to identify the PST skills that you believe you need to improve your performance, and then choose the PST methods that you believe are the most appropriate for your PST needs. Don't try to do too much too soon (e.g. don't work on all the PST methods at once), otherwise you will struggle to find the time and commitment necessary for effective PST practice.

As stated above, PST is designed to help you with:

➤ Performance enhancement

➤ Enjoyment and satisfaction in participation

➤ The development of life skills

Finally, keep in mind that PST is not just for elite players, and that it is only one part of rugby performance. You must have realistic expectations of it. Psychological skills will not replace a lack of physical skills or fitness. Nor is it a 'quick fix' — PST takes time and effort.

———

Psych skills training for mental toughness is vital
in the modern game of rugby.

———

You can fatigue someone's body, but the thing that will crack them is the mind. You should train the way you mean to play. If you know you can push yourself, that you've got a certain toughness that you've shown on the training field, it means that you're going to handle a pressure situation or a personal challenge on the sports field a whole lot better.

**Zinzan Brooke (All Black 1987–97)**

# PST methods

The following are practical guidelines for implementing the major PST methods of mental preparation, self-talk, centring/relaxation, and imagery (for greater detail see Hodge & McKenzie 1999, Hodge 1994 or Orlick 1986).[10] At the end of the chapter there is a 'case study' example of a complete PST programme for Ben, our flanker, which will help you to understand how you can design a PST programme for yourself.

## MENTAL PREPARATION

Mental preparation is a useful method of developing the PST skills of peak physical activation, peak mental activation, and peak concentration. Quality mental preparation is a key element of rugby success.[11] Mental preparation strategies are used to organise a consistent and systematic 'psych-up' period before the game.

There is no perfect mental preparation plan.[12] Each plan is dependent on your needs and preferences, and on the level of rugby you are playing.

### Performance plans

There are three types of performance plans that are designed to help you achieve peak mental preparation.[13] These are the pre-game plan, game focus plan, and coping plan (distraction control). Planning sheets for developing these plans are included at the end of the chapter. Make your own photocopies for writing out your ideas and plans.

To develop these plans you need to ask yourself the following questions. What kind of preparation do I like — how much, when, and why? What do I like and dislike about events leading up to game day, 24 hours before the game, once I get to the ground, and during the game itself? Do I already have an organised warm-up routine for game day? Does the team have a clearly defined game plan going into each game? What, if anything, makes me anxious and uptight before a game? How disciplined am I about my mental preparation and my focus for each game? Do I like to use other PST methods (e.g. self-talk, imagery) in my mental warm-up?

Once you have developed mental plans that you are happy with, be prepared to modify them as your rugby career continues. Like many things, mental plans can become a bit boring unless you keep looking for ways to keep them fresh and meaningful. Be wary of hanging on to a good mental plan that has worked well for you in the past but has lost some of its meaning — if you simply go through the motions during your mental preparation you are likely to play the same way!

Everyone has their own way of getting ready, it's just a matter of making sure your personal motivation doesn't intrude on those around you because it is an individual thing. Everyone is different and it has to be managed that way.

**Sean Fitzpatrick (All Black 1986–97; Captain 1992–97)**

### Pre-game plan

Plan, organise, and structure your thoughts and actions on game day. That is, you need to develop a 'mental warm-up' to go with your physical warm-up. Often this is referred to as 'segmenting', since you organise your mental warm-up into distinct 'segments' that give your mental preparation a sound structure. You might include self-talk, imagery and centring in your plan (these PST methods are outlined later in the chapter). See also the pre-game planning sheet at the end of this chapter (page 119), as well as Ben's example (page 120).

### Game focus plan

Plan and organise how you want to think, feel and focus during the game. If you like clear structure, it often helps to do some 'segmenting' so that you organise your thoughts during the game. For example, you may segment your game into the first five minutes of the half, last five minutes of the half, etc. See the game focus planning sheet at the end of the chapter (page 121).

### Coping plan (distraction control)

Plan and organise the strategies and thoughts that will help you deal with distractions and hassles before, during and after the game. For example, you may choose to include self-talk, imagery or centring as part of a coping plan. See the coping plan sheet at the end of the chapter (pages 122–123).

## SELF-TALK

### What is self-talk?

Self-talk may be described as conscious or intentional thinking, or as an inner conversation.[14]

Self-talk/thoughts $\longrightarrow$ Feelings $\longrightarrow$ Behaviour

Your level and type of self-talk is linked to your concentration, self-confidence and anxiety. Confident players 'think' they can, and they do! They imagine themselves being successful, and they focus on positive things such as successfully mastering a task rather than worrying about negative things and performing poorly. On the other hand, players with low self-confidence think that they can't perform well and invariably they don't. The effect of positive versus negative self-talk will be obvious to you if you complete the following exercise.

*Have a friend read the following instructions to you:*

Close your eyes. I am going to ask you to NOT think about some things, so whatever you do, DO NOT think about them. First, DON'T think about an orange. Second, DON'T think about a rugby ball. Finally, DON'T think about a nice cold glass of your favourite drink on a scorching hot summer's day.

Most people listen to the instructions, tell themselves NOT to see the object mentioned, but usually end up *thinking* about and seeing the object anyway! Imagine the consequences of negative self-talk if you give yourself instructions like 'Don't panic!' or 'Don't worry about the weather or ground conditions.'

Self-talk does not mean having a long conversation with yourself during the game, because you simply don't have time! Rather, self-talk words and phrases need to be brief and precise so that their effect can be experienced in the shortest possible time. In addition, the self-talk words or phrases that you use only need to be meaningful to *you*! It's like having your own cassette player in your head; you make your own 'tapes' and play them when you need them!

## Uses of self-talk [15]

### Skill learning

'Cue' or 'key' words are very useful in learning and practising physical skills. For example, 'head down, follow through' may help you to learn a punting or goal-kicking routine. Remember to keep the instruction brief but precise, and work towards 'automatic' execution of the skill(s).

### Concentration

Use a specific set of self-talk cues to 'hold' the appropriate focus on the task at hand (i.e. in the present tense). For example, self-talk like 'here and now!' may help some players to stay focused on what they have to do *right* now!

### Creating 'mood'

Use clear and specific words or phrases to create a particular mood or emotion. For example, 'go' or 'explode' may be useful for a sprint start from a defensive scrum, and 'smooth', 'easy' or 'rhythm' can be useful for goal-kicking, kick-offs and 22-metre dropouts.

Concentration shows on the players' faces as the front rows prepare to engage.

### Controlling effort

Use phrases to maintain energy and persistence, such as 'go for it', 'push it', 'pick it up', 'hold onto the rhythm', or 'keep going'.

### Mental preparation

Use cue words or phrases to assist with pre-game mental preparation. For example, 'boots on, switch on' could be a phrase to use as a cue to develop a more intense 'game focus'.

> As I run out — I'm busy talking to myself, and flashing images through my head. I may chant repetitive things like, 'First tackle, first tackle, make a big tackle, big tackle. First one on the ball, good hands, clean hands, watch the ball.' I'll remind myself to watch my D [defence]. I'm sure that by talking to myself this way before every game, before I come out and then while running out, it helps the fine tuning. I like to be flushed over, release an adrenalin rush beforehand so I can do my final couple of stretches out on the ground before kick-off.
>
> **Josh Kronfeld (All Black 1995– )**

### Affirmations for building self-confidence

Affirmations are statements that reflect positive attitudes or thoughts about yourself. They help you believe in yourself and develop self-confidence. For example, a player might say to him/herself, 'I've worked really hard. I deserve to play well.'

*Techniques for controlling self-talk* [16]

Once your awareness of negative vs positive thoughts and feelings is heightened, you need to learn techniques to eliminate negatives and to focus on positive thoughts. [17]

### Key word or phrase list

Develop a list of key words and phrases that have specific purposes (e.g. self-instruction, creating mood, holding focus, affirmation statements). See the example of a self-talk list at the end of the chapter (page 125).

### Changing negative thoughts to positive thoughts

Make a list of typical negative and self-defeating thoughts, then design a substitute positive thought for each negative thought. Many players couple this process with centring to help them relax. For example:

'I don't want to fail; I don't want the responsibility of this goal-kick' could be changed to '. . . relax . . . just give it your best shot; enjoy the challenge!'

'I hate the rain, I never play well in the rain' could be changed to '. . . relax . . . no one likes playing in the rain, but it's the same for them as it is for me, and I can handle it better!'

*Remember:* Confident players *think* they can, and they do!

## CENTRING AND RELAXATION

In sport, being relaxed allows you to become physically and mentally free from uncontrolled activation, tension, anxiety and negative thoughts. Relaxation is characterised by feelings of ease, looseness, and readiness. This involves physical and mental relaxation. [18]

———

Calm the body and clear the mind.

———

You can use relaxation/centring to calm the body physiologically by decreasing muscle tension, heart rate and breathing rate. It helps to shift attention from anxiety-provoking thoughts to a relaxed, focused mindset. Finally, you can use centring to help you reach your optimal level of physical and mental activation, before and during the game (i.e. it may be linked to mental preparation).

> When we get the knock on the door saying that we've got to be out on the ground in one minute, I try to relax my muscles and focus entirely on the job. Jiggling my muscles as I run out is part of it . . .
> **Josh Kronfeld**

Two relaxation techniques — centring and progressive muscular relaxation (PMR) — are described below.

### Centring

Centring is a relaxation and concentration exercise where you focus on breathing from your centre of gravity, which is just behind the navel/stomach for most of us. Centring combines abdominal breathing and key words, and once learned it is a quick relaxation technique that can help you reduce unwanted tension, stay loose under pressure, and focus your attention. Learning to centre helps keep you in control.

Everyone can centre to some degree right now. However, being able to centre under the pressure of high-level competition requires practice. The following two-phase learning process can help you to learn and practise centring.[19]

**Phase 1. Breathing skills and centring of attention**

1. The easiest way to learn this technique is to stand at ease with your legs shoulder width apart. Place one hand on your stomach just below your navel and rest the other hand on top of it.

2. Focus on a point just behind your navel. Concentrate on this point and then feel your entire body in relation to it. Remind yourself that your strength, power, balance and control all come from this point.

3. Breathe in through your nose and out through your mouth. Feel your stomach expand and contract as you breathe. Remember to breathe using your stomach and not your chest. Keep breathing in and out in this manner with your attention totally focused on your breathing and nothing else.

4. Make each inhalation and exhalation last the same amount of time. The transition between the two should be very natural and unforced.

5. Every time you breathe out repeat the word 'one' silently to yourself. If your mind drifts just refocus on your breathing and your concentration word (eventually replace the word 'one' with a word that is meaningful to you).

6. At first spend about ten minutes on this exercise each day. Eventually decrease the time to three to five minutes, and be able to practise the exercise in a position that is relevant to your playing position.

Build in self-talk as a mental cue for centring. As you breathe in, silently repeat a cue word (e.g. 'centre') to remind yourself to centre. As you exhale say another cue word (e.g. 'relax') to remind yourself to stay loose. At the end of one breathing cycle many players like to cue their attention towards their opponent or the next task while staying centred (a word like 'focus' or 'action' works well). See the centring training logsheet at the end of the chapter (page 126).

The entire sequence might be:

ACTION:     Breathe in (nose)    ⟶    Breathe out (mouth)

THOUGHTS:   'Centre'           'Relax'   'Action'

### Phase 2. Centring during practice or training

Practise centring between drills or between periods of practice. Later, make it a habit to centre each time you enter set pieces (e.g. scrums, lineouts). Use cue words to reinforce the centring drill. As your skill improves, try centring in low-pressure games, then gradually work up to more important games. The more automatic your centring skills become, the more they can be used before or during important games as part of your mental preparation. The better-centred player will have better timing, concentration and confidence. Centring helps you switch on your 'automatic pilot'.

### Progressive muscular relaxation (PMR)

PMR is a physical relaxation exercise that may be necessary if you are unable to effectively control your activation and anxiety levels with centring alone. PMR also allows you to relax to a much deeper level than centring. This depth of relaxation is useful for controlling insomnia, which is a common problem for many players before games. PMR is a muscle-to-mind relaxation technique, whereas centring is a mind-to-muscle relaxation technique. See Hodge and McKenzie (1999) for information on utilising PMR in rugby.[20]

> I'm quite relaxed before games. This is another aspect of finding the right balance. Once upon a time, before test matches I used to think you had to sit in your room getting yourself all worked up and tense about it . . .
> I feel I'm ready to play better if I'm relaxed, not tense, beforehand . . .
> I think that the ability to relax and keep your balance mentally could be the x-factor that lets you perform better than your opposition.
> **Zinzan Brooke (All Black 1987–97)**

There are four phases to learning PMR effectively so that you can use it before or during a game. The time frame for moving through these four phases depends on individual abilities and the time available to practise. Use the PMR relaxation log sheet at the end of the chapter to record your PMR practice.

### Phase 1. Tense-relax cycle

This learning phase relies on the overshoot principle — when a muscle is tensed it will then relax below the initial level of tension. Allow 15–20 minutes to do this exercise; you may wish to record the following 'script' onto an audiotape to use with a walkman. See the PMR relaxation logsheet (page 127).

*Phase I script:*

1. Lie down and relax your entire body. If you hear noises don't try to block them out, but focus on your breathing: inhaling, then exhaling slowly. If you want to move slightly, that's okay. Close your eyes, take it easy and relax. Focus on your breathing. Breathe in through your nose and out through your mouth.

2. Tense the muscles of your right lower leg and foot by pointing your toe. You'll tense for 5–6 seconds and then relax. You should be able to feel the tension in your foot and calf and then totally relax. When you relax feel the warmth in the muscles as the tension drains away. Focus on the differences between tension and relaxation. Repeat this procedure again on the right leg and then repeat it twice for the left leg.

3. Think to yourself 'LOOSE' and 'RELAX' every time you release the tension. Focus on your breathing again as you do so.

4. After tensing and relaxing the lower leg and foot, tense (for 5 seconds) and relax the thigh and buttocks region (twice for each leg). Tense the buttocks and thighs by pushing down with your butt.

5. Tense and relax the forearm and hand by making a fist. Do this twice for each arm.

6. Tense and relax the biceps of each arm by bending at the elbow and pretending you are doing a chin-up. Repeat twice for each arm.

7. Tense (for 5 seconds) and relax the back muscles by arching the back up. Tense and relax the back twice.

8. Tense the stomach and chest muscles by breathing in deeply and then releasing/relaxing. Do this twice.

9. Tense the neck and shoulders by shrugging your shoulders (pulling them upwards) and then releasing them and relaxing. Repeat this twice.

10. Tense the face and forehead by gritting your teeth and pulling your eyebrows together, then relax. Do this twice.

11. When you have completed this whole sequence, mentally check your body for any tension. Release it if you find any. By now you should be completely

relaxed (after 15–20 minutes of tense/relax). Focus on the feelings of ease and looseness in your muscles, the deep-breathing cycle you are in, and the calm, focused thoughts of your mindset.

To a degree your peak level of activation should also represent a calm, focused, semi-relaxed state. The script above is a general example of a PMR sequence; you should modify the wording of the script and the sequence of muscle relaxation to suit your personal needs and preferences.

### Phase 2. Relax-only cycle

Relax the same muscle groups without tensing. Begin to use a cue word or phrase to signal relaxation (e.g. 'loose and easy', 'calm and ready'). Allow 10–15 minutes each time you practise this phase. Progress to a sitting and then a standing position (which is probably more like the position you will be in during a game when you have the opportunity to use the technique).

### Phase 3. Centring-relaxation

Move toward centring by learning to relax the muscle groups more quickly. You can start by dividing the body into fewer parts. The ultimate goal is to learn to relax deeply in the time it requires to take a deep breath, and to use your cue word/phrase (i.e. the centring procedure). Practise this about ten times a day.

### Phase 4. Utilisation stage

Begin to use centring in anxiety-provoking situations. Practise first in low-stress conditions (e.g. practice), then under moderately stressful conditions and finally in highly stressful situations.

*Basic relaxation training principles*

Relaxation and centring are techniques that require sustained practice. You need to create the right physical and mental climate to learn and practise relaxation. It is useful to have a quiet environment, a comfortable position, and to use a mental cue word or phrase. As you become more adept at relaxing, you should practise the techniques under conditions that are more like rugby practice and game situations.

The amount of time needed to learn relaxation and centring depends on individual abilities. Relaxation is typically used in conjunction with other PST methods (e.g. self-talk, imagery). Additional techniques for lowering activation levels include physical stretching, relaxing music, schedules and routines (see 'Mental preparation', above), mental imagery, and self-talk. The same relaxation training procedure is not best for everyone. Modify your procedure to suit your personal needs and style.

## IMAGERY/VISUALISATION

Imagery is a PST method that involves the ability of a player to mentally recreate objects, people, skills and situations while not actually being involved in these situations. Imagery is more than visualisation ('movies in the mind'); it should involve all the senses. With practice you should be able to see the image, hear it, smell it, taste it, and feel it. It is a mental and physical 'blueprint' of sport performance.[21]

Imagery can be used for setting goals, controlling emotions, coping with unexpected events or problems, and developing self-awareness. It is also useful for improving concentration and mental preparation, and as a supplement to physical practice.

### *Stages in imagery development*

#### Begin with guided practice

Use an instructor (e.g. sportpsych consultant, coach, team-mate) to guide the imagery session. Have them take you through an imagery session or record their instructions onto your walkman. Remember to focus on all the senses, not just the visual. Work on developing vivid and clear images — hear the crowd, smell the grass, feel the ground and the ball, feel the movement and contact.

#### Practise self-directed imagery

Develop an imagery 'script' that is relevant to your playing position, record it on audiotape and use a walkman to practise it. Aim to be able to develop clear, vivid, and controlled images. Eventually you should be able to practise imagery without the use of the tape and walkman. Practise controlling your images by imaging the correct execution of simple skills, then moving to more complex ones. Controlling images is very important because uncontrolled imagery (e.g. seeing yourself fail or make errors) can increase anxiety and stress.

#### Use imagery during training or practice

Use the imagery training logsheet at the end of the chapter to record your imagery practice (page 128).

#### Begin using imagery before and during competition

Use imagery for your pre-game mental preparation, or for concentration routines (e.g. goal-kicking or lineout throwing).

## Case study: Ben Mills (flanker)

Ben, our openside flanker, is on the edge of provincial selection. To improve his overall performance, and therefore his chances of selection, he has decided to implement a PST programme. Throughout his rugby career Ben has spent considerable time working on his physical and technical skills, but he has not systematically worked on improving his psychological or tactical skills. Like many players he has used imagery on occasions, and likes to use a regular physical warm-up routine before games. However, he has frequently experienced problems with poor concentration and negative self-talk during games and in training, and sometimes felt a lack of motivation towards skill training. Ben feels that this has negatively affected his performances in the past, and wants to perform more consistently and achieve regular peak performances.

After seeking advice from a sport psychology consultant, Ben and his club coach, Rick, separately completed a peak performance profile, as described on page 115. This profile formed the basis for a discussion of his abilities in each of the identified skill areas. Ben and Rick felt the profiling process alone was useful from the perspective of improving their coach-player communication, and had enabled them to get onto the same wavelength in terms of the focus and direction of Ben's future training.

The peak performance profile identified several skill areas that Ben (and Rick) felt he needed to improve, and after deciding which of these were of most immediate importance, the following goals were set using the goal achievement worksheet (see pages 117–118):

**Physical goal:**   To increase his speed over 10–15 metres by 0.5 seconds by 27 April 2000.

**Psych goal:**   To maintain the use of positive self-talk, cue and mood words throughout an entire game — improve his concentration. This goal to be achieved by 27 April 2000.

Once these goals had been achieved, Ben planned to set goals in further skill areas after re-evaluating his abilities in each aspect of his peak performance profile.

To achieve the goals they had set, Ben and Rick decided to implement the following strategies.

### PHYSICAL GOAL: SPEED

1.  To complete a one-hour sprint practice session under the guidance of a local sprint coach each week.

2. During sprint training, Ben was to practise using the mood and cue words 'power', 'explode' and 'quick feet'.

3. Between sets in sprint training, Ben was to use imagery to practise the use of these words, and to imagine good technique (relaxed shoulders, straight arm swing, quick strides).

4. To practise sprint drills for 20 minutes on Tuesdays and Thursdays after training, with a sprint coach.

### PSYCH GOAL: CONCENTRATION

1. To compile a list of mood words, cue words, and positive self-statements to implement during team training sessions, pre-game preparation, and games (see page 125).

2. To use imagery to practise using these statements/phrases/words during team training, pre-game preparation, and games (five minutes of imagery training per day).

3. To keep a training log of self-talk statements/phrases/words used during team training, pre-game preparation, and games. A rating scale of 0–10 to be used to monitor self-talk during these sessions (0 = totally negative self-talk, 5 = half-negative, half-positive self-talk, 10 = totally positive self-talk).

Progress towards the achievement of each goal was evaluated at the end of each month, and further peak performance profiles were completed each month to determine if goal progress had influenced other skill areas (e.g. self-confidence, motivation).

After two months, Ben reported that he had improved his 15-metre sprint time from 3.0 to 2.5 seconds, and that his motivation and concentration had improved and become more consistent as a result of the increased use of positive self-talk. His third peak performance profile (see page 116) revealed improvements in several skill areas, and Ben felt that the process of completing the peak performance profiles, setting goals, and implementing the goal-achievement strategies (self-talk, imagery, sprint training) had significantly improved his overall performance. He was on target to achieve his overall goal of selection for the provincial team, but believed that further improvements were still possible. He was now looking to set goals in the areas of (i) tackling around rucks/mauls; (ii) reading running lines on defence, and (iii) pre-game psych-up, which he had identified as the other important aspects of his performance that needed improvement.

**# 1**

## PEAK PERFORMANCE PROFILE (II)

**Name:** *Ben Mills*      **Playing position:** *Openside flanker*

List the skills, and rate yourself on the performance of these skills during your *best-ever (peak)* rugby performance, and on your *current (right now)* level of performance of each skill. Also rate the level of improvement needed, and the consistency of each skill. Rate yourself according to the following scale:

|  | 0 | 1 | 2 | 3 | 4 | 5 | 6 | 7 | 8 | 9 | 10 |
|---|---|---|---|---|---|---|---|---|---|---|---|
| *Current + best:* | Poor | | | | | Average | | | | | Excellent |
| *Improvement:* | Improvement needed | | | | | | | No improvement necessary | | | |
| *Stability:* | Very unstable | | | | | | | | | | Very stable |

| | Current | Best-ever | Improvement | Stability |
|---|---|---|---|---|
| **Technical:** | | | | |
| Body position at breakdown | 8 | 9 | 5 | 7 |
| Tackling; in general | 9 | 10 | 8 | 8 |
| Tackling around rucks/mauls | 5 | 7 | 4 | 7 |
| Passing/link play | 8 | 9 | 8 | 9 |
| **Tactical:** | | | | |
| Reading running lines on attack | 8 | 9 | 7 | 8 |
| Reading running lines on defence | 5 | 8 | 6 | 8 |
| Options: choosing runner moves | 8 | 9 | 8 | 9 |
| **Physical:** | | | | |
| Speed over 10–15 metres | 3 | 7 | 5 | 8 |
| Upper body strength | 10 | 10 | 10 | 10 |
| Aerobic fitness/endurance | 9 | 10 | 8 | 8 |
| Leg strength & lineout leaping | 8 | 9 | 7 | 8 |
| **Psychological:** | | | | |
| Pre-game psych-up (activation) | 5 | 9 | 3 | 2 |
| Commitment | 8 | 10 | 7 | 7 |
| Concentration | 4 | 8 | 3 | 5 |
| Motivation for training | 7 | 9 | 8 | 10 |

# **# 3** PEAK PERFORMANCE PROFILE (II)

**Name:** *Ben Mills* .................... **Playing position:** *Openside flanker* .....

List the skills, and rate yourself on the performance of these skills during your *best-ever (peak)* rugby performance, and on your *current (right now)* level of performance of each skill. Also rate the level of improvement needed, and the consistency of each skill. Rate yourself according to the following scale:

| | 0 1 2 3 4 5 6 7 8 9 10 |
|---|---|
| *Current + best:* | Poor          Average          Excellent |
| *Improvement:* | Improvement needed     No improvement necessary |
| *Stability:* | Very unstable                Very stable |

| | Current | Best-ever | Improvement | Stability |
|---|---|---|---|---|
| **Technical:** | | | | |
| *Body position at breakdown* | 9 | 9 | 6 | 7 |
| *Tackling; in general* | 9 | 10 | 8 | 8 |
| *Tackling around rucks/mauls* | 5 | 7 | 4 | 7 |
| *Passing/link play* | 8 | 9 | 8 | 9 |
| **Tactical:** | | | | |
| *Reading running lines on attack* | 8 | 9 | 7 | 8 |
| *Reading running lines on defence* | 5 | 8 | 6 | 8 |
| *Options: choosing runner moves* | 9 | 9 | 9 | 9 |
| **Physical:** | | | | |
| *Speed over 10–15 metres* | 7 | 7 | 8 | 8 |
| *Upper body strength* | 10 | 10 | 10 | 10 |
| *Aerobic fitness/endurance* | 9 | 10 | 8 | 8 |
| *Leg strength & lineout leaping* | 9 | 9 | 8 | 8 |
| **Psychological:** | | | | |
| *Pre-game psych-up (activation)* | 6 | 9 | 4 | 5 |
| *Commitment* | 8 | 10 | 7 | 7 |
| *Concentration* | 8 | 8 | 9 | 9 |
| *Motivation for training* | 9 | 9 | 8 | 10 |

## GOAL ACHIEVEMENT WORKSHEET

**Name:** Ben Mills (Openside flanker)

- **Specific statement of** *performance* **goal:**

    1. To increase my speed over 10–15 metres by 0.5 seconds.

    2. To maintain the use of positive self-talk, cue & mood words throughout entire game —
    improved concentration.

- **Target date for goal achievement:** 27 April 2000

- **What is the 'payoff' from achieving my goal?**

    Personal satisfaction for achieving goals

    Possible selection for provincial team

    Motivation to continue to improve my performance

- **What are the consequences of** *not* **achieving my goal?**

    Letting myself down — all the other hard work won't have paid off

    Not improving performances

    Not reaching my potential as a player

- **What is my** *strategy* **to achieve my goal?**

    Use of self-talk and imagery during sprint training sessions. ('quick feet', 'power', 'explode')

    Extra sprinting practice (20 minutes) on Tuesdays and Thursdays with sprint coach

*Continued*

- **Possible *obstacles* in the way of achieving my goal:**

  *Work commitments — not enough time*

  *Injuries*

- **Strategies for *overcoming* these obstacles:**

  *Time management — detailed training plan including work commitments.*

  *Listen to my body — back off when necessary. More disciplined in doing flexibility exercises.*

- **What *excuses* do I usually make?**

  *Not enough time*

  *I'm only going to get injured anyway!*

- **Is it worth the time, effort, and commitment to reach my goal?**

  **Yes** ✓    **No**        **Why?**

  *I love competing. I want to feel the sense of achievement that you gain from performing your*

  *best in the game you enjoy the most.*

## GOAL-SETTING CONTRACT

I      *Ben Mills*                              pledge that I am committed to achieving the goal that I have set out above. I will achieve this goal by following the goal achievement strategy that I have developed and outlined above. I am fully committed to this goal and my achievement strategy.

**Signed:** *Ben Mills*                          **Date:** *23 February 1999*

**Witness:** *Rick Dyson*                        **Date:** *23 February 1999*

# MENTAL PREPARATION: PRE-GAME PLAN

Write out your pre-game plan in the sequence that you want it to occur on game day. List your physical warm-up in note form and develop a mental warm-up to go with it. List stretches, drills, activities, self-talk, self-suggestions, imagery, centring, etc. in the sequence that you intend to do them.

| General Warm-up: Physical and Mental (approx. 45–60 mins before kick-off) | | Kick-off Preparation: Physical and Mental (approx. 10–15 mins before kick-off) | |
|---|---|---|---|
| Physical | Mental | Physical | Mental |
| | | | |

## MENTAL PREPARATION: PRE-GAME PLAN

Write out your pre-game plan in the sequence that you want it to occur on game day. List your physical warm-up in note form and develop a mental warm-up to go with it. List stretches, drills, activities, self-talk, self-suggestions, imagery, centring, etc. in the sequence that you intend to do them.

| 'General' Warm-up: Physical and Mental (approx. 45–60 mins before kick-off) | | 'Kick-off' Preparation: Physical and Mental (approx. 10–15 mins before kick-off) | |
| --- | --- | --- | --- |
| **Physical** | **Mental** | **Physical** | **Mental** |
| *FRIDAY NIGHT* • Video or movies | *FRIDAY NIGHT* *Keep my mind off the game: 'Don't play the game on Friday night.'* | • *30 min: Grids with team* — *upper body stretches* — *kick-off countdown* | • *Psyching-up: focus on MY goals & MY standards* |
| *SATURDAY MORNING* • Read the paper • Go for a walk • Pre-game meal • Check gear, mouthguard | *SATURDAY MORNING Think over my goals for today; focus on standards* | • *15 min: 2nd pee stop* — *re-check gear & mouthguard* — *put boots on: 'Boots on, switch on.'* | • *Think : MUST TACKLE everything!, be physical, but be smart — stay focused on accurate technique; do MY jobs, 100% effort every time* |
| *AT THE GROUND* • 60 min: Team talk — coach/captain | *AT THE GROUND* • *Take it in, but keep psych-up under control* • *Build psych-up toward kick-off* | • *12 min: Jogging on spot & stretches* — *stay warm & loose* | • *Use imagery & self-talk to replay key jobs to be done: supporting backline, backrow moves, 2nd phase.* |
| • 50 min: Change gear — strapping — rub down (1st pee stop) | • *Think a/b opposition* — *their weaknesses & strengths* — *our game plan against them: backline & back-row moves; runners, etc.* | • *5 min: Last pee stop* • *4 min: 'Stay warm & loose'* — *stretches/jog* | • *Use imagery to psych up if needed; OR use centring to calm down if needed* |
| • 40 min: Stretching — hamstrings — neck & shoulders at same time — calves — groin | • *Scrum thinking* — *backrow moves* — *running lines from scrum in attack, support backs* • *Lineout thinking* — *support of 6 jumper* — *lineout defence* | • *2 min: Take warm-up gear off* | • *Avoid talking to others until on the field: 'Stay inside my bubble.'* • *Enjoy the adrenaline!* |
| • 35 min: Jogging on spot for 3–5 mins | • *Support play & lines* — *accurate lines* — *speed & urgency* — *backline targets* | | • *Briefly review general game plan* • *After the toss: focus solely on my first job at kick-off* • *'Be focused & disciplined.'* |

**Ben's plan: Flanker**

# GAME FOCUS PLAN

Write out your segmented plan of tactics, strategies, thoughts, cues, self-talk, imagery, centring, activities, etc. as you intend to use them during the game. For example:

- **First five minutes:**

.........................................................................................................
.........................................................................................................
.........................................................................................................

- **Last five minutes of first half:**

.........................................................................................................
.........................................................................................................
.........................................................................................................

- **First five minutes of second half:**

.........................................................................................................
.........................................................................................................
.........................................................................................................

- **Last five minutes of game:**

.........................................................................................................
.........................................................................................................
.........................................................................................................

- **Critical skills or critical moments, such as before set plays, actions:**
  **(e.g. lineout throw, scrum, backline move)**

.........................................................................................................
.........................................................................................................
.........................................................................................................

## COPING PLAN

Write out the coping plans that you intend to use if you are faced with distractions before and during the game. Identify things that could go wrong, then develop possible solutions to help you deal with them — to help you cope and refocus. List stretches, drills, activities, self-talk, thought-stopping, self-suggestions, imagery, relaxation, centring, etc. in the sequence that you intend to use them to help you cope.

Below are some possible sources of problems/distractions — use these as a basis for developing your coping plan(s).

- **Not psyched-up enough:**

. . . . . . . . . . . . . . . . . . . . . . . . . . . . . . . . . . . . . . . . . . . . . . . . . . . . . . . . . . . . . . . . . . . . . . . . . . . . . . . . . . . . . . . . . . . . . . . .

. . . . . . . . . . . . . . . . . . . . . . . . . . . . . . . . . . . . . . . . . . . . . . . . . . . . . . . . . . . . . . . . . . . . . . . . . . . . . . . . . . . . . . . . . . . . . . . .

. . . . . . . . . . . . . . . . . . . . . . . . . . . . . . . . . . . . . . . . . . . . . . . . . . . . . . . . . . . . . . . . . . . . . . . . . . . . . . . . . . . . . . . . . . . . . . . .

- **Overpsyched (i.e. overactivated):**

. . . . . . . . . . . . . . . . . . . . . . . . . . . . . . . . . . . . . . . . . . . . . . . . . . . . . . . . . . . . . . . . . . . . . . . . . . . . . . . . . . . . . . . . . . . . . . . .

. . . . . . . . . . . . . . . . . . . . . . . . . . . . . . . . . . . . . . . . . . . . . . . . . . . . . . . . . . . . . . . . . . . . . . . . . . . . . . . . . . . . . . . . . . . . . . . .

. . . . . . . . . . . . . . . . . . . . . . . . . . . . . . . . . . . . . . . . . . . . . . . . . . . . . . . . . . . . . . . . . . . . . . . . . . . . . . . . . . . . . . . . . . . . . . . .

- **Pre-game distraction:**

. . . . . . . . . . . . . . . . . . . . . . . . . . . . . . . . . . . . . . . . . . . . . . . . . . . . . . . . . . . . . . . . . . . . . . . . . . . . . . . . . . . . . . . . . . . . . . . .

. . . . . . . . . . . . . . . . . . . . . . . . . . . . . . . . . . . . . . . . . . . . . . . . . . . . . . . . . . . . . . . . . . . . . . . . . . . . . . . . . . . . . . . . . . . . . . . .

. . . . . . . . . . . . . . . . . . . . . . . . . . . . . . . . . . . . . . . . . . . . . . . . . . . . . . . . . . . . . . . . . . . . . . . . . . . . . . . . . . . . . . . . . . . . . . . .

- **Change in start time (earlier or later):**

. . . . . . . . . . . . . . . . . . . . . . . . . . . . . . . . . . . . . . . . . . . . . . . . . . . . . . . . . . . . . . . . . . . . . . . . . . . . . . . . . . . . . . . . . . . . . . . .

. . . . . . . . . . . . . . . . . . . . . . . . . . . . . . . . . . . . . . . . . . . . . . . . . . . . . . . . . . . . . . . . . . . . . . . . . . . . . . . . . . . . . . . . . . . . . . . .

. . . . . . . . . . . . . . . . . . . . . . . . . . . . . . . . . . . . . . . . . . . . . . . . . . . . . . . . . . . . . . . . . . . . . . . . . . . . . . . . . . . . . . . . . . . . . . . .

- **Non-ideal ground or weather conditions:**

. . . . . . . . . . . . . . . . . . . . . . . . . . . . . . . . . . . . . . . . . . . . . . . . . . . . . . . . . . . . . . . . . . . . . . . . . . . . . . . . . . . . . . . . . . . . . . . .

. . . . . . . . . . . . . . . . . . . . . . . . . . . . . . . . . . . . . . . . . . . . . . . . . . . . . . . . . . . . . . . . . . . . . . . . . . . . . . . . . . . . . . . . . . . . . . . .

. . . . . . . . . . . . . . . . . . . . . . . . . . . . . . . . . . . . . . . . . . . . . . . . . . . . . . . . . . . . . . . . . . . . . . . . . . . . . . . . . . . . . . . . . . . . . . . .

*Continued*

- **Early mistake by you in game:**

.............................................................................

.............................................................................

.............................................................................

- **Early mistake by team-mate in game:**

.............................................................................

.............................................................................

.............................................................................

- **Loss of ideal focus in game:**

.............................................................................

.............................................................................

.............................................................................

.............................................................................

- **Repeated mistakes during game:**

.............................................................................

.............................................................................

.............................................................................

.............................................................................

- **Poor performance in first half:**

.............................................................................

.............................................................................

.............................................................................

- **Poor overall performance (i.e. need to cope and re-focus for next game):**

.............................................................................

.............................................................................

.............................................................................

.............................................................................

## SELF-TALK LIST

| Statements I will use | When? | Purpose? |
|---|---|---|
| *Focus words/phrases* | | |
| *Mood words/phrases* | | |
| *Positive self-statements* | | |

## SELF-TALK LIST

| Statements I will use | When? | Purpose? |
| --- | --- | --- |
| *Focus words/phrases* | | |
| • 'Tackle hard with shoulder — at hip height' | • On defence, before the whistle to restart play | • To avoid having negative thoughts — I sometimes doubt my ability at front-on tackles |
| • 'I.C.E.' (Intensity, Concentration, Effort) | • Concentrate and focus my attention when I'm setting up at 1st phase ball | • To help with my mental prep during the phases of the game |
| • 'Smooth arm action' | • Technique reminder for sprinting | • To resist self-coaching during my sprinting from scrums and lineouts — simple self-talk to help me trust my sprinting technique |
| *Mood words/phrases* | | |
| • 'Calm and relaxed' or 'Ready, steady' | • At the start of each scrum or lineout | • To set the pace and mood for each re-start from 1st phase ball |
| • 'Boots on, switch on' | • 15 mins before kick-off | • To help kick-start my kick-off countdown prep |
| • 'Chop down the tree' | • Facing a big forward runner around rucks/mauls | • To help me focus on good tackling technique against the 'big boys' |
| *Positive self-statements* | | |
| • 'I've worked bloody hard, I deserve to play well' | • During my pre-game mental prep | • To remember one of my sources of self-confidence — all my training! |
| • 'I'm ripped and ready' | • During my 'kick-off countdown' part of mental prep | • To gee myself up for physical contact |
| • 'Stay in the PRESENT!' or 'Here and now!' | • After a mistake or a loss of concentration | • To cope with pressure and keep my concentration |
| • 'P.R.I.D.E.' (Personal Responsibility in Delivering Excellence) | • During my 'kick-off countdown' part of mental prep; and for staying focused after a mistake | • To play with pride and guts |

## TRAINING LOGSHEET FOR CENTRING

Use a scale from -10 to +10 (with -10 = extremely tense and +10 = extremely relaxed) to show your level of relaxation before and after the centring exercise.

Practise on five consecutive days. Each session should last only 10 minutes. Before training or before bedtime is a popular time. Practise in a quiet, warm environment where you will not be disturbed. Give yourself the opportunity to relax.

|  | Date of Practice | Time of Practice | Level Before Relaxing | Level After Relaxing |
|------|------|------|------|------|
| e.g. | May 8 | 10 p.m. | -7 | +5 |
|  |  |  |  |  |
|  |  |  |  |  |
|  |  |  |  |  |
|  |  |  |  |  |
|  |  |  |  |  |
|  |  |  |  |  |
|  |  |  |  |  |
|  |  |  |  |  |

After three days of centring training, try putting your new skill into practice at work or in social situations. When you feel yourself getting physically tense, your thinking rushed, or your emotions gaining control over your thoughts, stop and centre. Drop your shoulders, relax your facial muscles and focus on your stomach breathing. Close your eyes if you can. Remember, centring, like all the PST methods, needs consistent practice.

# PMR RELAXATION LOG SHEET

Use a scale from -10 to +10 (with -10 = extremely tense and +10 = extremely relaxed) to show your level of relaxation before and after the Phase 1 PMR relaxation exercise.

| | Date of Practice | Time of Practice | Level Before Relaxing | Level After Relaxing |
|---|---|---|---|---|
| e.g. | May 30 | 6 p.m. | -8 | +9 |
| | | | | |
| | | | | |
| | | | | |
| | | | | |
| | | | | |
| | | | | |
| | | | | |
| | | | | |

**1.  What physical changes did you experience as you practised?**

.............................................................................................................................

.............................................................................................................................

.............................................................................................................................

**2.  What mental changes did you experience as you practised?**

.............................................................................................................................

.............................................................................................................................

**3.  In what situations would you use PMR?**

.............................................................................................................................

.............................................................................................................................

# IMAGERY TRAINING LOGSHEET

Practise your imagery script regularly and record your imagery ability using the following rating scales. Rate your imagery *vividness* and your imagery *control*.

Practise on five consecutive days with the same imagery script, then change the script to a more difficult one. Each practice session should only last about 10 minutes. Before training or before bedtime is a popular time. Practise in a quiet, warm environment where you will not be disturbed.

Use a scale from 1–5 (with 1 = low vividness/control and 5 = high vividness/control) to show your level of imagery.

| | Date of Practice | Time of Practice | Vividness Level | Control Level |
|---|---|---|---|---|
| e.g. | May 30 | 6 p.m. | 3 | 2 |
| | | | | |
| | | | | |
| | | | | |
| | | | | |
| | | | | |
| | | | | |
| | | | | |
| | | | | |

**1. What *vividness* changes did you experience as you practised?**

**2. What *control* changes did you experience as you practised?**

## Case study: Enjoyment in Professional Rugby

A recent case study[22] on enjoyment in professional rugby has highlighted the integral role of enjoyment in a player's performance. Former Canterbury Crusaders and current All Black coach Wayne Smith is a strong advocate of this philosophy:

> I think that enjoyment is going to be the factor going into the next decade of professional rugby . . . players need more than just to run around and play for money. They need the security of money . . . but it's the intrinsic values that are the important ones and that was really brought home to me this year.

Several players from the 1999 Super 12 Champion Canterbury Crusaders took part in the season-long case study, aimed at determining the role of enjoyment in the professional game. A key feature of the study was integration of the enjoyment theme into the existing PST programme. This was accomplished by modifying Pinel's (1999) Enjoyment-Profiling intervention[23] to suit the current practices and activities of the team so that it fitted 'logically' into the programme. Gilbert Enoka, Canterbury Crusaders Sport Psychology Consultant, describes the process:

Enjoyment is what keeps Golden Oldies players in the game.

> Wayne is a strong advocate of PST initiatives . . . to this end, Enjoyment-Profiling was a natural extension to my programme regime and it was visited often. I have found that the key to successful implementation involves some degree of modification . . . there is never one best way.

The existing PST programme involved players completing various forms of peak performance profiles followed by discussions with the coaching staff (including the sport psychology consultant). As an extension of the performance focus of the profiles, the enjoyment aspect was added and players were also asked to identify important sources of enjoyment in relation to their performance. Based on the feedback given by the players, they felt that the enjoyment aspect complemented the other aspects of their performance. As one player commented, 'I was actually quite excited about it because it was something I feel I needed in my game to perform well . . . it just helps you stay a bit more focused.'

Five major themes emerged to describe the sources of enjoyment for these professional players (see table opposite). These themes highlight several areas that may help coaches to understand their players better. Therefore, it is important to acknowledge and try to identify the many different sources of enjoyment for players so that coaches can successfully plan to meet their needs.

> The greatest feeling I have ever had as a coach is walking into the changing rooms and seeing the grins on their faces and the enjoyment. That came about because we put a lot more effort into [finding out] what players' enjoy doing during the week and what they enjoy on Saturday [game day], and we work hard at [accomplishing] them.
>
> **Wayne Smith (All Black coach 2000–, Canterbury Crusaders coach 1997–99)**

**Major enjoyment themes (by ranking) and contributing sub-themes.**

| MAJOR THEME | ENJOYMENT SOURCES |
|---|---|
| **1. Social Factors** | *FUN & HUMOUR*<br>• Practical jokes, fun team activities, laughter during training and warm-up<br><br>*SOCIAL INTERACTION*<br>• Being with the boys, off-field social activities, being together while touring<br><br>'I'm looking at that [team] poster at the moment and I think, "You know, it's a good time to be sitting with those blokes, they're all good men and I enjoy my time with them." It's the camaraderie and all those sorts of things.' |
| **2. Performance Factors** | *FOCUSED TEAM TRAINING*<br>• Analysing team errors and aiming to correct them, developing team tactics as a group, training with a shared purpose, short and sharp training<br><br>*TEAM GOALS*<br>• Setting a team goal and working towards it, executing our game plan<br><br>*INDIVIDUAL GOALS*<br>• Analysing and correcting personal errors, striving for improvements, achieving personal goals<br><br>'. . . working out why I played well and things that I need to work on. That made training more enjoyable, although that is probably 'cos you are setting all these goals.' |
| **3. External Factors** | *PERFORMANCE OUTCOMES*<br>• Winning, achieving at this level<br><br>*EXTRINSIC REWARDS*<br>• More free time, travelling and sightseeing, getting paid<br><br>*SOCIAL RECOGNITION & STATUS*<br>• Fan support and praise, playing for the province<br><br>'Enjoyment is having people come to you and say, "Well played in the weekend, I really enjoyed the game." Getting support from all the fans . . . you get a bit of a buzz from that.' |
| **4. Emotional Factors** | *CREATIVE EXPRESSION*<br>• Freedom to run and create plays, personal expression on the field<br><br>*'BIG TIME' EXCITEMENT*<br>• Excitement of the game, hearing the cheer from the crowd, running through the tunnel with the music playing<br><br>'You're playing in front of a crowd and you're playing for your province. That certainly helps as far as motivation and enjoyment goes. It's a great feeling when you run through the tunnel, the music's going and the crowd's cheering.' |
| **5. Balanced Lifestyle** | *OTHER INTERESTS*<br>• Being able to get away from rugby, knowing when to 'switch on' and 'switch off', having other avenues of expression<br><br>'Being able to relax and get away from rugby and just chill out a bit and have other avenues to channel into.' |

# 7 The physics of footie

*David Pease*

> How do you steal the ball away from opponents who are dead set on
> making sure you don't? One is the speed with which you do it . . . The
> other . . . is the art . . . of changing the angle of attack on the player's
> grip on the ball . . . The same methods apply when you have the ball.
> Some guys are far superior to me in strength, so I try to keep changing
> the ball's position or angle so they can't get a good grip on it . . . It's all
> about getting the right angle of purchase. You need to know a bit about
> how levers and fulcrums work, a bit about torque.
>
> **Josh Kronfeld (All Black 1995– )**

When William Webb Ellis supposedly first picked up the ball and ran with it in 1823
he probably didn't think too much about the physics behind the movements he was
making at the time. Most likely, neither did you the first time you played the game.
However, all the movements involved in rugby rely heavily on the laws of physics, and
by understanding them you can learn how to perform them more effectively.

Everything from how fast a winger runs down the field to score a try to how far a
first five-eighth can punt a ball downfield is bound by the laws of physics. In fact,
most everyday movements, including those used in rugby, are based on three basic
laws that are known as Newton's Laws of Uniform Motion. In brief these laws are:

### Law #1

Any object that is either moving or stationary will tend
to stay that way unless a force acts upon it.

You can apply this to rugby by looking at a kick or a pass. In the absence of air
resistance and gravity, once the ball had left your foot or hands it would tend to move

in the same direction forever. But with air resistance and gravity, both of which are forces acting on the ball, you get the behaviour you see in a real game.

---

### Law #2

The force applied to an object is equal to the acceleration
of the objects involved multiplied by their mass.

---

This law can be expressed in the following equation:

F = ma    where F is force, m is mass and a is acceleration.

Now let's apply this to a player starting off running from stationary and accelerating up to a speed of 4 metres per second in about I second. Let's say the player weighs 100 kg. Based on this information we can see that the acceleration (or change in velocity) is 4 metres per second, and the mass is 100 kg. If you plug those values into the equation you'll get an answer for the force the player needs to generate with his or her legs in order to attain that kind of acceleration. In this case the answer works out to 400 newtons of force. A newton is simply a unit of force; if you divide that number by 10 you'll get an equivalent value in kg. So in this case the player needs to apply about 40 kg of force in the direction he or she wants to run in order to attain the required acceleration.

---

### Law #3

For every action there is an equal and opposite reaction.

---

This is probably the best known of Newton's three laws, in one form or another. Let's look at a player jumping in a lineout. For the purposes of this example we'll assume that other players are not assisting during the jump. The way this law works is that for every bit of force the player generates with their body against the ground, the ground pushes back against the player with exactly the same amount of force. This can seem a bit illogical at first glance but think about it as a leg press. When the player pushes the weights with their legs the weights tend to move away in the direction the player is pushing. What happens when the weight is too heavy for the player to budge? He or she tends to get pushed back into the seat. Translating this to our lineout example, if you look at the earth as a hugely heavy weight that the player can't move, since nothing is holding the player in place (as in the leg press chair) they will be pushed up into the air when they push against the earth. It is this 'reaction force' that actually causes the vertical motion. Therefore the greater the amount of force the player can generate against the earth, the greater the reaction force and the greater the height the player can attain.

As you can see these laws are fairly general, so in order to apply them to the basic skill areas of rugby we will use a few more easily applied principles that are based on Newton's laws. These principles are a bit easier to apply to particular movements than the laws themselves.

Later we'll go over some basic ways for you to analyse the techniques you use to perform the various skills involved in your position. If you can determine the physical cause and nature of any technical faults you may have, then you will have made a big step towards maximising your performance.

In this chapter we'll cover some of the basic physics of running, kicking, passing, tackling and scrummaging. The chapter is not designed as a specific technique guide, but will help you understand some of the underlying factors that affect your performance. Some of these will seem like common sense, which is good because it shows that you are already intuitively using physics to enhance your performance. Hopefully by explaining the physics involved you'll be able to analyse your movements more effectively, and improve your performance on the field.

## Basic terms

Before we get to the actual movements we should define some basic terms that will come in handy later on. The most basic term is *mass*. For the purposes of this chapter, you can think of mass as being the same as the weight of a given object, whether it is a person or a ball. In conjunction with mass we also have the term *centre of mass*. Centre of mass is also known as the centre of gravity, and is a single point

Centre of mass position.

that you can use to represent an entire object. This is very handy when you are dealing with an unusually shaped object like the human body. When a person is standing upright their centre of mass lies just around the area of the navel. Because centre of mass represents all the different parts of the body at once it moves according to the movement of various parts of the body. For example, if a person who is standing straight with their hands at their sides (centre of mass around their navel) lifts both arms over their head, the centre of mass will rise slightly because part of the body's mass (the arms) has risen. This is shown in the figure on the facing page, where you can see that the centre of mass (black dot) rises when the arms rise.

Another aspect of the centre of mass is that the object will always tend to rotate around its centre of mass as if it were an axle. This is very important, and we'll come back to it later on.

In order to describe the movement of a mass, we generally use the *velocity* and *acceleration* of the object's centre of mass. Velocity is essentially the same as speed and describes how fast an object is moving in a given direction. Acceleration is simply how fast the object's velocity is changing, either speeding up (accelerating) or slowing down (decelerating).

The next critical term is *force*. While you can probably write your own definition of force, for our purposes we'll say that a force is something that tries to generate movement of an object in a given direction. One of the characteristics of a force is that it tends to cause motion in a straight line. This is because a force's line of action, or the direction of a force at the point of contact with an object, passes through the centre of mass of the object the force is trying to move (see top figure below). Therefore there is no rotation around the object's centre of mass.

This is different to a *torque*, which is essentially a force, but instead of trying to create motion in a straight line, a torque tries to cause motion about an axis of rotation. Think of the axis of rotation as the axle of a wheel, and your hand spinning the wheel around the axle as generating torque. While a force acts through the centre of mass of an object, a torque is created any time the line of action of a force doesn't pass through the centre of mass of an object. This is shown in the bottom figure.

**Effect of a force.**

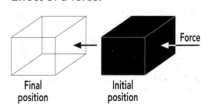

Final position    Initial position

**Effect of a torque.**

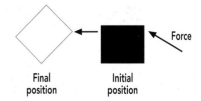

Final position    Initial position

The final term is *momentum*. At its most basic you can call momentum the amount of motion that an object has. It is determined by multiplying the mass of the object by its velocity. Therefore if you have a 100-kg player moving at 2 metres per second and a 50-kg player moving at 4 metres per second, they will have the same amount of motion or momentum. Momentum is also what is described in Newton's first law in that once an object has momentum in a given direction it is going to stay moving in that direction until a force acts on it to change its momentum.

There is one important aspect of momentum that will come in handy when we talk about some of the skills used in rugby. This is that momentum is *conserved*. A good example of this is a tackle situation. A player running down the field has an amount of momentum based on their mass and their velocity. Ahead of the player is a stationary defender who is waiting to make a tackle. Our ball carrier runs into the defender, who holds on in order to bring the ball carrier to the ground. If you watch this scenario unfold you'll notice that the velocity of the two players involved in the tackle decreases. This is because the mass of the ball carrier is increased because they're now also carrying the defender with them. However, if you determine what that new velocity is, as well as the combined mass of the two players, you'll see that the momentum of the two combined players is roughly equal to the momentum of the ball carrier before the tackle occurred. This relationship is shown in the following equations. Mass is shown in kilograms, velocity in metres per second, and momentum is in the unusual units of kilogram metres per second.

100 kg x 4 m/s = 400 kgm/s

This would be the equation for player one alone. Now, assume that player two also weighs 100 kg. Because momentum (in this case 400 kgm/s) is conserved after the tackle has occurred, the equation now looks like this:

200 kg x 2 m/s = 400 kgm/s

This principle applies to all instances where one object interacts with another, whether it's a collision, like the tackle just described, or one part of a player's body acting on another part of their own body. This will be discussed later.

## Pushing vs throwing type motions

One characteristic of almost all human motions is that they lie on a continuum which goes from a pushing type motion, where the entire body acts to exert force at the same time in a given direction, to a throwing type motion, where the segments of the body move in sequence rather than all at once.

The pushing type of motion is very good at generating force, and because all the force is aimed in a single direction it is also very good for tasks requiring accuracy. In rugby this would include scrummaging, and to some extent jumping and passing, although they tend to lie in about the middle of the continuum.

Throwing types of motions are very good at generating high velocities at the other end of the sequence of motion, but are not so good at accuracy when an object is projected at the end of the sequence. Throwing motions can best be described as whip-like in nature. In general these motions also proceed from the largest segments to the smallest (i.e. from the torso to the hand). In rugby this type of motion is involved in kicking and passing, and again to some extent in jumping and running. During a pure throwing type motion there is a very short period of time at which accuracy can be achieved when projecting an object such as a rugby ball, due to the curved path followed by the body segments.

The figure on the right shows the relative differences between the paths followed by a segment at the end of a pushing type motion (flatter path) and at the end of a throwing motion (curved path). Also notice the period indicated by the vertical lines during which accuracy can be achieved for each of these motions. Note that during the flatter path there is a longer period in which accuracy is achievable.

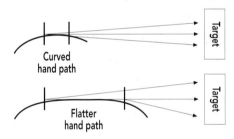

**Effect of movement path on accuracy.**

Because motions such as kicking and passing require different amounts of velocity and accuracy (depending on the circumstances), it is important to know how the motion should be produced differently for each of these circumstances; for example, comparing a normal punt to a 'grubber' kick. Some of these differences will be illustrated in the skill sections that follow.

# Stability

Another characteristic that is vital to all movements, whether you are running, kicking, passing, tackling or scrummaging, is stability. In general, if a player is not in a stable position while executing a skill, the success of that skill is usually compromised. Let's look at some of the characteristics of a stable position, which are described in the following principle.

---

### Principle 1

In order to maintain stability, establish a wide base of support when possible, maintain the centre of mass over the base of support, lower the centre of mass towards the base of support, and shift the centre of mass towards any expected force which may cause instability.

---

The most important of these factors is keeping the centre of mass over the base of support. If you look at the photo below you will see that if you draw a vertical line from the tackler's centre of mass to the ground, the line falls within his base of support, indicated by the horizontal line. For the moment pretend the ball carrier is not moving but is in a stationary position. If you look at the ball carrier and do the same thing as with the tackler, you see that the vertical line is well away from his base of support, shown by the short horizontal line. This means that the tackler is very stable in his position while the ball carrier, if he were not running, would fall over, making him ineffective at moving the ball down the field. Therefore, you can see that aligning the centre of mass over the base of support will keep you on your feet and better able to perform a skill like tackling.

**Stable and unstable positions.**

Now that we have some basic terms and concepts to work with, let's look at some of the skills we use in rugby.

## Running

The most basic skill in rugby is running, and to some extent walking. If you can't get around the field to be involved in the play then you're likely to be fairly useless. With regard to running in rugby, we are primarily interested in two things: straight-line speed and cutting/side-stepping, which is used to change direction. For this we'll consider three more principles.

---

### Principle 2

The amount of momentum you generate depends on the size of the force applied and the amount of time for which that force is applied.

---

In terms of running, the force we're talking about is the *ground reaction force* described above with regard to Newton's third law. This ground reaction force will come up throughout the remainder of this chapter because it is responsible for generating almost all human motion. The next principle is:

---

### Principle 3

Apply forces (i.e. ground reaction forces) in the direction of the desired change of motion (forward, sideways, up, down, etc.).

---

In order to maximise straight-line running speed and give ourselves the maximum amount of momentum, we need to generate large ground reaction forces for a relatively long time. This is done by finding the optimal combination of stride rate (how fast your legs are turning over) and stride length (how far you travel for every complete stride). The relationship looks something like that in the diagram to the right.

You can see that as velocity increases the player is able to increase both stride rate (dashed line) and stride length (solid

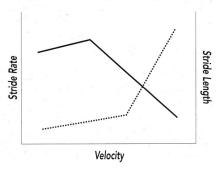

**Relationship of stride rate, stride length and running velocity.**

Christian Cullen lengthening stride as he moves into open space.

**Use of ground reaction force to cause lateral motion.**

Ground reaction force

line) to a point, but then stride length begins to fall off and stride rate begins to climb rapidly. Most players will use a stride rate that is rapid but not so rapid that there is a significant drop off in stride length. If you watch track sprinters you'll see that during the middle part of a race they travel a fairly large distance during every stride they take, while still having quite a rapid stride rate. They have learned through practice what stride rate they need to use in order to maximise their performance.

The problem when applying this to rugby is that with a long stride length, and therefore a relatively low stride rate (or turnover), you aren't able to reposition your foot back on the ground in order to change direction as quickly as if you had a quicker stride and a shorter stride length. If you're not trying to change direction, but simply trying to get from one end of the field to the other as quickly as possible, then a longer stride length is appropriate. However, when you watch players like Christian Cullen or Jeff Wilson running a weaving pattern through defenders they tend to shorten their stride. By quickening their stride they can get their feet back on the ground faster, and into positions that will generate sideways ground reaction forces which cause them to move sideways. It is this lateral force that provides the cutting motion characteristic of much of the running involved in rugby. In the photo at left you can see how the ground reaction force acting on Jeff Wilson's body passes right through his centre of mass, indicated by the white dot. The horizontal white line indicates the proportion of the ground reaction force that is moving him sideways and allowing him to change direction.

Another aspect of this type of movement involves the stability of the player, or their balance. It is important for the player who is about to execute a change of direction that they position themselves so that the ground reaction forces are moving them sideways rather than tipping them over. This is also shown in the photo of Jeff Wilson on the facing page. You can imagine that if the line of the ground reaction force did not pass through Wilson's centre of mass a torque would be created. Remember that objects tend to rotate about their centre of mass, when a torque is applied — the player would start to rotate, which may cause him to fall over. Therefore the best position when changing direction is to lower your body slightly or to lean it in the direction you want to go, so that the ground reaction force will push you sideways rather than tip you over. This is covered in the next principle.

----

### Principle 4

Position the body in such a way as to use
ground reaction forces efficiently.

----

Another important characteristic of high-speed running which is often overlooked is the role of the upper body. Remember when we talked about torque? Running is a prime example of torque generation in that the legs generate a large torque about the vertical axis of the player's body (think of this as a line travelling from the player's head to their feet) when they are driving their knees during the running stride. Therefore, since a torque tends to cause rotation, you would expect that the body would turn in the direction in which the player's legs were driving (i.e. left leg driving forward causing the player to turn to the right) because of the torque the leg was generating. However, we know that the player continues in a straight line rather than turning from side to side. This is due to the contribution of the upper body.

Have you wondered why track sprinters are so big in the arms and shoulders rather than just the legs? They need to have large

**Counter-rotation of arms and legs.**

strong muscles in the upper body in order to generate a torque in the opposite direction to the legs, in order to create a balance between the two halves of the body to keep it moving straight. This principle applies to rugby players as well as to any other athlete trying to sprint, and is nicely shown in the photo of the player on page 141. Note how his upper body is trying to rotate to his right while his legs are trying to rotate to his left. These opposite rotations actually generate the balance described above.

With all the different situations involved in a rugby game, it's important to understand how to modify your running technique to maximise your performance in any given situation, whether it calls for a high-speed sprint or a dramatic change of direction.

## Kicking

Now let's look at kicking. We'll look at both punting and place-kicking; although they require different skills many of the same principles need to be applied if they are to be performed successfully. The drop-kick will essentially be treated as a modified place-kick in terms of the principles involved.

First, let's cover some of the similarities between the different styles of kicking. The most obvious principle that applies to kicking is principle 2 (see page 139): the amount of momentum you generate depends on the size of the force applied and the amount of time for which that force is applied.

Simply stated, if you want to move something to the right, apply a force on it towards the right. This is probably the most basic of all the principles, but when dealing with a movement like kicking there are several factors that must be taken into account when determining the direction in which the force should be applied.

One characteristic of objects moving freely through the air is that they follow a curved path. The factors that determine the maximum height and distance travelled by the object are the height at which it is released, the angle relative to the ground, and it's velocity at the point of release. In terms of kicking, this means that the height a ball will reach and the distance it will travel depend not only on the velocity at which the ball leaves the foot, but also on how far off the ground and the angle at which the ball leaves the kicker's boot.

In the diagram on the facing page you can see the effects of different angles of release on the distance travelled and the height the ball attains. When the ball is kicked from and lands at ground level, the optimal angle of release for distance is about 45° and the optimal angle for height is 90°, or straight up.

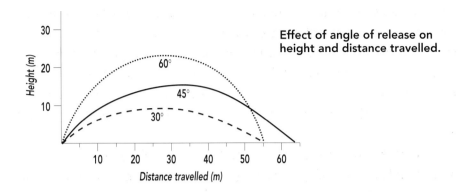

**Effect of angle of release on height and distance travelled.**

In the course of a rugby game kickers will need to determine, based on the situation, if the angle of release needs to be very small, as in a grubber kick, or very steep, as in a midfield bomb. Now that works fine for a place-kick that you're not trying to put through the goal posts, but when you're trying to clear the cross bar the ball needs to be released at an angle greater than 45° in order to attain maximum distance at the point where the ball clears the cross bar. Imagine that you are effectively trying to land the ball on the cross bar. This means that the ball is going to land at a height greater than the height at which it left the ground. In these situations the required angle of release is greater than 45°.

You can see this in the figure above if you imagine that the kicker is attempting a conversion from about 22 metres out from the goal posts: in order to reach the greatest height over 22 metres you need to kick the ball at about a 60° angle. Also notice that the further out from the goal posts you are, the lower the angle of release needs to be.

This is quite different to punting. When the ball leaves the kicker's foot at anything higher than ground level you get the maximum distance at an angle of release of less than 45°, depending on how high the ball is when it leaves the foot. The higher it is when it leaves the foot, the lower the angle. So let's say that a first five-eighth is clearing the ball from deep in his own territory by trying to kick it as far as he possibly can. Let's assume that the ball leaves his foot about 50 cm off the ground. In this case he wants the ball to leave his foot at an angle of somewhere around 44°. The distance travelled will also depend on how hard he kicks the ball and the velocity the ball has attained when it leaves his foot. The faster the ball is travelling, the further it will go for any given angle of release.

So, how does the kicker maximise the velocity of the ball in order to maximise the distance it travels? We already know from principle 1 (see page 138) that momentum is developed not only by the size of the force applied to an object but also the duration over which that force is applied. Therefore, to impart the maximum momentum to the ball (which equates to its velocity, since the ball has a constant mass), we want to apply as large a force as possible over as long a time as possible. We do this by properly sequencing the segments of the body so that the foot is travelling as fast as possible (thereby having a large amount of momentum of its own) when it comes into contact with the ball. The good thing about momentum being conserved is that it can therefore be transferred from one object to another (i.e. foot to ball). Momentum can even be transferred within the human body from one segment to the next as long as proper coordination is used.

In order to determine what the proper sequencing should be, let's take a look at the golf swing. If you play golf you'll know that in order to maximise the distance travelled by the ball you have to use your whole body to generate the necessary club speed at the point of contact with the ball. You know that your body doesn't all move at once, but instead the swing (we'll ignore the backswing) begins with movement of the hips, then the torso, shoulders, upper arms . . . all the way out to the club head. It is this sequencing of the motion that allows for the transfer of momentum from one body segment to the next. Exactly the same principle works with kicking and passing in rugby as well.

----

**Principle 5**

When trying to generate a high linear velocity at the end of a sequence
of rotating segments, the motion should start with the largest
segment in the chain (i.e. the trunk) and travel out to the
smallest segment in a coordinated series of motions.

----

From this principle we can see that the punting and drop-kicking motion should begin with generating motion in the trunk of the body by rotating the hips and shoulders. This is followed by the thigh, lower leg and foot. The trick is to have the motion of each successive segment begin when the previous segment is at its peak velocity. Proper and improper sequences are shown in the graphs opposite.

This figure shows the angular velocity of each segment involved in a kicking motion (i.e. how fast each segment is rotating). Notice that in the properly sequenced motion each segment accelerates when the one before reaches its peak velocity. By sequencing in this manner you are able to get the greatest amount of transfer of momentum between the body segments. In the improperly sequenced motion you will notice that each segment is accelerating at a point where the one before it is either speeding up or slowing down.

**Proper and improper examples of segment training.**

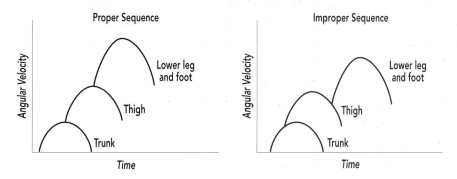

Notice that the peak velocity of the properly sequenced foot is much higher than the foot in the improperly sequenced example. This indicates that there was a more efficient transfer of momentum between the body segments. All other factors being equal, the player who uses the properly sequenced motion will be able to contact the ball with a higher velocity and will therefore generate greater momentum in the ball, which in turn helps the ball travel further.

One trick to this segmental sequencing is that, in order for the kick to be as good as it could possibly be, you must think of the ball as another segment in the chain running from your trunk to your foot. This means you want to contact the ball at the point where your foot is travelling at its peak velocity. In order to achieve this you need to have a good follow-through with your leg, in order to give it time to slow down after contact with the ball. If you don't have a good follow-through your foot will already be slowing down when it makes contact with the ball, which will reduce the distance the ball will travel. A good follow-through will also allow you to maintain contact with the ball for longer (remember momentum depends on force *and* time). This is normally termed 'kicking through the ball', and it is important for maximising the effectiveness of the kick. This is shown in the photo at right.

**Andrew Mehrtens kicking through the ball.**

In the case of goal-kicking, all of the previous discussion applies, with the addition that because of the run-up, you need to transfer the momentum of your entire running body to the ball. Positioning the plant foot firmly and effectively stopping it does this, thereby transferring its momentum to the lower leg and thigh of the plant leg. Each of these segments in turn stops its motion, and the momentum is transferred along the remainder of the sequence described on page 145, beginning with the trunk and continuing out to the ball.

### ACCURACY vs DISTANCE

Up to now we've been primarily concerned with the distance the ball will travel when kicked. When looking at accuracy in kicking, particularly in goal-kicking, we need to modify this a bit. Remember when we talked about pushing vs throwing motions, we said that throwing motions are usually less accurate than pushing type motions. When kicking for optimal distance we are trying to use as pure a throwing motion as we can, therefore we are sacrificing some accuracy. For this reason, when accuracy is desired in a kick and distance is not such a concern, then the kicking motion may tend to be slightly less sequential so that the foot is moving in a straighter line when it contacts the ball. This gives the kicker a longer period of time during which they can accurately direct the ball. As kickers become more skilled and their technique more solid, their kicking motion, regardless of the accuracy requirement, will become more and more sequential, thereby allowing them to be just as accurate from greater distances as they are when close to the posts.

# Passing

In terms of the biomechanics of passing, you can apply virtually all the principles covered under kicking to passing technique. The concept of proper sequencing, beginning with the torso and continuing out to the ball, is exactly the same for passing. In general, however, passing requires a greater amount of accuracy than kicking. This means that the motion of the arms will tend to be slightly more push-like. However, in order to achieve a high-velocity pass the passer must sacrifice some accuracy by employing a more throw-like motion.

### THE DIVE PASS

Due to the similarity in the physics behind both kicking and passing, we won't spend much time on passing. However, as an interesting application of the above principles, let's look at the dive pass.

Dive pass (left) vs standard clearing pass.

In order to investigate the effectiveness of the dive pass, which is primarily used by halfbacks, a small study was conducted using several first-grade halfbacks.[1] In this study a dive pass was compared to a standard clearing pass in terms of velocity at release, time to a target 10 metres away, and accuracy. It was found that the velocity at release was essentially the same, as was time to target. Accuracy was found to be slightly less for the dive pass.

Based on these findings it would seem that the only real advantage of the dive pass is that it is more effective at avoiding oncoming defenders, due to the movement of the halfback. Therefore this seems to be more of a tactical manoeuvre than an enhancement of the pass itself. Using the principles discussed previously, let's see if we can explain why this would be the case.

First let's look at velocity. The primary reason for the lack of an advantage is that in a standard pass the halfback is able to sequence their body segments and transfer their momentum to the ball. In the dive pass the halfback is not able to do this as effectively because they are airborne, and therefore unable to sequentially stop each segment, which in turn limits the amount of transfer of momentum to the ball. To compensate for this the halfback uses the initial velocity gained from the dive to give the ball some initial velocity prior to the actual passing motion of the arms. Time to target is therefore no different because the velocities are quite similar. As for accuracy, we need to look at the next principle, which is an extension of principle 3.

---

### Principle 6

When trying to achieve accuracy, have as many segments moving in the desired direction of movement as possible while limiting any motion in other directions.

---

During the dive pass there is a much greater potential for movement out of the line of motion of the ball, due to the highly unstable position the halfback is in. One thing the above principle doesn't say is that it is very important to have a solid base of support when trying to achieve accuracy. During the normal clearing pass the halfback is usually fairly low to the ground and has his or her legs spread wide. This is a very stable position and gives a firm base from which to direct the necessary forces on the ball. It also allows for more effective transfer of the ground reaction forces than during the airborne phase of the dive pass. Therefore, the dive pass can be much more effective when under pressure from the opposition, while the standard pass is generally a more accurate method of passing the ball.

## Tackling

As with the skills discussed above, tackling is highly variable in nature due to the wide variety of situations in which a tackle occurs. Therefore we'll just touch on some basics.

In order to be most effective a tackler needs to be able to generate sufficient momentum in his or her own body to counteract the momentum of the player with the ball. Probably the most important of the principles above in terms of tackling is principle 1 (page 138), which influences a tackler in two ways. First, starting a tackle from a stable position allows the tackler to adjust to any changes in direction by the ball carrier. If the tackler is not in a stable position, such as when they are overcommitted to a tackle, they are not able to change direction and the ball carrier can more easily avoid the tackle. Second, if you are not in a relatively stable position when you go into a tackle, you won't be able to utilise the ground reaction forces effectively to generate momentum. In order to achieve this stability it is important for the tackler to keep his or her centre of gravity low to the ground and to lean towards the oncoming ball carrier.

The reason for leaning into the tackle is that it gives more time for the tackler to apply force from a stable position because, even if they are pushed back by the ball carrier, their centre of gravity is still over their base of support. This also allows for a decrease in the force required at a given instant in time. If the tackler doesn't lean into the tackle then in order to get the same result, according to principle 2, they will need to apply a much greater force over a shorter period of time, which tends to cause the jarring impacts sometimes seen on the field. The generation of these very high forces is not only harder to achieve but it also greatly increases the risk of an injury to both the tackler and the ball carrier. This leads us to the next principle:

## Principle 7

When involved in an impact situation, use proper
techniques and equipment to minimise the forces involved.

Again, this is a general rule of thumb. Obviously this could be taken to extremes where a tackler applies an absolute minimum of force and the ball carrier is still able to travel 20 metres. The trick is finding the middle ground, where the impact forces experienced by the body are lower but are still at a level where the tackler is able to stop the ball carrier. However, it is particularly important for young and inexperienced players to be instructed with this principle in mind.

Now let's get back to principle 7. As well as technique, the other factor mentioned was equipment. In general this means padding of some kind. In recent years there has been a marked increase in the use of shoulder pads by players. While they are very effective at absorbing some of the forces involved in collisions, there is one factor of which both players and coaches must be aware.

Research has found that when players use padding to absorb forces, they tend to overestimate the cushioning effect of the pads.[2] As a result they fail to use the techniques of limiting forces and end up actually absorbing higher forces in their body than if they weren't wearing pads.[3] Again, this is particularly important for young players; it is vital that coaches instruct players in the proper techniques and don't let them 'overuse' the pads. When used properly, padding is very effective at reducing the rate of injury to players. When used improperly, there is potential for severe injury, which could end a player's career before it gets started.

So far we've mainly been looking at the tackler. Now let's take a quick look at the ball carrier. The same principles in terms of collisions apply to the ball carrier as to the tackler, but the ball carrier's goal is to get the defender into an unstable position where they are less effective. They also want to have as little force acting on them as possible. This is where a side-step or swerve away from the

**Moving away from a tackle.**

tackler can be used. By moving away from the tackler the ball carrier is able to draw them into an unstable position, as mentioned previously. Don't forget, though, that to achieve this the ball carrier must also maintain a stable position by keeping their centre of gravity low and over their base of support. You can see in the photo on page 149 how the ball carrier is moving away from the tackler, drawing him into an unstable position while remaining fairly stable himself (the strong fend doesn't hurt either).

However, the ball carrier doesn't always want to try and avoid the tackler. If they are trying to set up a ruck to draw in more defenders or, in the case of Jonah Lomu, sometimes trying to run straight through the tackler, they need to apply the same technique as the tackler of leaning towards the expected impact. If you watch a player run into a tackle situation you will see that just before impact they have a tendency to lean towards the tackler. This enables them to remain in a relatively stable position for longer, which gives them more control to set up a ruck or maul, offload the ball to a supporting player, or continue running down the field (if they are powerful enough to break through the tackle). Hopefully, you're getting the idea that stability is one of the key factors in virtually all of the skills involved in rugby.

## Scrummaging

The last skill we'll talk about is scrummaging. This is a skill that obviously doesn't depend on a single individual, but rather a group of eight individuals acting as a single unit. The most important principle for scrummaging is principle 4 (position the body in such a way as to use ground reaction forces efficiently). Body position is all-important in scrummaging: small flaws in position can ruin the effectiveness of the scrum by not allowing a proper transfer of the ground reaction forces onto the opposing pack.

When the eight players are in the proper position, these ground reaction forces are channelled through them into a single horizontal force of significant magnitude. It is because of the magnitude of this force that players must maintain the characteristic flat-backed posture. This allows for a smooth transfer of force through a player's body. If the back is curved this force will tend to bend the player in half. Imagine hammering on a nail. When the nail is straight a considerable force can be applied without damaging the nail and it can be pounded flush. If the same nail is slightly bent and you try to pound it in, the nail bends more and is useless.

The same principle applies to the body. A curved back not only limits the amount of force that can be generated, but it also greatly increases the potential for injury to the players. This is why players involved in the scrum need to apply force to the players in front of them along a line that passes straight along their backs, so that no bending forces are generated. This is shown in the photo below.

Another principle that applies to scrummaging is principle 6. While you're not really looking for pinpoint accuracy in scrummaging, you want to limit any unwanted lateral motion so that all the force is applied forward. Of course, if you are attempting to wheel the scrum one way or the other for tactical reasons, you will have to apply this unified force slightly differently, by leading in one or the other of your props in order to create a torque in the opposition pack. Whether you are trying to engage straight ahead or are trying to wheel the opposition scrum, the players need to be tightly bound in the scrum so that they don't split apart when the scrum engages. By being tightly bound the scrum is more like a single force-generating unit than a bunch of individuals.

The other advantage of keeping the scrum functioning as a single unit is that by limiting extra, unwanted movement you can decrease the risk of injury. If there is some 'slop' in the scrum there is more potential for twisting and bending of the players' bodies.

Once again this all comes back to coaches teaching proper technique, particularly to young and inexperienced players. Everyone knows that, because of the very high forces involved in scrummaging, there is always the possibility of a player suffering a catastrophic injury. With better technique and the proper application and transfer of the forces involved, this risk can at least be controlled. Further scientific information on scrummaging can be found in a selection of literature.[4]

Proper scrummaging technique.

# Qualitative analysis

Now that we have covered some of the basic physics behind some rugby skills, let's look at how we can evaluate our performance of them on the field.

In biomechanics there are two different types of analysis commonly performed: qualitative and quantitative analysis. Qualitative analysis is essentially a description of the movement in terms of velocity, acceleration, position, etc. Most of this can be done using a video camera strategically positioned to capture the movement.

Quantitative analysis is more concerned with what is causing the observed motions. In other words, it examines the forces and torques involved in a given technique. Due to the fact that most quantitative analysis requires the use of very expensive specialised equipment, it is usually performed in a laboratory situation by a trained biomechanist. This doesn't do much for the everyday coach or player unless they have access to such facilities. Therefore we'll focus on qualitative analysis, because it can be performed by anyone with a video camera who understands what they're looking for.

## WHAT TO OBSERVE

The first step in performing a qualitative analysis is to determine exactly what you want to look at. For example, in the case of kicking you may want to look at the kicker's approach, kicking motion, or follow-through, depending on the requirements of that particular player.

In order to determine what the important characteristics are in each of these phases of the overall motion, it is sometimes helpful to establish a list of critical features for a particular skill. This type of list can take many forms, depending on who makes it. When preparing the list you should try to break down the overall skill into phases that can be looked at separately. For example, a place-kick can be broken down into the run-up, plant, leg swing, contact, and follow-through phases. Once you know what the physics are behind the motion, such as those we have looked at above, you can apply the physics to your list of characteristics. This will then allow you to make modifications, based on the physics of the movement, in order to enhance performance.

Once you have your list of significant features and a good idea of the aspects of technique which need to be examined, you need to be able to observe the player performing the skill. Normally a coach can do this by watching. However, the coach is not performing the skill, and often a player's interpretation of a coach's comments is very different from what the coach intends.

A good way to rectify this situation is to videotape the player and then to have the coach and the player watch the video together. This way the player can see exactly what they are doing, rather than getting it second-hand through the coach. Once the skill has been observed, the coach and player can then discuss what was observed and determine what can be corrected to improve performance. The player can work on making the corrections and then go through the videotaping process again.

One thing to remember when performing this or any type of analysis which may lead to technique alteration is that due to the complexity of most skills a change in one seemingly minor aspect of the skill can alter the entire movement. Therefore work on only one correction at a time until you see that you are getting the desired results. Remember, every player is different, and sometimes slight structural differences in a player's body can cause theoretically positive alterations in technique that actually decrease performance. By working on one aspect at a time you are more able to see what alterations are effective for that particular player.

It is also important to give the player sufficient time to adapt to any modifications in technique. It is not uncommon for performance to decrease immediately following a 'correction', but with practice performance will rebound and then become even better than it was before.

## VIDEOTAPING BASICS

It is surprising how few coaches and players use video to analyse performance when you consider the wealth of information that a single video session can provide. This is largely because a video takes a picture of the player 25 times a second: if the old saying 'A picture paints a thousand words' is true, a second of video is worth a whole lot of words from a coach. However, for the video to be most useful there are some factors that need to be taken into consideration.

1.  The most important factor is *camera position*. If you want to look at the angle at which the ball is leaving a kicker's foot you don't want to view the kick from in front or behind the kicker, you want to be looking from the side (i.e. perpendicular to the direction the ball is going to travel). However, if you want to look at the amount of tilt in the kicker's body, you may want to view them from behind. Again, it all depends on what aspect of the skill you want to analyse.

2.  The *environment* in which the filming takes place is also very important. Try to have few distractions around the player. You want the player to be focused on what they are doing and not on what other people are up to. Also, try to have the background behind the player as plain as possible. If there are a lot of

people or other things in the background it can distract your eye when you are trying to analyse the skill later. In addition, try to have as much light as possible so that you get nice clear images.

3.  The correct *camera set-up* will further enhance the quality of your videotape. This starts with keeping the camera still during filming. If possible use a tripod during the taping process. Also, use a sufficient shutter speed so that there is no blurring of the player's body when using slow-motion playback during analysis. Typically you should be able to use a 1/250th of a second shutter setting, but this will depend on the amount of light available. On a sunny day you shouldn't have any problems but if it is overcast you may have to decrease the shutter speed to let sufficient light into the camera. In addition, always have the camera set to MANUAL focus. If you have the camera on AUTO, the image will likely go in and out of focus during the performance of the skill.

4.  The next factor is *image size*. Try to have the player as big in the view of the camera as possible while still being able to see the entire performance of the skill. For some skills this may mean that you have to use several cameras to cover the entire area the player uses during performance of the skill.

5.  *Image quality* can also be enhanced by using good quality VHS or SVHS tape.

6.  The way the *subject is dressed* is also a consideration. Try not to let the player wear baggy clothes that may limit your view of what their body is doing underneath the clothes.

7.  Finally, *keep a record* of what you are doing. This simply needs to be a sheet of paper where you keep track of the date, conditions, and comments on each trial in terms of its success, smoothness or some other characteristic. It is crucial that you do this so that when you go back and look at the video you know if there were any instructions given to the player or if something happened which may have affected their performance. It is also a good idea to indicate on the tape itself the trial number. This can be done by having numbered flash cards or even having the player hold up the appropriate number of fingers. This makes it much easier to compare the comments from the filming record with the video.

## ANALYSIS OF PERFORMANCE

In order to optimise the usefulness of the videotape watch it on as big a screen as you can find. The bigger the image is, the more clearly you can see things. Also, use a VCR that has a frame-by-frame mode or at least a slow-motion playback. By slowing the motion down you can detect aspects of the skill that you are unlikely to see when viewing at normal speed. Keep in mind the physical principles governing the particular skill you are looking at, so that you have a firm basis for making alterations to technique.

As mentioned above, a small change can have a huge effect on a skill. For this reason try to prioritise the corrections, from obvious flaws that must be corrected down to minor flaws for which correction may or may not improve performance. Once you have done this go and work on the technique corrections one at a time.

It is important to videotape the player again, particularly after any big changes have been made, to detect whether the correction of one fault has corrected any of the other faults that were seen earlier. Progress is made much more quickly if video sessions are conducted frequently, rather than with one-off sessions when the player doesn't see what their technique looks like after making corrections.

## Conclusion

Hopefully, from this chapter you have gained an insight into some of the basic physics of rugby skills. Remember that 'smart training' doesn't just mean physical training; biomechanics and technique in general are vital to the performance of any sport skill, so don't ignore technique evaluation. You'll be amazed by how effective regular videotaping of a skill can be at improving technique. By using the information provided in this chapter you can also begin to form a common language for communicating not only what changes need to be made, but the basis for those changes.

# 8 Eating smart

*Katrina Darry*

> Lunch at 11.30 consisted of mushroom soup, spaghetti with tomato sauce, pork chops, potatoes, salad and cold chicken legs followed by fresh fruit salad. Pre-match food of soup and sandwiches is available from 1 p.m.
>
> **Victor Ubogu (England prop 1992–99)**

For most people, the association of rugby and food conjures up visions of steaming meat pies, chips, and a can or three of beer. In fact, until a few years ago, this was exactly what rugby players were eating. The night before a game included eating a large steak, and a breakfast of bacon, eggs, toast and perhaps some spaghetti was eaten with gusto in anticipation of the big game ahead.

In the changing rooms of professional rugby players today you will not find beer, and most certainly not hot pies or chips. Instead you will find large amounts of sports drink, sandwiches, bananas, and other varieties of fruit. So what happened? What caused this change in the eating habits of today's rugby players?

With the growing need for rugby players to perform at a higher level than ever before, especially with the advent of professionalism, every aspect of a player's life that could improve their performance has been analysed. What a player eats has a major impact on their performance on the field. To compete at their best a player must incorporate the correct ratio of nutrients to provide them with optimal energy, eaten at the correct time of the day, in the appropriate amounts.

There are four different nutrients in food that give us energy. These are carbohydrates, protein, fat and alcohol. These nutrients are referred to as *macronutrients*.

During exercise our body accesses these nutrients from their various storage pools and breaks them down to provide energy for the contracting muscles. Of these

The meat pie —traditional rugby fare.

nutrients the main fuels for exercise are carbohydrate and fat. Only small amounts of protein are used as a fuel unless the body is starved of carbohydrate. Alcohol does not contribute energy to the exercising muscle.

When we exercise, carbohydrate and fat react with oxygen, and are broken down to produce a product called ATP (adenosine triphosphate), which provides our muscles with the energy they need to contract (see chapter 4). At moderate exercise intensities (up to 75 percent $VO_2$max) both fat and carbohydrate contribute equal amounts of energy to the contracting muscles. This is known as *aerobic* metabolism. Although many of us have large amounts of stored fat, it is difficult to mobilise fat fast enough to provide enough energy for higher-intensity exercise (greater than 75 percent of $VO_2$max). We therefore rely on carbohydrate, which can produce energy without oxygen. At exercise intensities greater than 75 percent $VO_2$max, carbohydrate is the main provider of energy. This is known as *anaerobic* metabolism. So what is the dominant fuel source for rugby players?

As we have seen, the *intensity* of the exercise dictates the key fuel that is used. Research indicates that rugby players, especially forwards, spend a large part of the game at exercise intensities higher than 75 percent $VO_2$max.[1] This suggests that the dominant fuel for rugby is carbohydrate. The *duration* of the exercise also dictates the choice of fuel.

All the carbohydrate we eat is broken down into the simple sugar unit of glucose and absorbed into the bloodstream. From here it is either stored in the muscle (79 percent of total) or liver (14 percent of total) in the form of glycogen (which consists of many glucose units joined together and is the storage form of carbohydrate), or it remains in the blood (7 percent of total) as glucose.

The body usually has enough carbohydrate stores to last for 30–90 minutes of exercise, depending on its intensity. In sports of long duration (>60–90 min), carbohydrate stores may be at risk of becoming depleted. Therefore, a rugby player runs a high risk of becoming low in carbohydrate stores (muscle glycogen) during a rugby game. Research has shown that fatigue sets in when carbohydrate reserves in the muscle become low. Studies have shown that soccer and rugby players who start a game with low carbohydrate stores do less running at high speed compared to those who have adequate carbohydrate reserves.[2]

To exercise at high intensities and delay the onset of fatigue you must either obtain high stores of carbohydrate *before* you exercise, or replace the lost carbohydrate fuel *during* exercise. This highlights the importance of eating adequate carbohydrate before, during and after exercise.

Fitness plays a significant role here. Regular training at moderate to high intensities enhances your ability to take up more oxygen and therefore utilise fat more efficiently as a fuel (see chapter 4). This helps to preserve your important carbo-hydrate stores. Consuming a high-carbohydrate diet encourages the muscles to store carbohydrate, and as a result you can exercise longer at higher intensities.

## The rugby diet

So let's pull all this information together to give us an idea of what a rugby player should be eating to achieve peak performance.

Due to the intensity and duration of practices and games, and the great deal of time spent at intensities above 75 percent $VO_2$max, we have seen that the nutrient that should be most commonly found in a rugby player's diet is *carbohydrate*.

## Carbohydrate

There is a wide range of carbohydrate foods for the rugby player to choose from. It is important to choose those that are nutritious or nutrient-dense (i.e. contain large amounts of vitamins and minerals), rather than those that are non-nutritious (i.e. contain low levels of vitamins and minerals).

## NUTRITIOUS CARBOHYDRATES

| | | |
|---|---|---|
| Breads | Cereals | Dairy products |
| Flour | Fruit | Fruit juice |
| Grains | Legumes | Low-fat baking |
| Low-fat muesli bars | Pasta | Rice |
| Starchy vegetables | | |

## NON-NUTRITIOUS CARBOHYDRATES

| | | |
|---|---|---|
| Cordials | High-fat baking | High-fat muesli bars |
| Honey | Ice blocks | Jam |
| Lollies | Pastries | Potato chips |
| Soft drinks | Sports drinks | Sugars |
| Syrups | | |

### DAILY CARBOHYDRATE REQUIREMENTS DURING TRAINING

The amount of carbohydrate a rugby player eats regularly is important. For most players, training lasts at least 60 minutes. It takes up to 24 hours to recover the carbohydrate used during such training sessions, and if there are consecutive training sessions within 24 hours there will be considerable strain on your carbohydrate reserves. Rugby players also perform some form of exercise most days of the week, so eating a high-carbohydrate diet seven days a week is absolutely vital to ensure recovery from all training sessions and games.

You should aim to get 55–65 percent of your total daily energy intake from carbohydrates. This can be described as the amount of carbohydrate in grams per kilogram of bodyweight. Rugby players need to eat about 7–8 g of carbohydrate per kg of bodyweight, most of which should be from the nutritious carbohydrate food group.

For example, Ben, our openside flanker from previous chapters, is hoping to play rugby at national provincial level this season. To ensure that his diet is optimal to support not only his own training but also the team training sessions, he wants to work out what his daily carbohydrate needs are. At present his bodyweight is 100 kg.

Carbohydrate assessment for Ben:

> 100 x 7 g = 700 g
> 100 x 8 g = 800 g

Ben's carbohydrate requirement is therefore between 700 g and 800 g each day.

To make it easier to work out how much carbohydrate you are eating, you can break it into 20-g portions (see page 191). Ben would need 35 to 40 portions each day. These should be evenly spread out over all meals and snacks. For example:

Breakfast      = 9 portions carbohydrate

Post-training = 5 portions carbohydrate

Lunch          = 9 portions carbohydrate

Pre-training  = 5 portions carbohydrate

Dinner         = 8 portions carbohydrate

Supper         = 4 portions carbohydrate

It isn't necessary to calculate your carbohydrate intake each day, but it does help to do it every so often to get a good guide. Here are some tips to help you eat enough carbohydrate each day.

## EAT-SMART TIPS TO ENSURE A GOOD CARBOHYDRATE INTAKE

Nutritious carbohydrates should form the basis of all meals and snacks. These can include bread, cereals, pasta, rice, fruit and starchy vegetables.

➤ Eat a variety of fruits, such as dried, stewed, tinned and raw fruit.

➤ Eat starchy vegetables such as potatoes, kumara, taro, yams, peas and corn regularly with meals.

➤ Try different varieties of bread, such as fruit, pita and mountain bread, rolls, bagels and crumpets.

➤ Try different varieties of pasta and rice as a side or main dish. Make sure you use low-fat sauces.

➤ Make use of low-fat carbohydrate desserts, such as fruit with cereal and yoghurt or milk, milk puddings using trim milk, and low-fat fruit crumbles.

➤ Try fruit smoothies (milk, fruit and yoghurt blended together) as a snack or a quick meal replacement.

A basic guide is to have about 75 percent of your meal plate taken up by nutritious carbohydrate foods.

You may find you have difficulty eating all the carbohydrate that you need, due to the bulk of the foods. Here are some tips to help you boost your intake.

## EAT-SMART TIPS TO BOOST YOUR ENERGY INTAKE

➤ Choose low-fibre foods (e.g. white bread, white rice).

➤ Eat little and often. This will reduce the bulk of each meal.

➤ Use liquids that are high in carbohydrate (e.g. fruit juice, trim milk, fruit smoothies, sports drinks, high-carbohydrate meal replacements such as Gatorade).

➤ Use simple sugars (e.g. use jam and honey on toast, add sugar to foods, eat jubes).

## EXERCISE AND CARBOHYDRATE INTAKE

One very important feature of carbohydrate foods that has a strong influence on rugby performance is the speed at which carbohydrates are broken down into glucose, absorbed into the bloodstream, and cause a rise in blood glucose levels. This is indicated by a food's glycaemic index (GI). This is a rating that indicates the extent to which a particular food raises blood glucose above normal levels. Bread and simple glucose give the greatest increase and are given a rating of 100. That is, their glucose is released quickly into the blood and is available to use as a fuel source. Factors that slow down a food's absorption, and thus decrease its GI rating, include the protein, fibre and fat content. The form of the carbohydrate food — whether it is dry, a paste, raw, or cooked — will also affect the rate of absorption. New Zealand foods for which a glycaemic index has been identified are listed below.

*Foods with a high glycaemic index (rating 70–100)*

Bread (white, wholemeal, Fibre White, and Molenberg)

| | | |
|---|---|---|
| Broad beans | Calrose quick rice | Carboshotz |
| Cornflakes | Glucose | Golden Fruit biscuits |
| Jelly beans | Kumara | Lucozade |
| Parsnip | Potato, baked and mashed | Pumpkin |
| Rice bubbles | Sports drinks | Squeezies |
| Sunbrown quick rice | Swede | Tinned spaghetti |
| Watercrackers | Watermelon | Weet-Bix |

*Foods with a moderate glycaemic index (rating 55–75)*

| | | |
|---|---|---|
| Bananas | Beetroot | Cordials |
| Couscous | Crumpets | Honey |
| Ice-cream | Maize | Miniwheats |
| Nutrigrain | Pineapple | Potatoes, new |
| Puffed wheat | Ryvita | Sao crackers |
| Soft drinks | Sucrose | Sustain |

*Foods with a low glycaemic index (rating <55)*

| | | |
|---|---|---|
| All-Bran | Apple | Apple bran muffins |
| Apple juice | Apricots, fresh and dried | Baked beans |
| Basmati rice | Blueberry bran muffins | Bulghur wheat |
| Bürgen mixed grain bread | Bürgen rye bread | Carrots |
| Cherries | Chickpeas | Chocolate |
| Dates | Fructose | Grapefruit |
| Grapes | Green beans | Kidney beans |
| Kiwifruit | Lactose | Lentils |
| Maggi 2-minute noodles | Mango | Milk (all varieties) |
| Mother Earth muesli bars | Muesli (all varieties) | Oatbran bread |
| Orange juice | Oranges | Pasta (all) |
| Peaches | Pears | Peas |
| Pita bread | Plums | Popcorn |
| Porridge | Raisins | Rice (long-grain) |
| Rice (parboiled) | Rockmelons | Rolled oats |
| Soya beans | Special K | Sultana Bran |
| Sultanas | Sustagen | Sweetcorn |
| Taro | Yams | Yoghurt |

The glycaemic index of a carbohydrate food can help you identify the role the food may play in enhancing your rugby performance when taken before, during and after exercise. You must remember that these foods have all been tested as individual foods, and the glycaemic index of a mixed meal is different. For example, when you add milk to cornflakes you lower the glycaemic index of the cornflakes. Adding protein, fibre or fat to a food also lowers the GI.

*Before exercise*

Carbohydrate foods eaten before exercise top up the supply of muscle glycogen and blood glucose. About 200–300 g of carbohydrate food should be consumed 3–4 hours before exercise, or 50–100 g 2 hours before exercise. To get the most benefit, this food should be low in fat, protein and fibre, and be well tolerated. Some research suggests using moderate to high GI foods for this meal/snack.[3]

**Example of a pre-training or pre-game meal (230 g carbohydrate)**

3 pieces toast + 3 tsp butter/margarine

1 x 440 g tin spaghetti

1½ cups mashed potato (2–3 baked potatoes)

1 banana

1 litre sports drink

**Example of a pre-training or pre-game snack (50 g carbohydrate)**

1–2 cups cereal and trim milk

2 pieces toast and mashed banana

honey sandwich using 2 pieces bread

creamed corn toastie pie

½ tin baked beans on 2 pieces toast

1 iced fruit bun and 1 banana

750 ml sports drink

1 fruit smoothie (1 glass trim milk blended with 1 banana and 4 tbsp yoghurt)

Of course, you can make up your own meals or snacks using the 20-g portions on page 191.

In the 10–15 minutes before exercise you should try to drink about 500 ml of 5–8 percent glucose concentration sports drink. This will give you a top-up of 30–40 g of glucose, which will help maintain or elevate your blood glucose levels and increase the glucose available as a fuel during the exercise session or game. Be careful, however; some people's stomachs cannot tolerate this, or they feel lightheaded and dizzy with the changes in blood sugar levels. Try it at training sessions first.

*During exercise*

Consuming carbohydrate during exercise can delay the onset of fatigue by anywhere from 30 to 60 minutes, and increase sprinting ability towards the end of the game.[4] This carbohydrate not only acts as a source of energy but it also helps to maintain blood glucose levels in the later stages of exercise. Since your carbohydrate stores will start to run low after about 60 minutes of exercise, it is advisable to consume high GI foods or fluids during any training session or game. Fluids are probably the easiest to consume, and you also kill two birds with one stone by consuming both carbohydrate and water (see Fluids, page 175).

Your muscles need about 30–60 g of glucose for every hour of exercise, which equates to 500–1000 ml of sports drink per hour. So that the drink has time to be absorbed and the glucose made available to the muscles, you must start drinking it as soon after the start of exercise as possible. This means that you must make the most of every break in play to drink.

### After exercise

Following a heavy training session or game your carbohydrate stores will be fairly low. It takes about 24 hours to reload your muscles if you eat a high-carbohydrate diet; if you do not, then the recovery period is longer. It is critical for rugby players who are doing some form of heavy training every day, if not twice a day, to ensure there is a rapid recovery of the carbohydrate stores.

#### Type of carbohydrate

The most appropriate carbohydrates to take after exercise appear to be moderate to high GI foods or fluids.

#### Amount

You should have at least 50 g (up to 1 g per kg of bodyweight) of carbohydrate immediately after any exercise, and then 50 g every two hours after that. The list on the facing page gives some examples of 50 g of moderate to high GI foods/fluids that you could consume immediately after a training session or game.

#### Timing

You should eat carbohydrate foods as soon as possible after exercise, while the muscles are still warm and receptive to reloading carbohydrate. This will promote a rapid recovery.

#### Proteins to aid recovery

Protein eaten with your carbohydrate recovery foods helps to repair any muscle damage that may have occurred either from the type of exercise performed or from contact damage. The protein also aids the passage of glycogen into the muscle cells. The recommended amount is 10–20 g taken with your recovery carbohydrate food (see page 193 for protein portions).

### Ideal recovery foods

➤ 50 g of high to moderate GI foods or fluids with 10–20 g protein (choose at least one of these options). Note: it is important to ensure that these foods have no added fat.

➤ 1 ham or chicken sandwich (2 slices of bread) with 1 cup sports drink

➤ Banana sandwich and a pottle of yoghurt

➤ 1 cup cornflakes or ricies + 1 cup trim milk

➤ 3 medium baked potatoes or 1 cup mashed potato and a glass of flavoured milk

➤ 2 pieces toast, 1 tin spaghetti and a milk Milo

➤ 1 cup calrose rice, 50 g tuna and vegetables

➤ 2 crumpets with honey or jam and a pottle of yoghurt

➤ 100 g jelly beans or jubes and 250 ml flavoured milk

➤ 800–1000 ml sports drink and a pottle of yoghurt

➤ 6 Golden Fruit biscuits with 250 ml flavoured milk

➤ 2 fruit bread buns and 250 ml flavoured milk

Over the next 24 hours you should eat at least 600 g of carbohydrate, or about 8 g carbohydrate per kg bodyweight. In particular, for the first 24 hours after a game the fat and protein content of your meals should be kept to a minimum. The following is an example of a meal outline for the 24 hours after a game.

### Meal plan for 24 hours containing >600 g carbohydrate

AFTER GAME:    500 ml sports drink

Jam or honey sandwich or 2 fruit bread buns

MEAL 2 HOURS    120–150 g lean meat, chicken or fish (palm size)
AFTER GAME:
4–5 baked or mashed potatoes or 2–3 cups calrose rice (cooked)

1–2 cups vegetables or salad including high GI vegetables

2 slices white bread + 2 tsp butter or margarine

500 ml fruit juice

*Dessert:* 1 cup cereal + fruit + milk/yoghurt,
*or* fruit and 1 cup low-fat ice-cream

BREAKFAST:    2 cups cereal

1–2 cups milk

1 cup fruit

2 slices toast + 2 tsp butter or margarine + jam or honey

MID-MORNING:    1 banana + 4 Golden Fruit biscuits + 1 cup fruit juice, *or* 2 slices toast + 2 tsp butter or margarine + jam, honey or banana

LUNCH:    3 slices toast + 3 tsp butter or margarine

1 x 440g tin spaghetti or baked beans

Fruit muffin, scone, or slice of fruit loaf

Fruit

1 cup milk

MID-AFTERNOON: Banana sandwich

Fruit smoothie

Unfortunately, many rugby players tend to drink large amounts of alcohol in the twelve hours following a game. This has a drastic effect on their recovery.

## Effects of alcohol on recovery

➤ Alcohol is a diuretic, therefore it dehydrates you at a time when you should be rehydrating.

➤ It slows down the muscles' ability to reload lost carbohydrate stores.

➤ It causes increased swelling and pain to injury sites.

➤ It causes hangover, which induce you to eat high-fat, low-nutrient foods that do not aid recovery.

If you are going to drink alcohol, you must have your post-exercise snack and a meal before consumption begins (at least two hours post-game). Drink plenty of water and sports drink to ensure that you have clear urine. You must also ensure that you eat the recommended 600 g of carbohydrate in the 24 hours after the game.

You may find that the breakfast and mid-morning snacks that are typically eaten the day after a game will be eaten together as a type of brunch, which is fine, but you must continue eating as suggested for the remainder of the day.

# Protein

Protein plays an important part in a rugby player's diet. It is used as the building blocks for muscle and tissues; as a component of many different hormones and enzymes it helps to maintain an active immune system; and it makes a small contribution to muscle fuel.

Because rugby players regularly take part in resistance training, and because rugby is a contact sport with a high injury rate, the protein requirements of players are greater than those of people who live a more sedentary lifestyle.

Protein should provide 12–15 percent of your total daily energy intake. For a rugby player this would translate to between 1.4 and 2.0 g of protein per kg bodyweight. The upper end of the range is for those who take part in three or more weights sessions a week, while the lower end is for those doing none.

For example, Mark is a prop who weighs in at 105 kg. He does two weights sessions a week as part of his weekly training. He should therefore be consuming about 1.5–1.7 g protein per kg bodyweight a day.

105 x 1.5 = 157.5 g   105 x 1.7 = 178.5 g

Mark's protein needs are therefore in the range of 155–180 g protein each day.

As with carbohydrate, we can use protein portions to help keep track of our intake. In Mark's case, 10-g portions are ideal (see page 193 for 10-g portions of protein). Mark's protein intake should be 15–18 portions each day, spread evenly through the day.

Breakfast     = 3 portions protein

Post-training = 2 portions protein

Lunch         = 3 portions protein

Pre-training  = 2 portions protein

Dinner        = 4 portions protein

Supper        = 2 portions protein

Not only is the amount of protein important, but so is the quality. Proteins can be broken down into amino acids. Of the twenty known amino acids, eight are known as 'essential amino acids', and we must obtain these on a daily basis from our food. Foods that contain all eight of these essential amino acids are called 'high-quality' or 'complete' proteins. These proteins are more easily utilised by our bodies.

*High-quality protein foods include*

| Cheese | Eggs | Fish | Meat |
|--------|------|------|------|
| Milk | Poultry | Yoghurt | |

'Low-quality' or 'incomplete' protein foods contain only six or seven of the essential amino acids and are not easily utilised by the body. Therefore, their protein is less able to meet your body's needs.

*Low-quality protein foods include*

| Bread | Cereals | Grains | Legumes |
|-------|---------|--------|---------|
| Nuts | Seeds | | |

# Fat

Although fat can make a significant contribution as a fuel during low-intensity exercise, it is not necessary to have a generous intake, as most of us have the ability to store ample amounts of fat. In fact, even the leanest of athletes will have enough fat stores to run continuously for several days.

Fat is very energy-dense. It provides 37 kilojoules (kJ) of energy per gram, compared with carbohydrate and protein which provide 16 and 17 kilojoules per gram respectively. This means it is very easy to consume large amounts of fat and calories in a small mouthful. Compare:

| I tbsp cream = 6 g fat | 0.5 g carbohydrate | 238 kJ |
|------------------------|---------------------|--------|
| I tbsp yoghurt = 0.I g fat | 1.I g carbohydrate | 45 kJ |

There are other reasons why we need to limit our fat intake.

1. *Athletic performance.* If you eat too much fat you often replace the essential fuel, carbohydrate. Consequently, the lack of carbohydrate will impair your peak performance.

2. *Health reasons.* A high fat intake has been related to an increased risk of heart disease, stroke, obesity and some cancers.

New Zealand guidelines suggest that we limit our fat intake to 25–30 percent of our total energy intake. This may need to be lowered to 20–25 percent to allow for your high carbohydrate requirements. Unfortunately the foods often associated with rugby contain a lot of fat —pies, chips, steak sandwiches, crisps, etc. If you wish to succeed and compete well as a rugby player, you will need to take extra care to keep your fat intake down. Here are some tips that might help you.

## EAT-SMART WAYS TO LOWER YOUR FAT INTAKE

➤ Limit your use of high-fat spreads (e.g. butter, margarine, peanut butter, cheese spreads). Use 1 tsp per slice of bread, and only butter one slice of bread in a sandwich instead of two.

➤ Trim all visible fat from meats, including skin on chicken.

➤ Use low-fat cooking methods. It's a lot faster and cleaner to microwave, steam, bake, grill, or lightly boil food than it is to shallow- or deep-fry it. Your taste buds will adjust!

➤ Use low-fat dairy products (e.g. trim milk, Edam or Gouda cheese, yoghurt).

➤ Choose low-fat snack foods such as fresh fruit, yoghurt, vegetables, sandwiches or muesli bars instead of chocolate biscuits or crisps.

➤ Fill sandwiches with only one protein food (e.g. ham or cheese, not ham and cheese).

➤ Avoid pink, processed meats such as salami, luncheon, saveloys and sausages.

➤ Watch out for hidden fats in chocolate, nuts, ice-cream, pastries, chips, quiche, croissants and avocados.

➤ Always take your own food to eat after training or a game, so that you are not tempted by the high-fat foods in the clubrooms or at the shop on the way home.

➤ While it is important to try and reduce your fat intake, it is equally important not to eliminate it completely. Fat is a very important source of vitamins A, D, E and K, and is vital to the structure of cells.

## A WORKING EXAMPLE

Let's pull it all together and give you an example of a typical training diet for a rugby player.

Tony, who plays lock, weighs in at 110 kg. At present, as part of his club season, he has two team practices a week, one game, three weights sessions, a sprint session, a recovery session, and a day off. He trains at the gym at lunchtime and has team training after work.

Tony's carbohydrate requirement = 7–8 g per kg bodyweight = 770–880 g

Choose 800 g = 40 x 20 g carbohydrate per day

Tony's protein requirement = 1.5–2.0 g per kg bodyweight = 165–220 g

Choose 200 g = 20 x 10 g protein per day

To make sure Tony has the maximum amount of carbohydrates stored for each training session and to ensure a quick recovery, as well as fit in with his training and nutrition goals and his work commitments, the following spread of carbohydrate and protein portions throughout the day was planned:

Breakfast = 7 portions carbohydrate and 3 portions protein

Post-training = 4 portions carbohydrate and 4 portions protein

Lunch = 7 portions carbohydrate and 3 portions protein

Pre-training = 4 portions carbohydrate and 2 portions protein

Dinner = 7 portions carbohydrate and 4 portions protein

Supper = 4 portions carbohydrate and 4 portions protein

Plus 3 carbohydrate portions taken as 1 litre of sports drink at each training session.

Tony's meal plan is now as follows:

**Breakfast**
Cereal and toast as usual
Only 1 tsp butter per slice instead of two
Honey or jam as a spread
Include 250 ml fruit juice

**Mid-morning**
Sandwiches as usual; 1 tsp butter per sandwich instead of 4
1 serving of meat per sandwich instead of 2
Could include a fruit smoothie or protein shake

**Lunch**
Sandwiches as usual, or beans or spaghetti on toast, changes as above for butter
Add fruit, yoghurt, 250 ml fruit juice or flavoured milk, and 2 plain biscuits
Could include a fruit smoothie or protein shake

**Pre-training**
Add a sandwich with banana and fruit or fruit juice

**During and after training**
Sports drink during and immediately after training
Honey sandwich and banana after training

**Dinner**
Reduced serving of meat
Use low-fat cooking methods
Rice and pasta as usual with low-fat sauces; increase amount
Add fruit juice or milk to the meal
Have a low-fat milk pudding for dessert such as custard, fruit and yoghurt or
rice pudding

**Supper**
Fruit smoothie, cereal and yoghurt, etc., or fruit and sandwich

Your weight and body fat percentage (measured using calipers) are good ways of
determining whether these guidelines are meeting your needs. This can be done by
a sports dietitian or qualified gym instructor.

# Vitamins and minerals

Although you may be getting sufficient energy from carbohydrate to fuel your
exercise, this does not mean that your diet is ideal. It is crucial that your diet is also
*balanced*.

Although micronutrients — vitamins and minerals — are not a source of energy
for our muscles, they are involved in many of the processes that convert carbohydrate,
fat and protein to energy. They are also vital to the transport and utilisation of
oxygen, red blood cell formation and tissue repair.

Rugby players often feel their diet is inadequate to meet their vitamin and mineral
needs. When they feel tired or unmotivated, or fail to improve their fitness, they often
blame their diet, rather than considering other reasons such as inadequate sleep,
overtraining, excessive alcohol consumption, or stress related to other aspects of
their lives.

Players who train regularly have increased needs for vitamins and minerals, but
these can usually be met with a well-balanced diet that supplies the extra energy
needed for exercise. Any vitamin and mineral supplements taken over and above the
recommended intakes do not enhance performance. Before you diagnose a lack of
vitamins or minerals as the reason for your poor performance, seek the help of a
sports dietitian or physician to identify any possible deficiency. Unsupervised
consumption of extra vitamins and minerals can lead to toxicity.

The following table lists a number of micronutrients, their function in the body,
and what foods they are found in.

## VITAMINS

| Nutrient | Recommended Intake | Function | Food source |
|---|---|---|---|
| Vitamin A | 750 mg | For maintenance of cell surface, for sight, and for normal growth | Dairy foods, butter, margarine, liver, green and yellow fruit and vegetables |
| Vitamin B1 (Thiamin) | Males: 1.1 mg<br>Females: 0.8 mg | Required for carbohydrate metabolism | Meat, yeast products, whole grains, vegetables, nuts |
| Vitamin B2 (Riboflavin) | Males: 1.7 mg<br>Females: 1.2 mg | Involved in fat and protein metabolism. Needed for growth and development | Dairy products, yeast products, eggs, organ meats, whole grains, green leafy vegetables |
| Vitamin B6 (Pyridoxine) | Males: 2.0 mg<br>Females: 1.6 mg | Involved in protein and glucose metabolism | High-protein foods, yeast products, whole grains and cereals, peanuts, vegetables, bananas |
| Vitamin B12 | 2 µg | Development of red blood cells and genetic material | Dairy products, liver, meat, oysters, sardines |
| Folic acid | 200 µg | Involved in formation of genetic material and normal red blood cell production | Liver, meat, fish, orange juice, green leafy vegetables |
| Pantothenic acid | 4–7 mg | Involved in carbohydrate, fat and protein metabolism | Meat, poultry, fish, whole grains, yeast, legumes, egg yolk |
| Biotin | 30–100 µg | Involved in carbohydrate, fat and protein metabolism, and nerve cell growth and function | Meat, fish, egg yolk, nuts, vegetables |
| Vitamin C | 40 mg | Helps with iron absorption, aids muscle and tissue healing, protects against oxidants, maintains tissue, cartilage, tendons and bones | Green leafy vegetables, parsley, peppers, citrus fruits, berry and tropical fruits, currants, tomatoes |
| Vitamin D | 10 mg | Required for bone mineralisation, helps absorption of calcium and phosphorus | Eggs, butter, fortified margarine, fish oils, liver. Also from sunlight |
| Vitamin E | 10 mg | Protects cell membranes, important for red cell production | Vegetable oils, margarine, nuts, wheatgerm, wholegrain products, green leafy vegetables |
| Vitamin K | Males: 65–80 µg<br>Females: 55–65 µg | Important in blood clotting, and some bone and kidney proteins | Meat, liver, green leafy vegetables, soya beans, cabbage, cauliflower |

| MINERALS | | | |
|---|---|---|---|
| **Nutrient** | **Recommended Intake** | **Function** | **Food source** |
| Calcium | 800 mg | For bone structure, blood clotting, muscle contraction and nerve impulse transmission | Milk, cheese, yoghurt, green leafy vegetables |
| Iron | Males: 7 mg Females: 12–16 mg | Essential in aiding the transport and utilisation of oxygen | Red meat, liver, chicken, fish, mussels, kidney beans, dried apricots, green leafy vegetables |
| Chlorine | 270 mg | To maintain fluid and electrolyte balance | Common table salt |
| Magnesium | Males: 320 mg Females: 270 mg | Involved in protein synthesis, muscle contraction, body temperature regulation, and energy production | Most foods, especially wholegrain products, green leafy vegetables, fruit |
| Sodium | 1.2 g | Has a co-role with potassium and is involved in muscle function, nerve transmission, carbohydrate and protein metabolism, maintenance of body fluids and acid/base balance of the blood | Soy sauce, table salt, seafoods, dairy products, Marmite, Vegemite, processed foods |
| Potassium | 2.5 g | As above | Most foods, especially meat, fish, poultry, cereals, oranges, bananas, fresh vegetables |
| Phosphorous | 1000 mg | In bone and teeth formation, essential for vitamin B functions, important in delivery of energy to cells as part of ATP | Milk, poultry, fish, meat |
| Iodine | Males: 150 µg Females: 120 µg | As part of thyroid hormone helps regulate metabolic rate | Iodised salt, seafood |
| Zinc | 12 mg | Aids in wound healing, involved in protein and fat metabolism | Meat, eggs, oysters, wholegrain products, legumes |
| Selenium | Males: 85 µg Females: 70 µg | Important in the protection of cells from oxidation by free radicals | High-protein foods, wholegrain products |
| Fluorine | 1.5–4.0 mg | Prevents tooth decay and possibly also osteoporosis | Most water supplies, tea, some small fish |
| Manganese | 2–5 mg | Involved in bone structure and nervous system activity, and carbohydrate metabolism | Green leafy vegetables, wheatgerm, nuts, wholegrain cereals, bananas |

How do we know whether we are getting all the nutrients we need, in particular the micronutrients listed on pages 172–73? A good way to assess your diet for nutritional adequacy is to compare it to that outlined in the healthy food pyramid below, which provides suggested quantities of servings of the main food groups.

The foods at the bottom of the pyramid include carbohydrate foods such as breads, cereals, pasta and rice (six servings a day), fruit and vegetables (two and three servings a day respectively). The protein foods in the middle section include meat, chicken, fish, eggs, nuts, seeds, legumes (one serving a day) and dairy products (two servings a day). The foods at the tip of the pyramid should be eaten sparingly, and include fat, oils, sugar, salt and alcohol. Examples of serving sizes for each food group can be found on page 190.

**The healthy food pyramid.**

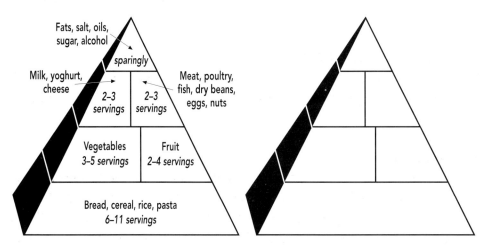

Courtesy of NZ Heart Foundation

Using the blank food pyramid provided, rate your own food intake. Beside the pyramid, write down everything you ate yesterday (or on a typical day). Using the portion sizes provided on page 190, calculate how many servings you have eaten from each food group. These should be the same as, or in a similar ratio to, the suggested servings in the completed pyramid. To comply with the guidelines you should then ensure that all your carbohydrate foods are low in fat and high in fibre, and that the protein foods are low-fat choices.

To help put it all together, some meal ideas are provided on pages 193–94. You should have one food item from each of the options at each meal.

# Fluids

Despite the fact that much rugby is played in cooler weather, your body temperature still increases due to the heat generated by your muscles, which in turn causes you to sweat. Sweating is the mechanism your body uses to keep your body temperature down. If too much fluid is lost from the body as sweat or in the air you breathe out (which increases in moisture content in cold temperatures), a fluid deficit, or dehydration, will occur. Dehydration can severely impair your performance.

## PHYSIOLOGICAL RESPONSES TO DEHYDRATION [5]

Dehydration causes a decrease in the amount of blood being pumped around the body, which causes a decrease in your sweat rate, and an increase in heart rate. This, in turn, causes your exercise intensity to drop, and also interferes with your coordination and decision-making ability. All of these factors are vitally important to your on-field performance.

## EAT-SMART GUIDELINES FOR FLUIDS

You should aim to start all exercise well hydrated, and replace fluid as you lose it during exercise. The guidelines for fluids are therefore the same for training as for a game.

### Before exercise

A good plan of attack is to start all exercise fully hydrated. You must ensure that you have recovered all the fluids lost during your previous training session, and drink well in the 24 hours prior to your next exercise session. The best way to monitor this is by the colour of your urine. If you are well hydrated your urine will be nearly clear in colour (unless you have taken a multivitamin supplement, which gives a very bright yellow urine). In addition:

➤ With your last meal or snack, drink about 500–1000 ml of fluid.

➤ In the 15 minutes before you start, try to consume a 500-ml preload drink. The larger the volume of fluid in the stomach, the faster consecutive intakes of fluid will be absorbed. However, 500 ml is about the maximum you will be able to tolerate without feeling nauseous or getting stomach cramp. If you use a 5–8 percent glucose concentration drink you will also meet the guidelines for carbohydrate ingestion immediately before exercise.

### During exercise

The amount of fluid you need varies between individuals. The greater your muscle mass, the higher your fluid needs will be because you will sweat more. Hot, humid conditions and a high-intensity game will also increase your needs.

A general rule of thumb is to drink 800–1000 ml for every hour of exercise. Where possible, this should be drunk at regular intervals (150–200 ml every 10–15 minutes). A good way of determining your individual requirement is to weigh yourself before and after a training session (wear the same clothes and dry off the sweat). A loss of 1 kg equates to the loss of 1 litre of fluid. You need to drink about 80–100 percent of this loss to prevent dehydration (i.e. 800–1000 ml). Do not rely on thirst as a good indication of when to drink; by the time you are thirsty you are well on the way to being dehydrated.

Unfortunately the nature of a rugby game means it is often difficult to get many chances to drink. Forwards especially lose high amounts of fluid, even in the cold (up to 6 litres in a game), so always be on the lookout for opportunities to drink during the game, and drink at least 300–400 ml at half-time.

### After exercise

Try to drink about 500–1000 ml in the first hour after exercising, and the same again in the second hour. Consuming a moderate to high carbohydrate concentrated sports

**Drinking during and after the game is vital for maintaining performance.**

drink (5–25 percent) will ensure that you are reloading fluid and carbohydrate. *Drinking alcohol will NOT achieve this!*

———

**Eat-Smart tip**

Always have your own drink bottle at training and start drinking during your warm-up.

———

## SPORTS DRINKS

Players often ask whether a sports drink is needed during training or for a game. The question to ask yourself is: will my glycogen stores be challenged during the exercise?

Since most rugby training sessions, practices and games last longer than 60 minutes, your carbohydrate reserves will be at risk of being depleted. It is therefore advisable to use a sports drink. The type of drink you choose is very important.

There is a wide range of sports drinks on the market, and they are often promoted for reasons other than the specific use for which they were intended, which is *for exercise*. Sports drinks are made up of a combination of glucose, sucrose, malto-dextrins and a small amount of fructose. The first three are easily absorbed and utilised as a fuel during exercise, whereas fructose is mainly added to sweeten the drink. For the fastest rate of fluid and carbohydrate absorption, a sports drink should contain a carbohydrate concentration of 5–8 percent (5–8 g glucose per 100 ml).

Sports drinks also contain small amounts of the electrolytes sodium and potassium, which:

➤ Help facilitate the absorption of glucose.

➤ Stimulate thirst.

➤ Replace the small amounts of these electrolytes that are lost in sweat.

Sports drinks often contain a variety of other ingredients, which are usually to make them more palatable to drink while you are exercising.

Fruit juices and cordials diluted to one part drink to two parts water may be just as effective, but again, try them out in training.

Outside of their role during exercise, sports drinks are just the same as cordial-type drinks, and their use should be kept to a minimum. The new 'smart drinks' are also just glorified soft drinks, with some nutrients and often caffeine and guarana (a herb that contains natural caffeine) added. These are totally inappropriate for use before, during and after exercise. They are too highly concentrated in glucose, and the caffeine and guarana, although stimulants, are both diuretics and will make you very dehydrated if taken in conjunction with exercise.

### DAY-TO-DAY FLUID NEEDS

Generally, you should try to drink 1500–2000 ml over and above your training requirements. This can be taken as water, fruit juice, herbal tea, or milk or milk drinks. To achieve this, try to have one or two glasses of fluid at each meal and get through 1–2 drink bottles over the course of a day. Try to limit tea and coffee to fewer than four cups a day.

# Eat-Smart game plan

The players who put in the best performance during a game are usually those who have achieved their recommended nutritional goals during the week before the game. A good training diet is therefore vital. Acts such as skipping meals, eating junk food and drinking alcohol will undoubtedly lead to a dismal display on the field.

Good nutrition for your game is about eating foods that enable you to play to your potential on the day. So make sure that a poor diet doesn't let you down. Always make sure that all your food plans for the game have been well rehearsed in training.

### EAT-SMART GOALS FOR THE RUGBY GAME

➤ To have maximum muscle and liver glycogen stores.

➤ To be well hydrated.

### PRE-GAME NUTRITION

The extent to which you have to nutritionally prepare for your games will depend on:

➤ How much your glycogen stores will become depleted.

➤ The potential risk of dehydration.

In the two to three days before your game you should make sure you recover well from your last training session by eating the high-carbohydrate diet outlined earlier. You should then maintain your normal high-carbohydrate, low-fat diet while having the day off before the game. This will boost the amount of carbohydrate stored in your body. Continue to drink plenty of fluids to ensure that you are well hydrated. Alcohol should be avoided during these three days.

*Pre-game meal*

The purpose of your pre-game meal is to top up glycogen and fluid stores, and to prevent hunger developing during the game. It most certainly is not the time to make up for a poor carbohydrate intake during the week.

Your last big meal should be 14–16 hours before the game, i.e. the evening meal the night before, with your last small meal or snack two to three hours before. Timing is very important as you must allow time for the food to digest before playing.

### Early afternoon game
Normal breakfast, light pre-game snack/meal two hours out from the warm-up for the game. Have water or a sports drink at regular intervals to hydrate yourself.

### Mid-afternoon game
Normal breakfast and pre-game meal three to four hours out from the game. Light snack two hours out from the start of the warm-up. Have water or a sports drink at regular intervals to hydrate yourself.

### Evening game
Normal breakfast and lunch followed by pre-game meal three to four hours out from the game. Light snack two hours out from the start of the warm-up. Have water or a sports drink at regular intervals to hydrate yourself.

All meals and snacks prior to the pre-game meal should be high in carbohydrate and low in fat and protein.

## EAT-SMART TIPS FOR THE PRE-GAME MEAL

➤ Always eat foods you are familiar with. You don't know how you will react to a new food.

➤ Choose high-carbohydrate, low-fat, low-protein foods.

➤ Keep the meal low in fibre. This will reduce its bulk.

➤ Avoid foods that cause gas or have spices in them. They may upset your stomach.

The meal can be either solid or liquid. Some players find they are too nervous to eat solid food. A high-carbohydrate sports drink is just as suitable.

*Suggested pre-event meals*
Low-fibre cereal such as cornflakes, trim milk, fruit and yoghurt
Bread, toast, rolls, fruit bread, jam, honey (no butter)
Spaghetti, baked beans or creamed corn on toast
Low-fat pasta dishes

Low-fat rice dishes

Low-fat muffins

Fruit buns

Vegetable soups (not cream based) and buns

Pancakes and syrup

Fruit

Fruit juice

## DURING THE GAME

You must ensure that you are adequately hydrated throughout the game and have enough carbohydrate to play the full 80 minutes. When planning your carbohydrate and fluid intake you should consider the following factors.

### Amount of carbohydrates

Aim to consume about 60 g carbohydrate per hour.

### Type of carbohydrates

Since you require fluids during exercise it is often a good idea to use a sports drink, which will meet both your fluid and your carbohydrate requirements. You can easily meet your carbohydrate requirements through fluids alone.

### Timing of carbohydrate intake

For carbohydrate intake to be effective in delaying fatigue, you must start eating at least 30 minutes before fatigue sets in. Since this is difficult to calculate, and the opportunity to consume fluids does not occur very often in a game, it is best to begin at the first possible chance.

Overall, the consumption of about 1.5 litres of 6–8 percent glucose concentration sports drink over the course of the game will meet both your carbohydrate and your fluid needs. You need to drink this a little at a time, and at regular intervals.

## Recovery

Eating is just as important to your recovery from a game as it is in any other part of your nutrition programme. How familiar does a pint of beer, chips or a Moro bar sound? What you eat after exercise is vital in the recovery of your lost carbohydrate and fluids. In fact, your recovery dictates how well you will train and play in the following days and weeks.

### EAT-SMART GOALS FOR GAME RECOVERY

➤ To replace all used glycogen and fluid stores.

➤ To repair muscle damage.

As with your training recovery diet, for a speedy recovery after a game you must consider the following.

### Timing of food intake

Remember your muscles are most efficient at restoring glycogen within the first 60 minutes after exercise. By making the most of this period, you will go a long way to restoring all your glycogen in 24 hours instead of 48 hours.

### Type of food

You should eat easily digested and absorbed carbohydrate foods that are low in fat, fibre and protein. Choose foods that have a moderate to high glycaemic index (see pages 161–62). Either solids or liquids are fine.

### Amount of food

Try to eat about 50 g of carbohydrate in the first 15–20 minutes after the game (see page 165 for examples of 50-g servings), and then 50 g every two hours until your next big meal. The next big meal will usually come about two hours after the game, then there will be limited food intake for several hours, so ensure that you have 100 g of carbohydrate at that meal. This should be a highly nutritious carbohydrate meal with a small amount of high-quality protein to aid muscle repair. You should then continue with your high-carbohydrate diet for the next 24 hours (8 g carbohydrate per kg bodyweight).

Fluid replacement should also begin straight away, and continue until your urine runs clear and your weight returns to normal. Again, do not use thirst as a guide.

You should not drink alcohol until at least two hours after exercise, and should be fully hydrated and refuelled before you start to do so. Try to drink in moderation, as alcohol delays fluid and glycogen recovery, increases swelling, and delays recovery from injuries.

### SUMMARY OF EAT-SMART TIPS FOR THE GAME

➤ Plan all your game needs and practise them well in training.

➤ Always take your own food and fluids with you. Do not rely on what may be provided after the game.

A good way of planning and keeping track of what you are eating is to keep a food diary, along with your training log (see chapter 11). You should regularly review this to see if you are continuing to meet your specific nutrition requirements.

# Ideal bodyweight

Your ideal bodyweight is one that you can maintain without compromising your nutrient intake or your performance. You should not have a set weight, but rather an ideal weight range that is appropriate for your height, body type, and playing position. A good method of assessing your ideal body composition for rugby is by assessing your body fat using skinfold calipers. A sports dietitian or physician can help you assess your ideal weight and body fat range for your position.

### MUSCLE TO GAIN

Because of the power and strength aspects of the game of rugby, many players want to build up their muscle mass. This can be of benefit to forwards in particular, who need the extra weight, power and strength. You can increase your muscle mass by consuming a high-energy diet, accompanied by resistance weight training. This is best done in the off-season.

People often associate muscle gain with high-protein diets, but the emphasis should still be on carbohydrate for energy.

*Eat-Smart ways to build muscles*

➤ You need an extra 2100–4200 kJ a day to achieve a 1–2 kg weight increase per month. Eating more complex carbohydrate foods that contain a moderate amount of protein and are low in fat should provide this.

➤ Protein should provide about 2 g per kg bodyweight per day. You can only build muscle at a given rate, regardless of how much protein you eat. A high-protein diet will result in inadequate carbohydrate to fuel exercise, and protein will then be used as a fuel.

➤ You should chose high-quality, low-fat protein foods such as fish, chicken without the skin, low-fat dairy products, and lean red meat.

➤ Your protein requirements can easily be achieved through a well-balanced diet, without the use of supplements. Not only is this cheaper, but foods provide other vital nutrients that supplements may not.

➤ Protein supplement drinks should only be used as a convenience food when you are in situations where you do not have access to your own food (e.g. while travelling).

➤ Have your body fat assessed regularly to ensure it is muscle and not fat that you are gaining.

**Examples of 2100 kJ of high-carbohydrate moderate-protein foods**
You can include at least one of these foods each day in your diet to aid muscle gain.

➤ 2 fruit smoothies

➤ 2 peanut butter, ham, or Edam cheese sandwiches

➤ 5 glasses of trim milk (plain or flavoured, or as Milo)

➤ 2 slices toast with 2 tsp butter or margarine and 440 g baked beans

➤ 2 cups cereal and fruit with milk/yoghurt

## LOSING WEIGHT

You may decide to lose weight to help achieve your peak performance. Ideally this should be done in the off-season, to prevent added stress on your body during the season itself. It is essential that the weight you lose is fat, not muscle. Since this does not show up on the scales, you should monitor your body fat regularly as a safeguard.

Your body can only lose fat at a certain rate (about 0.5–1.0 kg per week). Fad diets, crash diets and other practices that cause faster weight loss result only in the loss of precious muscle and fluid, not fat.

### Eat-Smart tips for weight loss

➤ Set a realistic monthly goal. Aim to lose about 1–2 kg a month.

➤ Focus on cutting down your fat intake. Every gram of fat has twice as many kilojoules as carbohydrate or protein. It is very energy-dense (see Fat section, page 168).

➤ Base all meals and snacks around high-fibre, nutritious carbohydrate foods. Try and cover 75 percent of your plate with these foods. The other 25 percent should be low-fat protein.

➤ Use fresh fruit, vegetables, and low-fat yoghurt as snacks.

➤ Avoid high-sugar foods and alcohol. They are low in nutrient value.

➤ Eat little and often and do not skip meals.

➤ Weigh yourself once a week, at the same time, in the same clothes.

➤ Keep a food diary to monitor your food intake.

## Eat-Smart summary

It is important to remember that since each player is an individual, these guidelines are just that — guidelines. If you feel that your nutrition is not helping you to achieve your rugby goals, contact your local sports dietitian, who will be able to give you a detailed assessment of your individual food requirements.

A good training diet must be as planned and detailed as your training programme in order for you to achieve your peak performance. It must take into consideration all your sporting, social, and occupational commitments, as well as your nutritional goals. It's all about *eating smart*!

## Consumer awareness

In order to make the most of the foods available to you it is important that you are 'consumer aware'. When you are supermarket shopping it is helpful if you understand what is written on food labels, and know how to assess the different marketing ploys used by companies to sell their products. This will enable you to select low-fat, nutritious foods, while being aware of the false advertising to be found on many food packages. It also enables you to evaluate any new product that comes onto the market and whether it has a place in your day-to-day diet.

The different types of information that help us to assess the nutrient value, and therefore the usefulness, of a food product include the following.

### 1. INGREDIENT LIST

All foods sold must have on the pack a list of their ingredients. These ingredients are listed in descending order from the greatest quantity to the smallest. Foods that are high in fat usually have fat or fat products in the top three ingredients.

### 2. NUTRIENT COMPOSITION

Many food manufacturers also include a nutrient breakdown of the product. This is usually done per serving size and per 100 g of edible product.

For example:

| Nutrient | | per 50 g | per 100 g |
|---|---|---|---|
| Carbohydrate | — total | 15 g | 30 g |
| | — sugars | 10 g | 20 g |
| Protein | | 5 g | 10 g |
| Fat | | 9 g | 18 g |
| Sodium | | 10 mg | 20 mg |
| Iron | | 1.2 mg | 2.4 mg |
| Calcium | | 110 mg | 220 mg |
| Energy | | 658 kJ | 1316 kJ |

### 3. 'PICK THE TICK'

Many food products have a 'pick the tick' symbol on them. This means that they meet the guidelines set out by the National Heart Foundation and are low in fat, saturated fat, and salt.

### COMMON SUPERMARKET FOODS

Let's work through some of the foods you would buy at the supermarket and what sort of nutritional information you should be looking for.

#### Canned fruit

There are many varieties of canned fruit, and they are a good source of both carbohydrate and vitamin C. Choose those that are canned in fruit juice or a light syrup to avoid the excess sugar in heavy syrup.

#### Soups

Most soups on the market today are acceptable, but watch for the sodium (salt) and fat content of soups from sachets and cans.

#### Sauces

Many of the prepared sauces sold in jars or cans are suitable. Choose those with a vegetable (usually tomato) base. Any sauce that looks thick and creamy should be avoided!

#### Breads

Bread makes a fantastic high-carbohydrate addition to any player's diet. In general the best breads are those that are high in fibre. Try to choose bread that has at least 6 g dietary fibre per 100 g.

### Crackers

Where possible, choose crackers that have less than 10 g fat per 100 g. This does tend to limit the variety that you can choose from, as cracker biscuits are generally fairly high in fat (15–20 g fat per 100 g).

### Biscuits

Most types of biscuit do not have a nutrient label on them because they are high in fat and have limited nutrient value. The most suitable biscuits to choose are plain ones or those with dried fruit in them. You may like to compare the nutrient composition of these biscuits with some of the crackers that are available. Any biscuits with a chocolate or yoghurt coating are high in fat and should only be eaten occasionally.

### Muesli bars

There are a wide variety of muesli bars on the market, many of which are high in fat. Fortunately there has been an increase in the number of low-fat bars (<5 g fat per 100 g) which taste good and are high in carbohydrate. These make excellent snacks and are great after a training session.

### Dressings

Most dressings or mayonnaises are oil-, egg- or dairy-based, and are high in fat. Choose dressings that are oil-free, low-calorie or have 5 g fat per 100 g or less.

### Breakfast cereals

The number of different cereals available seems to be expanding every day. Choose one that is low in fat and high in carbohydrate and fibre, i.e. 6 g fibre per 100 g or more, and less than 6 g fat per 100 g.

### Milk

Milk is an excellent source of calcium and protein. Try to choose the low-fat varieties. The fat content of milk ranges from 3.3 g fat per 100 g (homogenised) to 0.5 g fat per 100 g (trim milk). In general, the lower the fat content of the milk the higher the calcium content.

### Yoghurt

Yoghurt is an excellent source of calcium and protein while still low in fat. When selecting plain or fruit yoghurts try to choose those with 2 g fat per 100 g or less.

### Dairy products

Cheeses, cream cheese, sour cream and cream are high-fat dairy products (20–40 percent), but you will usually find lower-fat alternatives in the supermarket. Remember though that the low-fat varieties are only *lower* in fat, not *low* in fat, and should still only be used in moderation.

### Butter and margarine

Butter, margarine and oils all have (per teaspoon) exactly the same amount of fat (about 80 g per 100 g). However, lower-fat varieties of margarine are now available and are increasingly popular.

Don't be confused by the advertising for these products. Margarines are often marketed as being more 'healthy'. This is not because they are lower in fat, but rather that they are made up of a different type of fat. Butter is made up of saturated fats, which are reported to increase blood cholesterol, and is therefore regarded as less 'healthy', whereas margarines are made up of either polyunsaturated fats (most cooking oils and margarines) or monounsaturated fats (peanut, avocado, canola and sunflower oil), which do not elevate cholesterol levels.

### Meat portions

For the active athlete, a serving of meat, chicken or fish should be:

> females: 100–120 g per day
>
> males: 150–200 g per day

When you go to the supermarket look at the packaged meats to get an idea of how much you can eat as a serving. For example, how many chicken drumsticks can you eat?

Choose meats that are low in fat. A lot of white fat, or marbling, indicates that the meat is high in fat. Pink processed meats such as salami, belgium, luncheon, sausages, or saveloys are also high in fat.

## EAT-SMART GUIDE TO SPORTS SUPPLEMENTS

Foods and other substances have been used to enhance athletes' performances for many years. However, with the advent of professionalism in sport the hunt for the ultimate winning potion has become more intense. So how can you sort out fact from fiction and decide which ones really work?

There are two categories of sports supplements on the market: 'dietary supplements' and 'ergogenic aids'.[6]

*Dietary supplements*

➤ Contain nutrients in amounts similar to those specified in the recommended dietary intakes (RDI), and similar to the amounts found in ordinary food.

➤ Provide a convenient means of ingesting these nutrients, particularly in an athletics setting.

➤ Contain specific nutrient(s) in large amounts for treating known deficiencies.

➤ Have been shown to meet a specific physiological or nutritional need that improves sports performance.

➤ Their efficacy in improving sports performance is generally acknowledged by sports medicine and science experts.

**Examples of dietary supplements include:**

Sports drinks (5–8 percent concentration)

High-carbohydrate sports drink (20–25 percent concentration)

Liquid meal supplements

Sports bars

Vitamin and mineral supplements

Iron supplements

Calcium supplements

It is important to remember that dietary supplements are just that: supplements to a well-balanced diet. They will not replace a balanced diet of real food, and on their own they will not improve a player's performance.

———

It is advisable to use sports supplements only after consultation with a sports dietitian or physician.

———

*Nutritional ergogenic aids*

➤ Contain nutrients or other food components in amounts greater than the RDI levels, or in greater amounts than typically present in ordinary food.

➤ Propose a direct ergogenic (performance enhancing) effect on sports performance, often through a pharmacological rather than physiological effect.

➤ Often rely on theoretical or anecdotal evidence only, rather than on documented scientific trials.

➤ Are generally not supported by sports nutrition experts, except where scientific trials have documented a significant ergogenic effect.[7]

The number of ergogenic aids on the market changes constantly as many come and go with fashion. The following is an overview of the supplements available at present.

| Supplement | Proposed Function | Success |
|---|---|---|
| Amino acids and protein powders | Claim rapid absorption in free form. Also effects from individual amino acids | Further work required before any benefits can be decided |
| Caffeine | Reduces perceived effort of exercise, improves reaction time, and increases alertness. May free up fatty acids for exercise, thereby saving glycogen and increasing time to fatigue | Need to use 5–6 mg/kg bodyweight in the hour before exercise. Must be caffeine-free for some time to get benefit. Individual responses. Causes dehydration and is a banned drug |
| Bicarbonate | Buffers the build up of lactic and pyruvic acid during anaerobic exercise and therefore delays the onset of muscular fatigue in sprint-type exercise | 200–400 mg/kg bodyweight used. Can cause nausea and gastric upsets |
| Carnitine | Aids the transport of fatty acids into the cells for oxidation, thus enhancing the energy supply from fat during exercise, aiding weight loss | Not enough research yet to confirm this effect |
| Creatine | Used to regenerate ATP, which is the most important energy source for muscles during short bursts of high-intensity exercise lasting 1–10 seconds | Taken in the form of Creatine monohydrate, involves a loading phase then a maintenance phase. Some benefit has been shown for resistance training and sprint-type exercise |
| Chromium picolinate | Promises to increase body mass by enhancing insulin activity | At present there is little evidence to support the role of chromium in increasing lean muscle mass |
| Ginseng | A Chinese root plant, claimed to reduce fatigue and improve strength, mental ability and recovery | Very little research conducted to prove its positive benefits |
| Bee pollen | Reported to improve immunity and athletic performance | Majority of studies fail to find any ergogenic effect |
| Medium-chain triglycerides (MCT) | More rapidly absorbed and oxidised than other fats. Claimed to increase energy and reduce body fat | Not very palatable. No evidence of ergogenic effect in athletes |

## Examples of single serving sizes

### VEGETABLES

1 medium-sized potato
½ cup root vegetables
1 cup cooked vegetables
½ cup salad
1 tomato
¼ avocado
1 small corn cob
1 cup vegetable-based soup

### FRUIT

1 apple, pear, banana, orange
2 small apricots or plums
½ cup fresh fruit salad
½ cup stewed or canned fruit
½ cup fruit juice
¼ cup dried fruit
½ cup berries (all varieties)

### BREAD AND CEREALS

1 small roll
1 small muffin or scone
1 medium slice bread
½ round pita bread
1 cup cornflakes, rice bubbles, porridge
½ cup muesli
2 Weet-Bix
1 cup rice, noodles, pasta (cooked)
1 cup popcorn (cooked)
½ cup baked beans
3 plain crackers
2 plain sweet biscuits

### MILK AND DAIRY PRODUCTS

250 ml milk
150 g yoghurt
2 slices cheese (50 g)
75 g cottage cheese
2 scoops ice-cream (140 g)

### MEAT, CHICKEN, SEAFOOD AND PULSES

60 g cooked meat, chicken, fish
½ cup mince, casserole
1 sausage, saveloy
1 slice ham, bacon
½ cup mussels, salmon, tuna
½ cup cooked legumes, beans
1 egg

### FATS, SWEETS

1 tsp butter, margarine, peanut butter
1 tsp salad dressing, mayonnaise
1 tsp sugar, jam, honey, syrup
2 sweets
1 tsp cream, cream cheese, sour cream

# Examples of 20-g servings of carbohydrate

The following foods each provide 20 g of carbohydrate.

HF = high fat

## FRUIT

| | |
|---|---|
| I apple | ⅓ cup dried apricots |
| I small banana | 4 (30 g) dates |
| I grapefruit | 5 dried prunes |
| 2 kiwifruit | ¼ cup sultanas |
| 2 nectarines | ¼ cup raisins |
| 2 small oranges | 500 ml tomato juice |
| 2 peaches | 200 ml fruit juice |
| 2 pears | ⅔ cup fruit in juice |
| 2 cups strawberries, raspberries | ⅓ cup fruit in syrup |

## VEGETABLES (COOKED)

| | |
|---|---|
| ⅔ cob of corn | 200 g baked beans |
| ⅔ cup kernel corn | ⅔ cup haricot beans |
| 2 cups peas | I cup kidney beans |
| ½ cup yams | I cup chickpeas |
| I¼ cups mixed veges | I cup lentils |
| 200 g pumpkin | I medium-sized potato |
| ⅔ cup mashed potato | ⅔ cup instant potato |
| 100 g kumara | ⅔ cup taro |

## CEREALS

| | |
|---|---|
| 2 Weet-Bix | ⅔ cup canned spaghetti |
| I cup cornflakes | ⅔ cup cooked pasta |
| I cup rice bubbles | ⅓ cup cooked rice |
| ⅔ cup honey puffs | 2 cups puffed wheat |
| ¾ cup Nutrigrain | I½ cups puffed rice |
| ⅔ cup Sultana Bran | I cup porridge |
| ¾ cup All-Bran | ½ cup Sustain |
| ¾ cup Special K | ⅓ cup toasted muesli (HF) |
| ⅓ cup natural muesli | |

## BREAD AND BAKED PRODUCTS

2 medium slices white
1½ toast slices white
2 medium slices wholemeal
1½ toast slices wholemeal
1 (32 g) muesli bar (HF)
½ doughnut (HF)
1 crumpet
2 plain digestives (HF)
2½ gingernuts (HF)
½ (40 g) fruit scone
1 cabin bread
½ Mother Earth bar

2 chocolate biscuits (HF)
5 cream crackers (HF)
1½ icing-filled biscuits (HF)
½ wholemeal roll
1 (35 g) small roll
⅔ pita pocket
2 thin pancakes
1½ pikelets
1 (40 g) scone
½ (70 g) bran muffin
½ power bar

## DAIRY PRODUCTS

400 ml trim milk
400 ml homogenised milk
200 ml flavoured milk
5 tbsp skim milk powder

150 g fruit yoghurt
200 g natural yoghurt
200 g yoghurt dairy food
⅔ cup ice-cream (HF)

## SUGAR PRODUCTS

25 g (5) boiled sweets
35 g (7) fruit gums
30 g Liquorice Allsorts
20 g peppermints
25 g marshmallow
2 tbsp sugar
2½ tbsp icing sugar
2 dsp jam
1 tbsp honey/golden syrup
4 tbsp Complan
2 tbsp Quik

⅔ Bounty bar (HF)
½ Mars bar (HF)
35 g plain chocolate (HF)
5 filled chocolates (HF)
5 toffees (HF)
¼ cup jelly
1½ ice blocks
200 ml soft drink
200 ml Raro
3 tbsp Milo

## SPORTS SUPPLEMENTS

150 ml Lucozade
250 ml Replace
350 ml Gatorade

4 tbsp Sustagen
100 ml Gatorlode
250 ml Powerade

# Examples of 10-g servings of protein (cooked weights)

| **HIGH-QUALITY PROTEINS** | **LOW-QUALITY PROTEINS** |
|---|---|
| 60 g grilled fish | 5 medium slices bread |
| 50 g tuna or salmon | 2½ toast slices bread |
| 40 g lean beef or lamb | 3 cups cereal |
| 40 g chicken flesh | I cup natural muesli |
| 2 eggs | 2 cups pasta or rice |
| 40 g cheese | ¾ cup dried beans |
| 70 g cottage cheese | 200 g baked beans |
| 250 ml trim milk | 60 g nuts |
| 200 g low-fat yoghurt | 60 g seeds |

# Suggested meal outlines

## BREAKFAST

Cereal (low fat)

Trim milk

Low-fat yoghurt

Fresh, tinned or stewed fruit

Toast (I tsp fat spread per slice)

Jam, honey, Marmite, Vegemite, peanut butter, tomato or banana topping

Baked beans, spaghetti, creamed corn

Fruit smoothie

Water, fruit juice, milk, flavoured milk

## LUNCH

Bread rolls, pita bread or sandwiches

I meat, chicken, cheese or fish serving per roll or sandwich
  (e.g. I thin slice of cheese or meat)

Pita bread and beans

Doner kebabs

Soup and bread

Baked potatoes with bean, creamed corn, spaghetti or salad filling

Baked beans, spaghetti, creamed corn on toast or as toastie pie

Rice or pasta meals

Raw fruit

Yoghurt
Water, fruit juice, milk, flavoured milk

## DINNER

Moderate meat, chicken or fish serving (low-fat cooking method)
Plenty of potato, rice, pasta, tortillas, etc. (low-fat sauces)
Vegetables
Water, fruit juice, milk, flavoured milk

## DESSERT

Fruit
Ice-cream
Trim milk custard
Rice pudding or semolina made with trim milk
Jelly
Ice blocks
Fruit crumbles (lots of fruit)
Pancakes and syrup

## SNACKS

Fruit — raw or dried
Bread, toast or crumpet with small fat spread and toppings
Plain or fruit rolls
Fruit biscuits or plain biscuits
Fruit smoothie
Low-fat muesli bars or breakfast bars
Low-fat crackers and low-fat cheese
Cup of soups or home-made soup
Low-fat yoghurt
Popcorn
Noodles or rice
Baked beans
Spaghetti
Creamed corn
Low-fat sandwiches
Flavoured milk
Low-fat fruit muffins

# 9 Preventing and managing injuries

*David Gerrard*

## Introduction

Until recently, rugby in New Zealand has been a traditional male contact sport typified by the physical confrontation of vigorous rucking, mauling and high-impact tackling. The advent of women's rugby has done little to dispel this image, and women players have embraced the game with all the enthusiasm of their male counterparts. The current New Zealand women's rugby team — the Black Ferns — is the best in the world.

Today, larger and decidedly fitter players are less constrained by the traditional stereotypes that used to predetermine positions in the team. Tight forwards with explosive speed are indistinguishable from 100-kg three-quarters. Second-row forwards kick goals, midfield backs begin their careers as loose forwards, and the halfback is no longer the team's smallest member. Expansive coaching styles have also contributed to a contemporary game that places greater emphasis on ball retention and the athleticism of larger players. These are among the changes that have brought rugby union into the current era of professionalism, and although only a small proportion of players become fully professional, most serious rugby players have elite aspirations.

Professional rugby has also spawned an expansion in team staff to include doctors, physiotherapists, fitness advisers, massage therapists, nutritionists, strength trainers, podiatrists and other related health professionals. Behind every successful team is an insightful coach who has assembled the correct mix of support staff, each mindful that sickness or injury is the frequent rate-limiting factor for any athlete.

To the professional rugby player these factors equate directly to their ability to work, and contracted players are expected to take greater responsibility for their health and general well-being. They need to become more knowledgeable about injury prevention, banned and permitted drugs, and aspects of nutrition.

The focus in this chapter is on physical preparation, injury, rehabilitation and general health issues, including drug misuse and policy matters relating to responsibilities for spinal injury and blood-borne infections. While the elite player is taken as the model, these issues are equally important for players at all levels of the game.

## Injury and rehabilitation

The average rugby player is often regarded as an accident 'just waiting to happen'. Considering the demands of contemporary elite sport, this is not an unreasonable assumption: premature retirement from sport is frequently the consequence of chronic injury. While some consider injury in rugby as inevitable, sports medicine practice points to a number of ways to minimise the risks.

According to the 1997 statistics from the Accident Rehabilitation and Compensation Corporation (ACC), injuries sustained in New Zealand as a result of recreational activities accounted for $86 million.[1] These data need to be interpreted in the light of our national romance with sport and physical recreation. Heading the table of sports injury claims is rugby union, which accounts for nearly 25 percent of the total cost to the ACC fund. This is not surprising when one considers not only

Dangerous tackles not only draw penalties but also are a recipe for serious injury.

the physical characteristics of the game, but the fact that there are an estimated 200,000 registered players in New Zealand, from junior school teams to Golden Oldies.

Representatives from the ACC and the New Zealand Rugby Football Union (NZRFU) have been enthusiastic in their development of injury research. The Rugby Injury Prevention Project (RIPP) study identified a group of 356 Dunedin rugby players and determined their risk profiles, physical and psychological preparedness and other factors contributing to injury. These players were followed up at regular intervals throughout the season.[2]

This research highlighted the tackle as being responsible for around 30 percent of all injuries. It also emphasised that there are frequent pressures on players to return to the game before they are fully fit, often with the indiscriminate use of painkillers to mask their injuries.

As an outcome of the RIPP study, several initiatives have been introduced by the NZRFU including the compulsory use of mouthguards, a standardised management protocol for concussion, a policy for sports first aid, and the establishment of a panel to monitor the implementation of safety messages to players at all levels of the game.[3] Responsibility for monitoring injury issues in rugby rests with the NZRFU medical panel, which has direct contact with the International Board of the Rugby Union (IRB).

Injury in any sport has been described as an occupational hazard. There may be collision with a stationary object, or impact between two bodies that happen to be moving in opposite directions. In such cases fractured limbs, dislocated joints, ruptured ligaments, head or spinal injuries or concussion are common. These injuries are often very serious, and usually demand urgent medical intervention and special investigations including x-ray or bone scans.

Repetitious forces generated by ballistic, bouncing and weight-bearing activities are responsible for the large number of overused muscles, inflamed tendons and stress reactions in bone. Although such injuries are less dramatic, they are no less troublesome to the enthusiastic competitive athlete. These are overuse injuries, and they represent the largest group of injuries seen by sports doctors and physiotherapists.

## KEY FINDINGS FROM RUGBY INJURY RESEARCH [4]

➤ For every 100 games played in 1998, 5.7 injuries occurred (reduced from 9.9 injuries in 1993).

➤ Sprains and strains are the most common rugby injuries.

➤ Knees, shoulders and ankles are the most frequently injured body parts in rugby.

➤ Over one-third of all rugby injuries occur in tackles.

➤ In tackles both the ball carrier and the tackler are at risk.

➤ 88 percent of all players surveyed in 1998 wore mouthguards, while 26 percent wore headgear.

## THE ACUTE MANAGEMENT OF INJURY IN RUGBY

With any injury, management begins with appropriate first aid. There is a simple acronym that forms the basis of any first aid programme. It includes the principles of Prevention, Rest, Ice, Compression, Elevation and Diagnosis (PRICED). These are simple yet effective measures that set the scene for more elaborate management after the acute situation has been controlled. It is well within the ability of any sports first-aider to apply these principles before handing the management of the injured player to someone with advanced skills.[5]

———

### P R I C E D

is a simple first aid measure for treating soft tissue
(muscle, tendon, ligament) injuries.

**P** = Prevention

Prevent further injury by immediately ceasing activity. Practise the skills and maintain levels of physical and mental fitness appropriate to your sport or activity.

**R** = Rest

Rest prevents further damage and reduces uncontrolled bleeding, thereby reducing excessive pain and swelling.

**I** = Ice

Ice cools tissues and reduces pain, swelling and bleeding. It should be applied to the injured area crushed and wrapped in a damp towel. The pack should be kept in place for approximately 20 minutes, and this treatment may be repeated every three to four hours for 48 hours after an injury has been sustained.

**C** = Compression

Compression helps to stop bleeding and reduce swelling. It may be introduced via a firm compression bandage when moulding the ice pack over the injured area. Between ice treatments, a firm compression bandage should be maintained.

**E** = Elevation

Elevation also helps to stop bleeding and reduce swelling, through support and by raising the injured area to a comfortable position. Limbs left hanging are affected by gravity and soon become swollen and uncomfortable.

**D** = Diagnosis

Because all injuries cause some degree of tissue damage it is absolutely essential for an accurate diagnosis to be made.

> *If any injury fails to improve significantly within 48 hours,*
> *despite the use of the sports first aid measures described,*
> *consult your doctor or physiotherapist.*[6]

## THE PREVENTION OF INJURY

Injury prevention begins with adequate preparation, correct technique and adherence to the rules of the game.

A legacy of New Zealand rugby of the late 1970s and early 1980s was an unacceptable number of spinal cord injuries. Concern was expressed at all levels of the game, and as a consequence rule changes to scrummaging were implemented. These changes signalled a significant shift in policy that New Zealand administrators can proudly claim to have promoted. Meanwhile in Australia, research into the biomechanics of the scrum provided further scientific argument for the potential risks of poor technique and the need to instil these into front-row forwards from an early age.[7]

A referee calling in a scrum engagement.

No less important was the teaching of the correct tackling technique. Coaches and referees were also willing contributors to other safety initiatives that reduced the risk of injury. The implementation of the 'crouch — pause — engage' technique for packing scrums is now widely adopted from junior games to international matches.

At a time when we are exposed to extensive media coverage of sport, any attempts to eliminate unnecessary injury must be applauded. Examples include the introduction of the 'sin bin' and severe penalties for players whose 'over-vigorous' behaviour is often beyond acceptable standards. The 'blood bin' acknowledges the potential spread of blood-borne infection,[8] and there is also a more serious approach to head injury and consistent penalties for foul play.[9] These are all examples of good preventive practices that have an application to rugby at all grades.

### THE QUESTION OF REHABILITATION

Rehabilitation begins with appropriate first aid and an early, accurate diagnosis. It should really begin at the moment of injury, and by definition, rehabilitation aims to restore structure and function to as near normal as possible.[10]

In simple terms this means that the injury must be skilfully assessed and treated in accordance with best clinical practice, in order to have the player back on the field in the minimum amount of time. Several members of the team's medical staff are usually involved, with the doctor providing the initial diagnosis. The rehabilitative process is only complete when the injured player is capable of carrying out a full range of functional movements without discomfort.

Persisting pain is a sure signal that tissues are still not healed. Pain reduces confidence, the player underperforms and the risk of re-injury escalates. There are innumerable examples of players returning to the game too soon or having to rely on the unacceptable use of painkillers. This is an area of significant debate, where the relationship between the coach and the medical staff is vital. It is totally inappropriate for a coach to make excessive demands on the team doctor, whose responsibility is for the long-term health of the athlete.

Rehabilitation is traditionally divided into the following four distinct phases.

### 1. Acute first aid and primary assessment

This generally occurs on the field of play or the sideline. It involves the primary decision of whether to allow the player to remain in the game or to be taken off. It sets the scene for the stages that follow, and may involve some immediate intervention such as the application of ice or a compression bandage. Trivial injuries may permit a return to play, while more serious problems demand further care.

## 2. Secondary assessment and investigations

Under the grandstand or back in the clubrooms, the player is reviewed by medical staff who may require further specialist opinion or investigations such as an x-ray. Additional elements of treatment are normally added and at this point more definitive measures such as splints, slings or bandages are used to rest the injury and comfort the patient. There is also a place for pain-relieving medication at this time.

## 3. Diagnosis and treatment plan

The following day, in the light of x-ray reports and other contributing information, a clearer diagnosis should be established. The treatment plan may include more permanent splinting and ongoing medication. At this point the physiotherapist takes over the physical aspects of treatment, and in consultation with the patient and doctor should develop an appropriate time-frame with definable points of assessment that will result in a pain-free return to training.

## 4. Advanced rehabilitation and return to sport

During this period, other members of the medical team are likely to become involved. Elements of fitness are maintained through aerobic activities involving non-injured parts, and the injury is regularly assessed. Through the combined knowledge of all staff, an appropriate test of fitness to return to play should be established. This requires the collaboration of player, coach and medical staff to ensure realistic goals are achieved. A successful rehabilitation programme must address both physical and psychological elements, and a return to training should precede full match fitness.[11]

**KEY POINTS**

➤ Injuries in rugby are either due to a single identifiable event or are the result of repetitive minor stress (overuse).

➤ Sudden impact, collision and the vigorous forces at scrum, maul and tackle account for most of the serious injuries in rugby.

➤ Forces severe enough to cause bones to break, ligaments to rupture and joints to dislocate are not uncommon in rugby at all levels.

➤ Broken bones, spinal injuries, concussion and dislocations represent the serious end of the injury spectrum.

➤ Agencies like the ACC, the Hillary Commission and Sports Medicine New Zealand have a responsibility in maintaining the profile of sport and physical recreation in this country.

➤ Rehabilitation is a team effort that culminates in the player returning to full physical and psychological fitness. There are no short cuts, and at all times the welfare of players must override the desire for a premature return to the game.

# Drug misuse in sport

The universal abhorrence of drug misuse in sport is well publicised. The NZRFU abides by the standards that have been set by the International Olympic Committee (IOC) and includes in its list of banned substances those drugs and other prohibited practices that are listed by the IOC.[12]

The NZRFU has a strict constitutional requirement relating to the use of drugs and adherence to its doping regulations. In particular these regulations state that:

'. . . no participant or member union (or its employees) shall engage in any doping practice at any time.' And with specific regard to personal responsibility: '. . . notwithstanding the obligations on others to comply with these regulations, it is the personal responsibility of any participant to ensure that he or she does not engage in any doping practice'.

**(NZRFU Doping Regulations, 2.1 and 2.2).**

### BAN ON DOPING PRACTICES

In rugby union, as in other sports throughout the world, penalties for infractions of the drug laws are severe. Depending on the substance detected, players may be banned for periods ranging from three months to two years. Repeat offenders may be banned for life.

The IOC's medical code lists substances under various categories.[13] It is no defence for a rugby player to plead ignorance of a drug's inclusion on that list. Neither is it a defence for a player to plead that he or she did not know a banned substance was being taken. Coaches and managers are also responsible for ensuring players are fully aware of doping regulations and of the consequences of breaches. They should also ensure players consult medical staff or other competent health professionals before taking any prescribed or over-the-counter (OTC) medicines.

*Players must accept the ultimate responsibility*
*for taking any substance.*

Breaches of the doping regulations, whether wilful or accidental, reflect on the individual, his or her team, the team support staff and in many instances the union concerned. In New Zealand the existence of the New Zealand Sports Drug Agency (NZSDA) makes access to lists of banned substances very simple. The NZSDA has a confidential telephone service that is available to any athlete, their coach or adviser, to provide updated information on substances banned in sport. Details of contact numbers appear at the end of this chapter, on page 209. A summary of the major categories of banned substances as declared by the IOC is also provided.

# The use of protective equipment in rugby

The use of various forms of external padding has become more common in all contact sports where impact and collisions are to be expected. IRB laws only permit rugby players to wear certain delineated forms of padding.[14] Such padding is permitted on medical recommendation, provided it is attached to the body or sewn into the jersey.

Padding will not prevent major injuries but it does help to lessen the force of an impact and the risk of soft tissue bruising. In this section we discuss the use of all forms of protective gear in rugby, and highlight the need to address this issue with respect to the increasing number of women now playing the sport.

Informed advice for women rugby players regarding the use of specific padding is not widely available at present. Current information is anecdotal and not confirmed by any well-conducted research. In these circumstances women rugby players should observe the same recommendations as their male counterparts, although there is a move in many contact sports today for women to wear chest and breast protection.[15]

### SHOULDER PADS

There is little evidence to show that shoulder pads decrease the incidence of severe shoulder injuries such as fractures or dislocations. However, well-fitting shoulder pads, constructed of materials that effectively absorb and disperse the force of impact, appear to reduce the potential for soft tissue damage.

The number of different commercial designs of shoulder pads is evidence of their increasing use, and in many sports they bear the endorsement of prominent players. Despite their increasing use, however, the debate continues over the real benefits of pads as protectors against soft tissue injury as opposed to their ability to prevent serious joint damage. The laws associated with wearing shoulder pads relate to the fact that padding is either attached to the body or sewn into the jersey.[16]

### SHIN GUARDS AND THIGH PADDING

The shin region is another area of potential impact. Shin guards that are made of light, soft, compliant materials are effective in reducing impact to the shin and thereby reducing the risk of bruising injuries.

The use of headgear and thigh protectors is still a point of discussion among some rugby people.

The use of shin guards is far more common in sports such as soccer and hockey, where direct blows to the front of the shin are more frequent and can result in significant damage. Shin guards are not widely used by senior rugby players, although there is some evidence to suggest that their use by junior players would be helpful in preventing bruising to the front of the shin.[17]

Similarly, thigh pads are able to modify the effects of direct contact forces to the front of the thigh, where deep bruises commonly occur. Little has been written about the use of thigh pads and few scientific articles have appeared to confirm their effectiveness, although American footballers and international cricketers are well aware of the benefits of wearing appropriate thigh protection.

Before recommending the use of any form of thigh protectors the IRB laws need to be studied. At the moment undergarments such as neoprene sleeves over thighs and calves are permissible, but these undergarments may not contain any form of padding.

## HEADGEAR

Headgear is most effective in protecting against cuts, lacerations and bruising. It provides little if any protection from the consequences of direct impact, and players must not be lulled into a false sense that concussion is prevented by the use of headgear. Physical forces may be altered by the combined use of head protection and an appropriate custom-designed mouthguard, but once again it is important to state that the protection is limited. Research has shown that most players who wear headgear do so because of previous injury.[18]

Anecdotal evidence also suggests that wearing head protection of any type may give the wearer a feeling of invincibility and inadvertently increase the risk of injury, rather than prevent it.

## MOUTHGUARDS

Mouthguards are most effective in protecting the teeth, gums and surrounding tissues from direct impact. They may be inexpensive thermoplastic types (boil and bite) or more expensive custom-fabricated mouthguards that are recommended for higher grade adult players. Their use in New Zealand is compulsory for all rugby players and they should be worn at all practices as well as during games.[19]

It is important to remember that children's mouthguards must be replaced regularly to accommodate growth. A correctly fitting mouthguard should not be uncomfortable to wear, or cause speech and breathing difficulties.

## KNEE AND ANKLE SUPPORT

No form of joint support should ever be used to mask pain. Knees and ankles are particularly vulnerable joints and the use of external supports or splints must only be used after you have received qualified advice.[20]

Preventative taping will only provide support for a few minutes of vigorous activity. Sweat and muscle activity will soon loosen the tape no matter how expertly it is applied. More complicated devices such as knee braces are designed to be worn as part of the rehabilitation process, and are not designed for playing rugby. They are usually constructed of rigid materials, and often hinged to allow for functional knee movements.[21]

Ankle braces may also be of rigid materials and their use is also generally limited to rehabilitation. Some forms of soft ankle bracing may be worn in conjunction with rugby boots, but their use generally indicates incomplete rehabilitation and should counter the decision to play.[22]

Generally speaking there is no substitution for the strength of the protective muscles that surround a joint. Their role is one of protection, and at all times this must be fully developed before continuation in any sport is encouraged. The best advice in these matters is obtained from a doctor and physiotherapist.

### KEY POINTS ABOUT PROTECTIVE GEAR

➤ Protective gear must be used correctly to reduce the risk of injury to players.

➤ Shoulder pads do not decrease the risk of severe shoulder injuries such as dislocation or fractures.

➤ Shin guards are effective in reducing the impact of forces and therefore reduce the risk of bruising injuries.

➤ Thigh pads are considered to be effective in modifying the effects of direct contact forces.

➤ The use of protective equipment in rugby must be seen as protective rather than offensive.

➤ In the case of women rugby players, the best advice available is to follow the same recommendations that apply to their male counterparts.

➤ Knee support must never be used to mask an injured joint because incomplete rehabilitation increases the risk of re-injury.

➤ Taping will only provide limited support for a joint, lasting for about 20 minutes of vigorous exercise.

➤ Mouthguards protect the teeth, jaw and surrounding tissues (it is compulsory for all rugby players in New Zealand to wear mouthguards).

## Infectious disease transmission in rugby

There is a potential for the spread of infectious diseases in any contact sport. Some infections are relatively harmless, while others may have life-threatening consequences. Nevertheless, attention to the principles of general hygiene are always worth promoting, and in sporting situations this ought to be a shared responsibility.[23]

Close physical contact can lead to the spread of bacterial, viral and fungal diseases. Skin infections, hepatitis and athlete's foot are examples of infections that may be spread by contact with infected blood, saliva, sweat or other body fluids such as urine.

There are serious community health problems associated particularly with the spread of hepatitis and HIV, and the sporting fraternity should be aware of the risks, however slight, and develop a responsible attitude. For example, in rugby players, all actively bleeding cuts and abrasions must be attended to immediately. Officials are within their rights to stop play to allow bleeding players to have their injuries attended to, and the use of the 'blood bin' for this purpose is encouraged.

Here are some simple guidelines to minimise the risk of infectious disease spread in rugby:

➤ All players should have fresh cuts and grazes covered with an impermeable dressing.

➤ Players should be vaccinated against hepatitis B.

➤ Clubrooms and changing facilities should be kept clean, with household bleach (diluted 1:10) used to clean up any blood spills.

➤ Contaminated clothing and equipment should be treated as if they are potentially infectious.

➤ Sharing towels and drink bottles greatly increases the risk of cross infection and should be strongly discouraged.

➤ Referees must insist that any bleeding player leaves the field, and only agree to their return when the bleeding has stopped and any contaminated clothing has been changed.

➤ Officials handling bleeding players should wear disposable gloves, and resuscitation should only be carried out using disposable face masks.

➤ Good education in the prevention of infectious disease spread is necessary for all team support staff, officials and players.[24]

## Head injuries in rugby (concussion)

By its very nature rugby involves collision and impact. These have the potential to cause head injury, and there is a real concern that serious damage may be overlooked as trivial. Head injuries range in severity from brief periods of confusion and semi-consciousness to significant periods of unconsciousness and the risks of convulsions, coma or even death.[25]

The soft, delicate brain is a particularly sensitive organ that sits within the bony box of the skull. Any sudden, violent movement of the head, due to collision or unexpected change of direction, has the potential to damage the brain tissue. Usually the damage is slight, and recovery is uncomplicated. But sometimes the injury is more severe and the damaged brain may take some time to heal. During this time, any further damage may have serious consequences.

Quite simply, the term concussion infers damage to the brain that will affect normal function. It is important to realise that to be concussed a rugby player does not necessarily have to be 'knocked out'. A very brief period of confusion, often accompanied by a short period of memory loss, is still considered to be concussion.

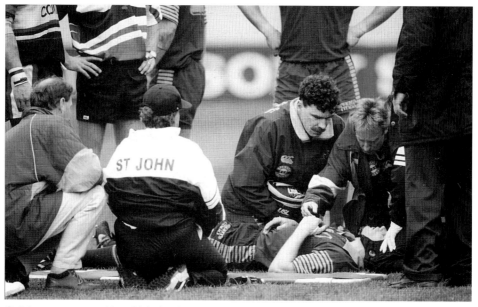

Quick assessment of head injuries is vital, and should be left to the specialists where possible.

Quite obviously there are various degrees of concussion, and the more serious the damage to the brain the more significant will be the period of unconsciousness and the loss of memory.

On the field of play it is necessary to make a quick assessment of any player with a head injury. This is best done by an independent agent, and certainly not the team captain or even the referee. Often it takes little more than a few quick questions (date, time, place, score, etc.) to establish whether the player has been significantly injured. Unsteadiness, confusion or uncharacteristic behaviour are further clues to possible concussion, and any player showing these symptoms should be removed from the game immediately for further assessment.

If the player is obviously unconscious they must be watched carefully and attention must always be paid to AIRWAYS, BREATHING AND CIRCULATION (ABC).

---

An unconscious player must never be shifted, for fear of
causing damage to an unrecognised spinal injury.

---

Once consciousness has returned, a careful assessment of the neck and lower spine must be made before the player is moved or allowed to move spontaneously. Where there is any doubt, qualified first aid assistance must always be sought.

The issue surrounding head injury that causes most concern in rugby is the decision regarding the time needed for recovery and full return to playing. This will obviously depend on the amount of damage done to the brain, and requires careful consideration. There are some general guidelines, but it is important to state that every case must be considered on the basis of age, player background and history of previous head injury. No two cases will ever be the same and no one should ever be criticised for adopting an attitude of caution when advising head-injured rugby players.

Generally speaking, a concussed rugby player should not participate in training or matches for at least three weeks and should return only with medical approval. If concussed twice in a season, a player should not play again that season. Obviously there are always going to be exceptions to these general rules, and the ultimate decision must rest with the doctor who will take into account the results of a medical examination and special tests for psychological evaluation.[26]

## IOC LIST OF BANNED SUBSTANCES

Five categories of doping agents are banned by the International Olympic Committee. These now apply to all major sports in New Zealand. The classes are stimulants, narcotic analgesics, anabolic agents, diuretics, and peptide hormones. A full explanatory list of these banned drugs together with a list of permitted alternatives is available from the New Zealand Sports Drug Agency (NZSDA).

In addition certain drugs are subject to restriction. These are alcohol, marijuana, local anaesthetics, corticosteroids, beta-blockers, and beta-agonist drugs. An explanation of the control of these drugs is also available from the NZSDA.

It is also illegal for any athlete to use blood doping methods or to manipulate their urine through physical or chemical means.

The NZSDA is an independent agency working to monitor drug use by athletes and to provide advice and educational material. A confidential Drug Hotline is available on 0800 378437. Anyone with drug-related concerns is advised to ring this number or to contact the agency at the following address:

NZ Sports Drug Agency, 71 Merton Rd, St Johns, Auckland

PO Box 18339, Auckland

Phone: 09 521 5706

Fax: 09 521 5726

Email: nzsda@nzsda.co.nz

Educational material and information on banned and permitted drugs is freely available. The responsibility lies with all athletes to become informed and follow the accepted guidelines. The objective is to make sport drug-free and above all else to help educate athletes.

# 10 Total programme planning

## Gordon Sleivert

Throughout this book we have largely been concerned with details. You have read about the mental aspects of the game and learnt how to develop mental skills to improve your rugby performance. You have hopefully evaluated your rugby fitness and set some training goals for yourself or your players, and thought about the factors that predispose players to injury and affect their rehabilitation. You have learnt that bacon and eggs is not a good pre-game meal, and identified some steps to improve your diet. Additionally, the skills associated with successful rugby performance have been presented and methods and principles of analysing and improving your skills have been discussed. All these factors make up the pieces of your rugby performance jigsaw.

It is now your mission to assemble the pieces in order to achieve peak performance. So where do you start? It is a challenge for most people to organise diverse goals and objectives; even though they may all have a common goal — improved performance — they seem to require quite different plans and strategies to achieve. We will now use the process of periodisation to facilitate and ensure that you reach your rugby potential!

## The four Ps

### 1. PERIODISATION

What is periodisation? It can be defined as the logical organisation of a training plan into periods of emphasis. The training plan is aimed at ensuring the player is performing at

The four Ps.

Philosophy

Prioritisation

$p^4$

Periodisation

Planning

peak potential at a specified time or times within the competitive rugby season. This is commonly referred to as peaking.

A player in club rugby may need to peak as often as every week to ensure their team has every chance of succeeding in the first round of the competition. If the team gets off to a good start, however, then they may not need to peak every week and can spend a bit of extra time working on weaknesses so they are better able to peak in round two or in the semi-finals or finals.

As a general rule of thumb, however, rugby players must be ready to perform at peak potential once a week for the duration of the rugby season. In club rugby this is usually a period of up to four months, but for top-class rugby players the season is much longer.

The process of peaking requires that physical and mental overload is balanced with recovery so the player feels fresh and ready to use their physical, mental, technical and tactical attributes to the best of their ability. For this reason a large part of the periodisation process is concerned with identifying periods of loading and unloading (recovery).

Another reason for periodising your training plan is to facilitate goal setting. As you know, goals are most readily achieved if they are performance based, realistic, and made up of a series of short-term objectives. Your periodised plan will be developed around the goals you have set yourself. In chapter 2 you were asked to complete a peak performance profile and a goal achievement worksheet. These tasks were designed so that you would not only have the opportunity to plan your season in advance of a particular training period, but you would also commit this plan to paper. Such planning will help you to think about what you are going to emphasise in your training at various times of the season and what you must accomplish by what date(s).

With the multitude of goals you have probably set, periodisation will also help you organise your goals and time into a cohesive training plan. Periodising your training can also help your time management, but you must be realistic in setting appropriate amounts of training time each week. Bear in mind that you still need to have a life outside training, and you will need to consider how your training fits into your work/school schedule. A balanced lifestyle is important; focusing exclusively on rugby is likely to lead to extra pressure and stress and reduce your enjoyment of the game.

We know that physical attributes must be overloaded so that they adapt and improve, and we know that mental and motor skills must be overlearned so that they can be executed properly and used automatically during competition. But if there is too much emphasis on overloading and/or overlearning, fatigue and overtraining is inevitable. Therefore, a final reason to periodise your training is that it will allow you to maximise your improvement.

For example, by laying all your training plans out on paper you will be able to identify periods of time when you might be trying to achieve too much, and can insert regular regeneration breaks to prevent fatigue. This proactive approach is certainly better than the reactive recovery breaks resorted to by the majority of players when they begin to feel overtired or overtrained, or have niggling injuries.

It can be a disadvantage to train too many performance factors at the same time because not only does the overload dominate the recovery aspects of training, leading to a reduction in performance, there are also benefits to training some factors before others. For example, it is desirable to have had some solid strength training before beginning plyometric training. Alternatively, it may be helpful to learn relaxation strategies in advance of mastering mental imagery techniques.

Periodisation is therefore critical to ensuring your training is optimised to suit your individual goals and time schedule, and to ensure a balanced, sensible and well-rounded programme.

## 2. PHILOSOPHY

Traditional periodised training programmes emphasise periods or blocks of training in which different performance factors are usually trained in sequence, not concurrently (see diagram A). For example, in laying out a physical fitness programme a sequential periodised programme would emphasise training aerobic fitness before training anaerobic fitness, and emphasise training strength prior to training speed.[1] Although there is little research supporting the use of this approach over others it is

Training programmes can be periodised sequentially (A) or concurrently (B).

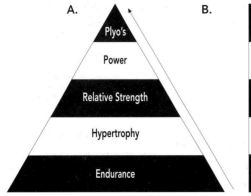

the most common type of programme, has largely arisen from tradition, and is widely accepted. In fact, for a novice trainer it is probably the most sensible approach.

Another approach to periodisation is to train a number of performance factors concurrently (see diagram B). That is, players may do a mixture of aerobic and anaerobic training each week, or a mixture of strength and power training each week.[2] This type of training programme — concurrent periodisation — appears to be better suited to team sports like rugby. This is particularly true during the competition phase, when games must be played every week and all the important performance factors must be maintained at an optimal level.

For elite rugby players with long training histories, concurrent periodisation may be the most suitable method of approaching training. These players have no need to spend large blocks of time working on a particular attribute or fitness component, since most are well developed or require just a little regular attention to improve or maintain that attribute.

Although in concurrent training multiple performance parameters are trained within the same period, there is still usually an element of sequencing training blocks. For example, the emphasis of an off-season training block may be to develop aerobic fitness, therefore aerobic workouts are performed three times a week, but anaerobic/functional fitness might still be loaded twice a week and strength could also be loaded twice a week. As the training programme progresses towards the competitive season less emphasis might be placed on aerobic fitness and more emphasis on anaerobic fitness, power and functional training. Thus the concurrent programme would have elements of game-specific training early in the off-season, but in the late off-season the training would be much more game-specific.

The third approach to training is a mixture of sequential and concurrent periodisation. In its most basic form this hybrid form of periodisation utilises traditional sequential periodisation in the off-season but concurrent periodisation in the competitive season (see diagram at right). For rugby players with little history of training the physical and/or mental aspects of the game, this is an appropriate method of periodisation; the major areas of weakness can be improved in the off-

**Hybrid periodisation.**

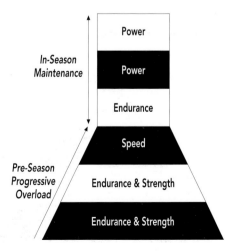

season using a simple sequential approach, and then maintained in-season using concurrent training.

Many players, coaches and even strength and conditioning specialists believe that a magic programme exists that can be used to develop the perfect rugby player; they are constantly searching for 'the answer'. Quite simply, the answer does not exist! Many excellent rugby players of equivalent performance levels have achieved their success in different ways. Different periodisation methods and different specific training methods can be equally effective. You must choose the training model and philosophy that seem to suit your individual characteristics and schedule best. Stick with them for a while so that you have a chance to determine their effectiveness at helping you reach your goals. Chopping and changing programmes every month or two will muddy the waters, making it difficult to determine how you are progressing and whether your training programme is working.

### 3. PRIORITISING

As a first step in your periodised plan you will need to identify the games you'll be playing in the first round, and project yourself into the 2nd round, semi-finals and finals. Although you can't predict whether your team will make it all the way to a final, you must ensure that you are ready if it does. It always pays to plan for success! You also need to indicate any representative games that you could play in. For example, if you are expecting to be called upon by the Black Ferns or the All Blacks in the near future then you should know their test schedule.

On worksheet I (facing page) list *all* competitions/games during your season and code them in chronological order (A = 1st competition, B = 2nd competition and so on). Secondly, rank the importance of these competitions/games on a Peak Index scale of 1–3 (1 = most important to 3 = least important). Page 216 contains an example for you to follow.

Transfer the letter-coded games and corresponding peaking ranking onto your periodised training plan (page 217) or the master periodised plan (worksheet 5, page 227). A periodised plan does not necessarily follow the calendar year, so you may want to place your most important games, such as finals, in one of the later weeks on the plan (see example). On worksheet 5 you should now indicate the major emphasis of the different blocks of time. Start by blocking off your competition phase(s) in the row marked 'Periods of Training'. In the same row you should also indicate off-season training and pre-season training blocks.

The off-season training block will be the time to develop your base fitness and work on fundamental motor and mental skills. This period may be from three to six

## WORKSHEET 1: COMPETITION SCHEDULE

| Date | Competition/Game | Code (A–Z) | Peak index (1–3) |
|---|---|---|---|

**Round 1**

| | | | |
|---|---|---|---|
| | | | |
| | | | |
| | | | |
| | | | |
| | | | |
| | | | |
| | | | |
| | | | |
| | | | |

**Round 2**

| | | | |
|---|---|---|---|
| | | | |
| | | | |
| | | | |
| | | | |
| | | | |
| | | | |
| | | | |
| | | | |
| | | | |

# WORKSHEET 1: COMPETITION SCHEDULE

| Date | Competition/Game | Code (A–Z) | Peak index (1–3) |
|---|---|---|---|
| **Round 1** | | | |
| 10th April | vs Heriot | A | 3 |
| 17th April | vs Gore | B | 1 |
| 24th April | vs Rakaia | C | 3 |
| 1st May | vs Wainouiomata | D | 3 |
| 8th May | vs Riversdale | E | 1 |
| 15th May | vs Naseby | F | 1 |
| 22nd May | vs Duntroon | G | 2 |
| 29th May | vs Waihi | H | 2 |
| 5th June | vs Waimakariri | I | 2 |
| 12th June | vs Ranfurly | J | 2 |
| 19th June | vs St Bathans | K | 2 |
| **Round 2** | | | |
| 26th June | 2nd Round Game 1 | L | 1 |
| 3rd July | 2nd Round Game 2 | M | 1 |
| 10th July | 2nd Round Game 3 | N | 1 |
| 17th July | 2nd Round Game 4 | O | 1 |
| 24th July | 2nd Round Game 5 | P | 1 |
| 31st July | Semi-finals | Q | 1 |
| 7th August | Final | R | 1 |
| | | | |
| | | | |

Example

# PERIODISED TRAINING PLAN

| | Game (A–Z) Weeks 1–52 | Peak Index (1–3) | | Game (A–Z) Weeks 1–52 | Peak Index (1–3) |
|---|---|---|---|---|---|
| **Off-season** *(General preparation)* | | | | | |
| | | | **Competition phase** | A | 3 |
| | | | | B | 1 |
| | | | | C | 3 |
| | | | | D | 3 |
| | | | | E | 1 |
| | | | | F | 1 |
| | | | | G | 2 |
| | | | | H | 2 |
| | | | | I | 2 |
| | | | | J | 2 |
| | | | | K | 2 |
| | | | | L | 1 |
| | | | | M | 1 |
| | | | | N | 1 |
| | | | | O | 1 |
| | | | | P | 1 |
| | | | | Q | 1 |
| | | | | R | 1 |
| **Pre-season** *(Specific preparation)* | | | **Time off** | | |

months long, depending on your individual situation. The attention to fundamentals may continue into the pre-season block but by this time your training should be of higher intensity and mimic all the demands that you will experience in a game. That is, you should be performing a great deal of functional, game-specific training. This period of specific training is usually six to eight weeks long.

Finally, it pays to schedule some time off at the end of your competition schedule. This three- to six-week period is an opportunity to relax, forget about rugby for a while and regenerate your body and mind for the upcoming season.

The next step in developing your plan is to decide which performance factors can be transferred to your training plan. You have already performed evaluation exercises in the physical, technical, tactical and psychological domains important to your rugby performance. You did this in chapter 2 using a peak performance profile and also followed it up by evaluating your fitness in chapter 4, your rugby skills in chapter 6 and your nutrition in chapter 8. It will pay at this time to review all the goals you have set yourself in these chapters and list them in worksheet 2 (pages 219 and 220). You should then prioritise these goals from most important to least important, as this will help you to decide which goals to tackle first, since it may be impossible to work towards achieving all your goals in one season.

## 4. PLANNING

Before transferring these prioritised goals to your master plan write down how much time you have available for training each week in each of the training periods. This task should be completed on worksheet 3 (page 221). This training time must include regular team or organised practice sessions as well as training you normally complete on your own. Remember to count competitions as part of your overall training time.

Now refer back to your *prioritised goals* and transfer these in order of priority to the appropriate training period (e.g. off-season) on worksheet 4 (see example, page 223). Make sure you start with your most important goals and calculate how much time your action plans will take each week. Stop listing goals on this worksheet if you reach your maximum allocated training time from worksheet 3.

As noted previously, the actions you have just listed must be realistic; there is a danger of setting too many goals in a particular training period and trying to do too much. If you have listed three or four goals in each training period you should now double-check to make sure that all the actions you have documented to achieve these goals can fit into your time schedule for training.

In the example provided, our rugby player has indicated that he can spend about six hours a week of individual training in both the general and specific preparatory

# WORKSHEET 2: GOAL PRIORITISATION

| Goals | Priority |
|---|---|
| **Technical** | |
| ................................................................................................ | ................ |
| ................................................................................................ | ................ |
| ................................................................................................ | ................ |
| ................................................................................................ | ................ |
| ................................................................................................ | ................ |
| **Tactical** | |
| ................................................................................................ | ................ |
| ................................................................................................ | ................ |
| ................................................................................................ | ................ |
| ................................................................................................ | ................ |
| ................................................................................................ | ................ |
| **Physical** | |
| ................................................................................................ | ................ |
| ................................................................................................ | ................ |
| ................................................................................................ | ................ |
| ................................................................................................ | ................ |
| ................................................................................................ | ................ |
| **Psychological** | |
| ................................................................................................ | ................ |
| ................................................................................................ | ................ |
| ................................................................................................ | ................ |
| ................................................................................................ | ................ |
| ................................................................................................ | ................ |

## WORKSHEET 2: GOAL PRIORITISATION

| Goals (Abbreviated) | Priority |
|---|---|
| **Technical** | |
| Goal-kicking accuracy | 1 |
| Passing accuracy | 10 |
| Tackling technique | 6 |
| General stability | 14 |
| | |
| **Tactical** | |
| Reading running lines on defence | 8 |
| Options – choosing runner moves | 9 |
| | |
| | |
| **Physical** | |
| Acceleration over 10 m | 3 |
| Aerobic fitness | 11 |
| Improve upper body strength | 5 |
| Improve leg strength | 7 |
| | |
| **Psychological** | |
| Improve arousal control | 4 |
| Improve positive self-talk | 2 |
| Improve concentration | 13 |
| Improve motivation for training | 12 |

Example

## WORKSHEET 3: AVAILABLE TRAINING TIMES

| Training period | Time (hours/mins) per week with organised team practice or competition | Time (hours/mins) per week with individual practice |
|---|---|---|
| General preparation | | |
| Specific preparation | | |
| Competition | | |
| Off-season | | |

| Training period | Time (hours/mins) per week with organised team practice or competition | Time (hours/mins) per week with individual practice |
|---|---|---|
| General preparation | *0 hours* | *6 hours* |
| Specific preparation | *4 hours* | *6 hours* |
| Competition | *6 hours* | *4 hours* |
| Off-season | *0 hours* | *4 hours* |

**Example**

# WORKSHEET 4: GOALS, TARGET DATES, ACTIONS

| Training period | Goal | Target date | Action |
|---|---|---|---|
| General preparation | | | |
| Specific preparation | | | |
| Competition | | | |
| Off-season | | | |

## WORKSHEET 4: GOALS, TARGET DATES, ACTIONS

| Training period | Goal | Target date | Action |
|---|---|---|---|
| **General preparation** | Physical: increase absolute strength in half-squats 25 kg to reach 'excellent' category | 30 Jan | Train leg strength 2 x week 3 rugby-specific strength exercises (1 hr/session) |
| | Physical: increase absolute strength in bench-press 14 kg to reach 'satisfactory' category | 30 Jan | Train upper body strength 2 x week using bench-press and dumbbell flies (1 hr/session) |
| | Technical: keep my head up and drive with my legs when making a tackle | 6 Feb | 1. Train body position using tackle bags machine with team mates 2 x week for 20 mins 2. Video body position every 2 weeks and have video reviewed by forward coach |
| | Psychological: decrease time to reach a complete state of relaxation by 30 s | 12 Dec | Practise centring 4 x week for 10 mins |
| **Specific preparation** | Technical: succeed with 90% of goal kicks within 40 m of goal posts | 10 April | 1. Extra instruction from a kicking coach before practice on Tuesdays and Thursdays for 45 mins 2. On Mondays, Wednesdays and Fridays spend 30 mins practising my kicking |
| | Physical: improve acceleration over 100 m by 0.2 s | 10 April | 1. Perform explosive jump squats 2 x week (20 mins) 2. Perform acceleration drills 2 x week (40 mins) |
| | Psychological: maintain use of positive self-talk behaviour throughout an entire practice | 1 April | 1. Compile list of cue words to implement during team training 2. Use imagery to practise these statements in game situations (5 mins/alt. days) |

Example for general and specific training periods

periods (worksheet 3). Adding up the hours required to action his goals in these periods it can be seen that he has budgeted 5 hours and 40 minutes of individual training in the general preparatory phase and about 5 hours and 45 minutes in the specific preparatory phase. He has had to leave out the seven lowest priority goals from a total of fourteen on worksheet 2, because he simply does not have the time to action them. Better to leave the low-priority goals for later than try to squeeze in too much too quickly and become overtrained, fatigued, injured or disillusioned because you have failed to achieve an unrealistic number of goals.

After reviewing the feasibility of your action plans, transfer your goals from worksheet 4 to your developing plan in worksheet 5 (page 227). The goals should be inserted under the appropriate headings (e.g. Fitness, Tactical). You will also want to insert other performance factors that require regular attention but have not necessarily been specified as goals.

Once you have finished transferring your performance factors to the training plan you must then determine loading, maintenance and regeneration periods for each factor. This can be achieved using a variety of approaches, and the exact pattern of loading will depend on the philosophy you ascribe to. The example provided uses the hybrid periodisation model described above. With this form of periodisation a sequenced approach to training is utilised in the off-season, but during the pre-season and during the competitive phase concurrent periodisation is used. Some general tips for laying out your training are provided below.

## General guidelines for rugby preparation

In rugby you must be fully game fit before the season begins as there is generally not enough time over the course of a regular competitive season to improve performance through targeted training. Most players now correctly undertake the majority of their physical training before the season starts, and even during this early stage there is a need for your physical training programme to be specific.

We have used the term 'general preparation' for the early off-season when constructing your training plan. However, during this period your physical training should still be as specific as possible so that you can maintain fitness in all the areas important to rugby performance. By maintaining fitness in all these components year-round you will not have to start from scratch again each year, and over your rugby career your performance level will gradually improve as a result of the cumulative training load (see figure opposite). Therefore you should think of specificity in your physical training year-round to get optimal benefits from your training programme.

**Cumulative training load.**

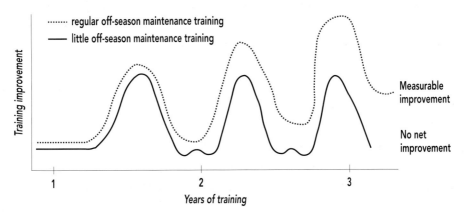

## SEQUENCING OF PHYSICAL TRAINING

As discussed previously, sequencing of different types of physical training is used so that you can concentrate on developing a particular fitness component with minimal interference caused by loading different fitness components simultaneously. In addition, sequencing ensures that the physical training conducted in one training period is completed before you change the emphasis of your physical programme in the next training period. However, when you move into each new training period you will want to maintain the levels of fitness you have obtained. To maintain fitness levels, training frequency of the old programme can be cut by up to two-thirds as long as the training load (volume and intensity) within the remaining sessions does not change.

For example, you may have just completed an eight-week general preparation period to develop muscular strength. During this period you normally trained three days a week. As your training emphasis changes to the development of muscle power in your specific preparation period, you would still perform one session per week for strength development on top of your new programme, which now concentrates on the development of muscular power. Maintenance programmes also allow you to concentrate on the other components of your training programme (e.g. psychological, technical, tactical).

In general, rugby players should concentrate on developing aerobic fitness early in the off-season since the aerobic system has potentially more room for improvement than the anaerobic systems and will take longer to fully develop. Also, a well-developed aerobic system can aid in the recovery from particularly strenuous training. Therefore a rugby player with little history of physical training is wise to develop

# PERIODISED TRAINING PLAN

| Periods of training | Off-season (General preparation) | Pre-season (Specific preparation) | Competition phase | Time off |
|---|---|---|---|---|

Game (A–Z) Weeks 1–52: A B C D E F G H I J K L M N O P Q R

Peak index (1–3): 3 1 3 3 1 1 2 2 2 2 1 1 1 1 1 1

**Skills**
- Goal-kicking
- Tackling
- Passing
- Stability

**Mental**
- Arousal
- Imagery
- Focus
- Self-talk

**Fitness**
- Speed
- Strength
- Aerobic
- Lactic acid
- Flexibility

**Tactical**
- Reading defence
- Reading options

**Assessment**
- Skills
- Mental
- Fitness
- Tactical

Legend: Evaluation · Maintenance · Overload/Overlearn · Regeneration

# WORKSHEET 5: PERIODISED TRAINING PLAN

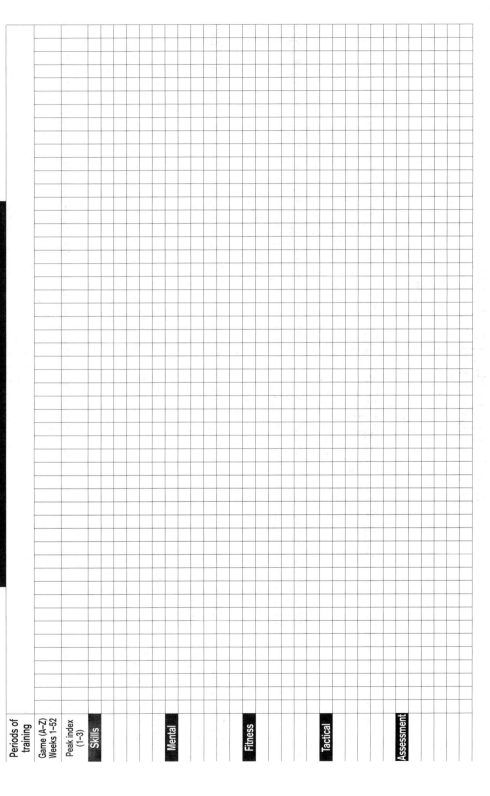

| Periods of training |
| Game (A–Z) Weeks 1–52 |
| Peak index (1–3) |
| **Skills** |
| **Mental** |
| **Fitness** |
| **Tactical** |
| **Assessment** |

some degree of aerobic fitness prior to more intense anaerobic-type training. Of course the time required to develop any fitness component will depend on how fit you are in that particular component when you begin training, and for many rugby players with adequate fitness a concurrent aerobic-anaerobic programme may be most suitable.

Sequencing for strength training follows a similar path of specificity. In the early stages (i.e. first eight weeks) of strength training, strength is increased due primarily to neural changes (i.e. your coordination improves), but small increases in muscle size (hypertrophy) also occur.[3] Thus, general strength programmes are required if you are relatively inexperienced with strength training. Once your muscles have become more efficient in strength training and adaptations in strength begin to plateau (usually around six to eight weeks), you should move to a more specific strength training programme. For example, if you have set a goal of increasing absolute strength, your programme should revolve around a few sets involving four to six reps of near-maximum strength exercises.

**VOLUME OF TRAINING**

Throughout this book we have reiterated that your training needs to be as specific as possible year-round. At the beginning of the season your training may involve a relatively small training load, but as the season progresses the load will increase. So, how do you know how much training to undertake during the various training periods and how much training is too much?

There is a fine line between being in excellent condition and performing well, and being just over the line and performing poorly because your training is hampered by niggling injuries, extreme tiredness, or viral infections. You want to be in the best condition possible at competition time, but the more you push yourself in training the more likely you are to open yourself up to illness and injury. Consequently there is a limit to how much of a training load you can sustain from day to day.

The classic warning signs of imminent overtraining are loss of confidence, mood swings (beyond normal), frequent depression or irritability, loss of appetite, or diminished quality of sleep.[4] You may also experience long-term medical problems (e.g. flu, colds, chest or throat infections). You may not notice any of these warning signs yourself, so it is vital that you listen to your coach, training partner, or family if they tell you they can see such signs. Physical stresses such as viral infections (e.g. colds, flu), increased mental stresses at work or with a partner, or financial problems all have the effect of lowering your overtraining threshold. If you are under greater stress than normal be prepared to reduce your training load so as not to overtrain.

## TAPERING

As discussed earlier, tapering is the process of physical 'fine-tuning' immediately prior to competition. In rugby your weekly in-season preparation should consist of a high training load at the beginning of the week which tapers off through to the next game at the end of the week. The emphasis of training sessions during the taper should shift from higher-volume physical sessions at the start of the week to shorter high-intensity skills sessions and mental/tactical preparation by the end of the taper. Note that the physical training that you perform in the taper should still be of competition intensity.

You can also devote more time to psychological preparation and tactics as you go through your taper. If your taper has an intensity equivalent to that of competition, but the duration of each practice session is decreased gradually, you can expect a three to five percent improvement in performance, as opposed to lesser gains from a taper that reduces duration while intensity is only moderate.[5]

## EVALUATION

It is essential that you evaluate your progress regularly to help you set realistic and measurable goals. There is room at the bottom of the training plan sheet for you to indicate where you will insert evaluation into your overall plan. Don't become a slave to evaluation, but instead view regular assessment as a way of motivating yourself to reach your goals and measure the success of your training.

## INSERT REGENERATION BREAKS

By now you have spent a great deal of time planning how to overload and overlearn various components important to your overall fitness. It is easy to get over-enthusiastic about this and plan to do too much for too long. As you know, this can lead to overtraining, and it is important that you now step back and decide on appropriate places to insert regeneration breaks into your training.

This can be done in a number of ways but generally light training weeks are inserted on a number of regular occasions to promote recovery and adaptation. In the off-season these may be inserted every four to six weeks, and they can be inserted even more frequently in the heart of the competition phase, where recovery becomes even more important to maintaining peak performance.

By regularly inserting regeneration breaks into your training programme you can avoid the feeling of flatness that comes with overtraining. Remember, however, that if you are feeling particularly tired for several days in a row it may pay to unload and recover for three or four days on the fly. Don't be a slave to your on-paper programme, but retain some flexibility and *listen to your body*. Insert your regeneration breaks now.

### OTHER FACTORS

It may pay to think through your training plan now and forecast any other significant events that are occurring in your life over the next year. Are you or any close acquaintances getting married? Do you have an important function or workshop to attend? What about a family holiday? These important events in your life may dictate when you need to schedule your regeneration breaks, and you may have to adjust your overall training schedule. I'm sure your spouse would not appreciate you popping out of the honeymoon suite for an hour or two to squeeze in your plyometrics workout!

## Details and more details

You should now have completed a year-long periodised training plan centred around your most important rugby goals. This is the blueprint that you will follow to guide your rugby preparation over the next year. You may feel that it lacks detail, and it does. This training plan provides you with a helicopter view of your approach to achieving rugby greatness. That is, it reminds you of the big picture and ensures that your specific training is generally targeted in the correct areas. Refer to it often and use it as a general guide when designing your weekly detailed training schedules.

## Summary

This book has provided you with all the tools necessary to improve your enjoyment and ability level in rugby. It is now up to you to implement these plans in order to improve. A wise old rugby coach once said that success is usually achieved when opportunity meets preparation. Achieving your peak rugby performance will depend on your commitment to holistic preparation, your training discipline and the opportunity to succeed in the exciting game of rugby. The challenge of performing well is always present and there is always another rugby challenge in the next game. Enjoy your rugby and Train Smart!

# 11 Training logbook

This chapter contains a number of training 'logsheets' for you to choose from in designing your personalised training logbook.

Throughout this book, we have emphasised the need to keep your own training logbook on a regular basis. A training logbook is not a diary in the sense of recording your general thoughts and feelings (although you may wish to do this). Rather, a logbook is a written record of your peak performance profile(s), goals, training methods, annual training plan, and daily practice sessions/workouts. These daily logsheets of your practice sessions/workouts are the core of your annual training plan, as they record your actual 'training work', your success or failure in achieving goals, and the effectiveness of your training plan. This information is vital for training motivation and commitment, and also for evaluating the overall success of your annual training plan. The information you record on the daily logsheets is objective evidence for you to use in modifying or adapting your on-going training plan(s).

In the following pages we have provided you with a selection of different logsheets for different types of training sessions/workouts. We encourage you to choose those that suit your style of recording information. For example, some players prefer to write general comments about a particular training session/workout, while others prefer to use rating scales and circle numbers or tick boxes instead of writing comments. The choice is yours, but the key point is that we regard a training logbook as absolutely vital to a successful training plan. We suggest that you choose the logsheet(s) that you prefer, or design one of your own, and photocopy multiple copies which you can file in a ring binder. We also suggest that you photocopy your peak performance profile (see chapter 2), goal achievement worksheet(s) (see chapter 3), and annual training plan (see chapter 10) and file them in your training logbook as well.

## GENERAL WORKOUT

**Week:** ........................ to ........................

**Goal:** ..................................................................

**Date:** ........................ **Time:** ........................ **Venue:** ........................

**Resting heart rate (HR):** ........................ beats per min (bpm)

**Daily goal:** ..................................................................

..................................................................

**Today's activities:** ..................................................................

**Activity intensity:** ..................................................................

**Activity duration:** ..................................................................

**Comments:** ..................................................................

..................................................................

..................................................................

..................................................................

..................................................................

..................................................................

**Daily goal achievement:** ..................................................................

..................................................................

..................................................................

..................................................................

# DAILY LOG

**Date:** .................. **Time:** ................ **Resting heart rate:** .............. bpm

**Goals for today:** ...........................................................

**Sleep:** ............. no. of hours    **Quality:**    1      2      3      4      5
                                                        sound       average       restless

**Physical** (Circle appropriate energy system)

*Aerobic*                           *Anaerobic:*     LACTIC     PHOSPHAGEN

**Duration** (mins): ...............     **Interval length/time:** .......................

**Intensity:** ...................... bpm     **Rest length/time:** ........................

 1      2      3      4      5     **Number of reps:** .........................

very easy     moderate     very difficult     **Intensity (% of effort):** ..................

**Other:** ...........................................................

**Assessment:** (Circle number)   Excellent session   1    2    3    4    5    Very poor session

**Why?:** **Energy**   Energised   1    2    3    4    5    Drained

        **Attitude**   Positive   1    2    3    4    5    Negative

**Mental** PST method (Circle one)    SELF-TALK    RELAXATION/CENTRING    IMAGERY    MENTAL PREPARATION

**Duration** (mins): ...............    **Type/content:** .........................

**Assessment:** (Circle number)   Excellent session   1    2    3    4    5    Very poor session

**Why?:** **Energy**   Energised   1    2    3    4    5    Poor

        **Attitude**   Positive   1    2    3    4    5    Negative

**Technical**   Skill #1 ..................    Skill #2 ..................    Skill #3 ..................

**Assessment:** (Circle number)   Excellent session   1    2    3    4    5    Very poor session

**Why?:** (Circle one)   PHYSICAL    MENTAL    OTHER

**Explain** ...........................................................

**Nutrition**   No. of servings

FLUIDS ................   CARBOHYDRATES ...............   FATS ...........   PROTEINS ..............

**General**   Hassle/distractions/injuries/illness/medications? ......................

.........................................................................

Comments .................................................................

.........................................................................

## DAILY RESISTANCE TRAINING LOG

Date: ........................  Time: ........................

Goals for today: ...................................................................
...................................................................................................

**Resistance training phase:** Endurance    Muscle building    Power    Relative strength
(Circle one)

| Exercise | PLANNED WORKOUT Intensity (reps max) | Reps | Sets | REPETITION X WEIGHTS Set number 1 | 2 | 3 | 4 | 5 |
|---|---|---|---|---|---|---|---|---|
| | | | | | | | | |
| | | | | | | | | |
| | | | | | | | | |
| | | | | | | | | |
| | | | | | | | | |
| | | | | | | | | |
| | | | | | | | | |
| | | | | | | | | |
| | | | | | | | | |

**Assessment** (Circle number)**:** Excellent session    1    2    3    4    5    Very poor session

**Why?** (Circle)**:**   PHYSICAL                     MENTAL                          OTHER

| | | | | | | |
|---|---|---|---|---|---|---|
| FOCUS | Totally focussed | 1 | 2 | 3 | 4 | 5 | Poor focus |
| ATTITUDE | Positive | 1 | 2 | 3 | 4 | 5 | Negative |
| ENERGY | Energised | 1 | 2 | 3 | 4 | 5 | Drained |

**Comments:** ...................................................................
...................................................................................................
...................................................................................................
...................................................................................................

# DAILY NUTRITION LOG

**Date:** ..................... **Time:** .....................

**Goals for today:** ..........................................................

..........................................................................

..........................................................................

| Meal | Nutrition record | | |
|---|---|---|---|
| | **Food** | **Food group** | **Number of servings** |
| | | | |
| | | | |
| | | | |
| | | | |
| | | | |
| | | | |
| | | | |
| | | | |
| | | | |
| | | | |
| | | | |
| | | | |
| | | | |

**Total number of servings**

**Fluids:** ........... **Carbohydrates:** ........... **Fats:** ........... **Proteins:** ...........

# Quote references

The authors gratefully acknowledge the support of the authors and publishers of the following works, from which they have sourced quotes in the text (page numbers refer to the location of quotes in *Smart Training for Rugby*).

## BOOKS

Kirk, D. (1997). *Black and Blue*. Auckland: Hodder Moa Beckett. 26, 28, 34.

Kronfeld, J., & Turner, B. (1999). *On The Loose: Josh Kronfeld*. Dunedin: Longacre Press. 32, 96, 106, 107, 132.

Fitzpatrick, S., & Johnstone, D. (1998). *Turning Point: The Making of a Captain*. Auckland: Penguin Books. 37, 104.

Gallaher, D., & Stead, W. (1906). *The Complete Rugby Footballer of the New Zealand System*. London: Methuen's Colonial Library. 66.

Palenski, R. (1982). *Graham Mourie: Captain*. Auckland: Moa Publications. 7, 24.

Parore, L. (1997). *Zinzan Brooke's Competitive Edge*. Auckland: Celebrity Books. 25, 102, 109.

## NEWSPAPERS AND MAGAZINES

*Newsweek*, Special Edition Oct/Nov 1993, Jordan, M. 17.

*North and South*, June 1999, Blackadder, T. 26.

*Otago Daily Times*, 8/11/99, Edwards, B. 9; 27/10/97, Blackadder, T. 27.

*Rugby Rave*, August 1997, Toomey, M. 18.

*Southland Times*, 3/1/98, Henderson, P. 12.

## INTERNET SITES

http://rwc99.scrum.com/columns/ubogu2.asp, Ubogu, V. 156

# References

## 1. INTRODUCTION

1. Hodge, K., & Sleivert, G. (1996). 'Introduction.' In K. Hodge, G. Sleivert, & A. McKenzie (eds.). *Smart Training for Peak Performance: A Complete Sports Training Guide for Athletes.* Auckland, NZ: Reed.

## 2. PEAK PERFORMANCE PROFILING

1. Hodge, K. (1994). *Sport Motivation: Training Your Mind for Peak Performance.* Auckland, NZ: Reed.
   Hodge, K., & McKenzie, A. (1996). 'Peak performance profile.' In K. Hodge, G. Sleivert, & A. McKenzie (eds.). *Smart Training for Peak Performance: A Complete Sports Training Guide for Athletes.* Auckland, NZ: Reed.
   Hodge, K., & McKenzie, A. (1999). *Thinking Rugby: Training Your Mind for Peak Performance.* Auckland, NZ: Reed.
2. Ibid.
   Butler, R., & Hardy, L. (1992). 'The performance profile: Theory and application.' *The Sport Psychologist* 6, 253–64.
3. Hodge, K. (1994). op. cit.
   Hodge, K., & McKenzie, A. (1996). op. cit.
   Hodge, K., & McKenzie, A. (1999). op. cit.
4. Butler, R., & Hardy, L. (1992). op. cit.
5. Hodge, K. (1994). op. cit.
   Hodge, K., & McKenzie, A. (1996). op. cit.
   Hodge, K., & McKenzie, A. (1999). op. cit.
   Butler, R., & Hardy, L. (1992). op. cit.
6. Ibid.

## 3. GOAL SETTING

1. Hodge, K. (1994). *Sport Motivation: Training Your Mind for Peak Performance.* Auckland, NZ: Reed.
   Hodge, K., & McKenzie, A. (1999). *Thinking Rugby: Training Your Mind for Peak Performance.* Auckland, NZ: Reed.
   Hodge, K., & McKenzie, A. (1996). 'Goal setting.' In K. Hodge, G. Sleivert, & A. McKenzie (eds.). *Smart Training for Peak Performance: A Complete Sports Training Guide for Athletes.* Auckland, NZ: Reed.
2. Gould, D. (1993). 'Goal setting for peak performance.' In J. Williams (ed.), *Applied Sport Psychology* (2nd ed.), (158–69). Palo Alto, CA, USA: Mayfield.
   Hardy, L., Jones, G., & Gould, D. (1996). *Understanding Psychological Preparation for Sport: Theory and Practice of Elite Performers.* Chichester, UK: John Wiley & Sons.
3. Gould, D. (1993). op. cit.
4. Hodge, K. (1994). op. cit.
   Hodge, K., & McKenzie, A. (1999). op. cit.
   Hodge, K., & McKenzie, A. (1996). op. cit.

Gould, D. (1993). op. cit.
5. Gould, D. (1993). op. cit.
Hardy, L., Jones, G., & Gould, D. (1996).
6. Kingston, K., & Hardy, L. (1997). 'Effects of different types of goals on processes that support performance.' *The Sport Psychologist* 11, 277–93.
7. Bull, S., Albinson, J., & Shambrook, C. (1996). *The Mental Game Plan: Getting Psyched for Sport.* Eastbourne, UK: Sports Dynamics.

## 4. FITNESS PROFILING

1. Green, H. (1991). 'Overview of the energy delivery systems.' In J. MacDougall, H. Wenger, & H. Green (eds.). *Physiological Testing of the Elite Athlete.* Champaign, IL, USA: Human Kinetics.
2. Spriet, L. (1995). 'Anaerobic metabolism during high intensity exercise.' In M. Hargreaves (ed.). *Exercise Metabolism* (1–42). Champaign, IL, USA: Human Kinetics.
3. Ibid.
Jacobs, I., Tesch, P., et al. (1983). 'Lactate in human skeletal muscle after 10 and 30s of supramaximal exercise.' *Journal of Applied Physiology* 55, 365–67.
4. Foss, M., & Keteyian, S. (1998). *Fox's Physiological Basis for Exercise and Sport* (6th ed.). Boston, USA: McGraw Hill.
McArdle, W., Katch, F., & Katch, V. (1996). *Exercise Physiology: Energy, Nutrition and Human Performance.* Baltimore, USA: Williams & Wilkins.
5. Thoden, J. (1991). 'Testing aerobic power.' In J. MacDougall, H. Wenger, & H. Green (eds.). *Physiological Testing of the Elite Athlete* (107–73). Champaign, IL, USA: Human Kinetics.
6. Leger, L., & Gadoury, C. (1989). 'Validity of the 20m shuttle run test with 1 min stages to predict VO$_2$max in adults.' *Canadian Journal of Sport Science* 14, 21–6.
7. Powers, S., & Howley, E. (1994). *Exercise Physiology: Theory and application to fitness and performance.* Dubuque, Iowa, USA: Brown & Benchmark.

## 5. IMPROVING FITNESS

1. Bouchard, C., Malina, R., et al. (1997). *Genetics of Fitness and Physical Performance.* Champaign, IL, USA: Human Kinetics.
2. Shepley, B., MacDougall, J., et al. (1992). 'Physiological effects of tapering in highly trained athletes.' *Journal of Applied Physiology* 72, 706–11.
Van Handel, P., Katz, A., et al. (1988). 'Oxygen consumption and blood lactic acid response to training and taper.' In B. Ungerechts, K. Wilke, & K. Reischle (eds.), *International Series on Sports Science: Swimming Science V* (269–75). Champaign, IL, USA: Human Kinetics.
3. Wenger, H., & Bell, G. (1986). 'The interactions of intensity, frequency and duration of exercise training in altering cardiorespiratory fitness.' *Sports Medicine* 3, 346–56.
4. MacDougall, J., Hicks, A., et al. (1998). 'Muscle performance and enzymatic adaptations to sprint interval training.' *Journal of Applied Physiology* 84, 2138–42.
5. Jones, D., & Rutherford, O. (1987). 'Human muscle strength training: The effects of three different regimes and the nature of the resultant changes.' *Journal of Physiology* 391, 1–11.
Komi, P. (1986). 'Training of muscle strength and power: Interaction of neuromotoric, hypertrophic, and mechanical factors.' *International Journal of Sports Medicine* 7, 10–15.
Kraemer, W., Fleck, S., et al. (1993). 'Changes in hormonal concentrations after different heavy-resistance exercise protocols in women.' *Journal of Applied Physiology* 75, 594–604.

6. Sale, D., & MacDougall, D. (1981). 'Specificity in strength training: A review for the coach and athlete.' *Science Periodical on Research and Technology in Sport*, March, 1–8.
   Sale, D. (1988). 'Neural adaptation to resistance training.' *Medicine and Science in Sports and Exercise* 20, S135–45.
7. Wilson, G. (1993). 'The optimal training load for the development of dynamic athletic performance.' *Medicine and Science in Sports and Exercise* 25, 1279–86.
8. Rimmer, E., & Sleivert, G. (in press). 'Effects of a plyometrics intervention program on sprint performance.' *Journal of Strength and Conditioning Research.*
   Delecluse, C., van Coppenolle, H., et al. (1995). 'Influence of high-resistance and high-velocity training on sprint performance.' *Medicine and Science in Sports and Exercise* 27, 1203–09.
9. Sleivert, G., Rimmer, E., et al. (1996). Strategies to improve speed and power. National Conference of Coaching New Zealand, Sport Science New Zealand, & Sports Medicine New Zealand, Wellington, NZ, National Conference Committee.
10. Ibid.
11. Fowles, J., & Sale, D. (1998). Time course of stress relaxation with repetitive stretching of human plantarflexors. Annual Meeting of the American College of Sports Medicine. Orlando, Florida, USA: Williams & Wilkins.

## 6. MENTAL TOUGHNESS TRAINING

1. Hodge, K. (1994). *Sport Motivation: Training Your Mind for Peak Performance.* Auckland, NZ: Reed.
   Hodge, K., & McKenzie, A. (1999). *Thinking Rugby: Training Your Mind for Peak Performance.* Auckland, NZ: Reed.
   McKenzie, A., & Hodge, K. (1996). 'Sport psychology.' In K. Hodge, G. Sleivert, & A. McKenzie (eds.). *Smart Training for Peak Performance: A Complete Sports Training Guide for Athletes.* Auckland, NZ: Reed.
2. Orlick, T. (1990). *In Pursuit of Excellence: How to Win in Sport and Life through Mental Training* (2nd ed.). Champaign, IL, USA: Human Kinetics.
   Williams, J. (1993). *Applied Sport Psychology: Personal Growth to Peak Performance* (2nd ed.). Palo Alto, CA, USA: Mayfield.
3. Hodge, K. (1994). op. cit.
   Hodge, K., & McKenzie, A. (1999). op. cit.
   McKenzie, A., & Hodge, K. (1996). op. cit.
4. Ibid.
5. Vealey, R. (1988). 'Future directions in Psychological Skills Training.' *The Sport Psychologist* 2, 318–36
6. Hodge, K. (1994). op. cit.
   Hodge, K., & McKenzie, A. (1999). op. cit.
   McKenzie, A., & Hodge, K. (1996). op. cit.
   Vealey, R. (1988). op. cit.
7. Hodge, K. (1994). op. cit.
   Hodge, K., & McKenzie, A. (1999). op. cit.
   McKenzie, A., & Hodge, K. (1996). op. cit.
8. Ibid.

9. Orlick, T. (1990). op. cit.
   Williams, J. (1993). op. cit.
10. Hodge, K. (1994). op. cit.
   Hodge, K., & McKenzie, A. (1999). op. cit.
   McKenzie, A., & Hodge, K. (1996). op. cit.
   Orlick, T. (1986). *Psyching for Sport: Mental Training for Athletes.* Champaign, IL, USA: Leisure Press.
11. Orlick T., & Partington, J. (1988). 'Mental links to excellence.' *The Sport Psychologist 2,* 105–30.
12. Hodge, K. (1994). op. cit.
   Hodge, K., & McKenzie, A. (1999). op. cit.
   McKenzie, A., & Hodge, K. (1996). op. cit.
   Orlick, T. (1986). op. cit.
13. Ibid.
14. Hodge, K. (1994). op. cit.
   Hodge, K., & McKenzie, A. (1999). op. cit.
   McKenzie, A., & Hodge, K. (1996). op. cit.
   Bunker, L., Williams, J., & Zinsser, N. (1993). 'Cognitive techniques for improving performance and building confidence.' In Williams, J. (ed.). *Applied Sport Psychology: Personal Growth to Peak Performance* (2nd ed.) (225–42). Palo Alto, CA, USA: Mayfield.
15. Ibid.
16. Ibid.
17. Bunker, L., Williams, J., & Zinsser, N. (1993). op. cit.
18. Hodge, K. (1994). op. cit.
   Hodge, K., & McKenzie, A. (1999). op. cit.
   McKenzie, A., & Hodge, K. (1996). op. cit.
   Horsley, C. (1991). *Relaxation Training for Athletes and Coaches.* Canberra: Australian Institute for Sport.
19. Ibid.
20. Hodge, K. (1994). op. cit.
   Hodge, K., & McKenzie, A. (1999). op. cit.
   McKenzie, A., & Hodge, K. (1996). op. cit.
21. Ibid.
   Vealey, R., & Walter, S. (1993). 'Imagery training for performance enhancement and personal development.' In Williams, J. (ed.). *Applied Sport Psychology: Personal Growth to Peak Performance* (2nd ed.) (200–24). Palo Alto, CA, USA: Mayfield.
22. Pinel, B., McKenzie, A., et al. (1999). 'Enjoyment in professional rugby: Getting the best from our players.' Presented at the 1999 Sport Science New Zealand Conference, Hamilton, New Zealand.
23. Pinel, B. (1999). *Enjoyment-Profiling: A Workbook for Youth Sport Coaches.* Dunedin, NZ: University of Otago Press.

## 7. THE PHYSICS OF FOOTIE

1. East, H. (1994). Comparison of the standard and dive rugby pass. Unpublished manuscript, University of Otago.

2. McNitt Gray, J., Yokoi, T., & Millward, C. (1993). 'Landing strategy adjustments made by female gymnasts in response to drop height and mat composition.' *Journal of Applied Biomechanics* 9, 173–90.

Gerrard, D. (1998). 'The use of padding in rugby union: An overview.' *Sports Medicine* 25, 329–32.

3. Milburn, P. (1995). 'The rugby tackle— a time for review.' *Journal of Physical Education New Zealand* 28 (1), 9–15.

4. Milburn, P. (1990). The biomechanics of rugby scrummaging: A report to the Australian Rugby Football Union and the New Zealand Rugby Football Union.

Jevon, M. (1996). 'The art of scrummaging.' *Rugby News and Monthly* 80–81.

Milburn, P. (1993). 'Biomechanics of rugby union scrummaging: Technical and safety issues.' *Sports Medicine* 16, 168–79.

Milburn, P. (1990). 'The kinetics of rugby union scrummaging.' *Journal of Sports Sciences* 8, 47–60.

Milburn, P. (1987). 'Biomechanics of rugby union scrummaging.' *Sports Coach* 11, 11–14.

Milburn, P. (1987). 'A comparison of the mechanics of hip and crotch binding techniques in rugby union scrummaging.' *Australian Journal of Science and Medicine in Sports* 19 (1), 3–9.

## 8. EATING SMART

1. Deutsch, M., Maw, G., et al. (1998). 'Heart rate, blood lactate, and kinematic data of elite colts (under 19) rugby union players during competition.' *Journal of Sports Sciences* August/October, 4–10.

2. Ibid.

3. Coyle, E. (1995). 'Substrate utilization during exercise in active people.' *The American Journal of Clinical Nutrition* 61, 968–79.

4. Ibid.

5. Murray, R. (1995). 'Heat stress and dehydration.' In *Endurance Training for Performance.* Barrington, IL, USA: Gatorade Sport Science Institute.

6. Burke, L., & Deakin, V. (1994). *Clinical Sports Nutrition.* Roseville, USA: McGraw-Hill.

7. Ibid.

## 9. PREVENTING AND MANAGING INJURIES

1. Accident Rehabilitation and Compensation Insurance Corporation (1997). *Injury Statistics 1997. Wellington: Accident Rehabilitation and Compensation Insurance Corporation.*

2. Bird, Y., Waller, A., et al. (1998). 'The New Zealand rugby injury and performance project: V. Epidemiology of a season of rugby injury.' *British Journal of Sports Medicine* 32, 319–25.

3. Chalmers, D. (1999). 'Rugby— reducing the risks.' *New Zealand Pharmacy*, February, 21–23.

4. Ibid.

5. Gerrard, D. (1996a). 'Sports medicine.' In K. Hodge, G. Sleivert, & A. McKenzie (eds.). *Smart Training for Peak Performance: A Complete Training Guide for Athletes* (116–29). Auckland, NZ: Reed.

6. Ibid.

7. Milburn, P. (1993). 'Biomechanics of rugby union scrummaging: Technical and safety issues.' *Sports Medicine* 16, 168–79.

8.  Sports Medicine New Zealand. (1996a). Policy statement on infectious disease transmission in sport. Dunedin, NZ: Sports Medicine New Zealand.
9.  Sports Medicine New Zealand. (1996b). Policy statement on head injury in sport. Dunedin, NZ: Sports Medicine New Zealand.
10. Gerrard, D. (1996a). op. cit.
11. Grove, J., & Gordon, A. (1995). 'The psychological aspects of injury in sport.' In J. Bloomfield, P. Fricker, & K. Fitch (eds.). *Science and Medicine in Sport* (194–203). Sydney, Australia: Blackwell Science.
    Brukner, P., & Khan, K. (1993). 'Principles of rehabilitation.' In P. Brukner & K. Khan (eds.). *Clinical Sports Medicine* (130–50). Sydney, Australia: McGraw-Hill.
12. Gerrard, D. (1996b). 'Drug misuse by athletes: What the GP needs to know.' *New Ethicals* 33, 9–15.
13. Ibid.
14. International Rugby Football Board (IRFB). (1993). *Laws of the Game of Rugby Football.* London, UK: IRFB.
15. Ibid.
    Gerrard, D. (1998a) 'The use of padding in rugby union: An overview.' *Sports Medicine* 25, 329–32.
16. Ibid.
17. Ibid.
18. Wilson, B. (1998). 'Protective headgear in rugby union.' *Sports Medicine* 25, 333–37.
19. Chalmers, D. (1998). 'Mouthguards, protection for the mouth in rugby union.' *Sports Medicine* 25, 339–49.
20. Hume, P., & Gerrard, D. (1998). 'Effectiveness of external ankle support, bracing and taping in rugby union.' *Sports Medicine* 25, 285–312.
    Gerrard, D. (1998b). 'External knee support in rugby union.' *Sports Medicine* 25, 313–17.
21. Gerrard, D. (1998b). op. cit.
22. Hume, P., & Gerrard, D. (1998). op. cit.
23. Sports Medicine New Zealand (Inc). (1996a). op. cit.
24. Ibid.
25. Sports Medicine New Zealand (Inc). (1996b). op. cit.
26. Ibid.

## 10. TOTAL PROGRAMME PLANNING

1.  Bompa, T. (1987). 'Periodisation as a key element of planning.' *Sports Coach* July/Sept, 20–23.
2.  Martin, D., & Coe, P. (1991). *Training Distance Runners.* Champaign, IL, USA: Human Kinetics.
3.  Sale, D. (1988). 'Neural adaptation to resistance training.' *Medicine and Science in Sports and Exercise* 20, 135–45.
4.  Belcastro, A., Dallaire, J., et al. (1991). Canadian Association of Sport Sciences: Overstress Study, CASS/ACSS.
    Fry, R., Morton, A., et al. (1991). 'Overtraining in athletes: An update.' *Sports Medicine* 12(1), 32–65.
5.  Shepley, B., MacDougall, J., et al. (1992). 'Physiological effects of tapering in highly trained athletes.' *Journal of Applied Physiology* 72, 706–11.

# Acknowledgements

The editors would like to thank the following people for their assistance in the preparation of this book: Mike Baudinet, Megan Harlick, Josh Kronfeld, Natasha McCarroll, Murray Pedersen, Bruce Pinel, Jamie Plowman, and Martin Toomey.

Thanks are also due to the *Otago Daily Times* for the generous help of their staff in sourcing photographs.

# Recommended reading and resources

## Sports Biomechanics

Carr, G. (1997). *Mechanics of Sport: A Practitioner's Guide*. Champaign, IL, USA: Human Kinetics.

Hay, J.G. (1993). *The Biomechanics of Sports Techniques* (4th ed.). Englewood Cliffs, NJ, USA: Prentice-Hall.

## Sport Psychology

Dugdale, J., & Hodge, K. (1997). *Psychological Skills Training: Practical Guidelines for Athletes, Coaches, & Officials*. Wellington, NZ: Sport Science New Zealand.

Hodge, K. (1994). *Sport Motivation: Training Your Mind for Peak Performance*. Auckland, NZ: Reed.

Hodge, K., & McKenzie, A. (1999). *Thinking Rugby: Training Your Mind for Peak Performance*. Auckland, NZ: Reed.

## Sports Nutrition

Burke, L. (1995). *The Complete Guide to Food for Sports Performance: Peak Nutrition for your Sport* (2nd ed.). Sydney, Australia: Allen and Unwin.

Howe, M., Hellemans, I., et al. (1999). *Sports Nutrition for New Zealand Athletes and Coaches*. Wellington, NZ: Sport Science New Zealand.

Pearce, J. (1991). *The Eat to Compete Cookbook: Food Power for Top Sports Performance*. Auckland, NZ: Reed.

## Sport Physiology

Anderson, R. (1980). *Stretching*. Bolinas, CA, USA: Shelter Publications.

Chu, D. (1992). *Jumping into Plyometrics*. Champaign, IL, USA: Human Kinetics.

Fleck, S.J., & Kraemer, W.J. (1997). *Designing Resistance Training Programs* (2nd ed.). Champaign, IL, USA: Human Kinetics.

Gascoigne, H. (ed.). (1996). *Smart Sport: The Ultimate Reference Manual for Sports People, Athletes and Players, Coaches, Parents and Teachers*. Canberra, Australia: RWM Publishing.

## Sports Medicine

*Drugs in Sport: Permitted over-the-counter Medications*. (1999). Auckland, NZ: New Zealand Sports Drug Agency.

*SportSmart: The 10-point Plan for Sports Injury Prevention*. Wellington, NZ: Accident Compensation Corporation.

Sports Medicine New Zealand policy statements:
Prevention of Head Injury in Sport.
Infectious Disease Transmission in Sport.

## General

Hodge, K., Sleivert, G., & McKenzie A. (eds.) (1996). *Smart Training for Peak Performance: The Complete Sport Training Guide for Athletes*. Auckland, NZ: Reed.

# Index

# Author profiles

*Katrina Darry*, MSc, is a private nutrition consultant who has worked with teams and individuals from a variety of sports, and is contracted to the Human Performance Centre at the School of Physical Education, University of Otago. She is the nutritionist for the Otago Highlanders, the Otago NPC team, and the Canterbury and Otago Rugby Development Squads, where her responsibilities include the development of individual nutrition programmes to enhance performance and training.

*Markus Deutsch*, BSc(Hons), is a doctoral student at the School of Physical Education, specialising in exercise physiology. He was principally responsible for the development of the GRUNT 3000 fitness testing system, and has conducted extensive research into the fitness demands of rugby players at various levels. He is a science advisor to the Otago Highlanders Super 12 team.

*David Gerrard*, MBChB, OBE, is an associate professor of medicine at the University of Otago. A former New Zealand Olympic swimmer and Commonwealth Games gold medallist, David was *chef de mission* at the Atlanta Olympic Games, and is a former Olympic team doctor. He is on the FINA (International Swimming Federation) medical committee, and is also a member of the New Zealand Sports Drug Agency Board and a former chairman of Sports Medicine New Zealand.

*Ken Hodge*, PhD, is a senior lecturer in sport psychology at the School of Physical Education. He has 27 years' rugby playing experience and 10 years' experience as a coach. He has been a staff coach for the New Zealand Rugby Football Union since 1989, specialising in psychological skills, and is a level III certified coach. He was the psychologist for New Zealand teams at the 1992 Olympic and 1994 Commonwealth Games, and is a sport psychology consultant for the Otago Rugby Football Union's Academy squad.

*Alex McKenzie*, PhD, is a senior lecturer in sport psychology at the School of Physical Education. He has 25 years' rugby playing experience and 8 years' experience as a coach and selector. He has been a staff coach for the Otago Rugby Football Union, teaching psychological skills to players and coaches. He is a co-editor (with Ken Hodge and Gordon Sleivert) of *Smart Training: A Complete Sports Training Guide for Athletes*, and co-author (with Ken Hodge) of *Thinking Rugby: Training Your Mind for Peak Performance*.

*David Pease*, MSc, is a doctoral student at the School of Physical Education, and a biomechanics consultant for the Human Performance Centre at the University of Otago. He has been a staff biomechanist for the United States Olympic Committee and United States Swimming. He has experience working on technique issues with athletes from many sports including rugby, where he has been involved in studies looking at passing, running, and testing of protective equipment.

*Gordon Sleivert*, PhD, is a senior lecturer in exercise physiology at the School of Physical Education, where he is also the director of the Human Performance Centre. He is the current chair of Sport Science New Zealand. He was recognised as New Zealand's Sport Scientist of the Year in 1998, and has been a fitness and training consultant to numerous individuals and teams for over 10 years.